CW00551423

BEAM BOMBERS

By the same author

Pathfinder Cranswick
The Powerless Ones: Gliding in Peace & War
The Starkey Sacrifice: The Allied Bombing of Le Portel,
1943

BEAM
BOMBERS

THE SECRET WAR OF No. 109 SQUADRON

MICHAEL CUMMING

SUTTON PUBLISHING

First published in the United Kingdom in 1998 by
Sutton Publishing Limited · Phoenix Mill
Thrupp · Stroud · Gloucestershire · GL5 2BU

British Library Cataloguing in Publication Data
A catalogue record for this book is available from the British Library

ISBN 0 7509 1998 1

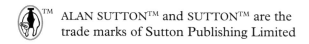

ALAN SUTTON™ and SUTTON™ are the
trade marks of Sutton Publishing Limited

Typeset in 10/12 pt Plantin Light.
Typesetting and origination by
Sutton Publishing Limited.
Printed in Great Britain
WBC Ltd, Bridgend.

CONTENTS

List of Plates

Acknowledgements

Researching any book about events that occurred during the Second World War more than half a century ago poses three particular problems: to confirm that the key participants are still alive, to establish their present whereabouts and to determine their capability and willingness to recount their role. Fortunately, while delving into one of the lesser-known inter-service operations of 1943, Operation Starkey, which Bomber Command entered with an understandable reluctance (Bomber Harris protested against the enforced involvement of his aircraft and crews in a strategy that he called 'play-acting'), I was introduced first to a member of No. 109 Squadron who flew an incredible 100-plus Oboe sorties and then, through him, to a member of the Oboe group at the Telecommunications Research Establishment (TRE) from its formation to disbandment.

A definitive account of No. 109's beam bombing activities and the close association which this squadron enjoyed with TRE and the Oboe ground-controlled blind-bombing system would be impossible to contemplate without the encouragement, assistance and continuing support of these two people: Squadron Leader Ronald E. Curtis DSO, DFC and Bar and John E.N. Hooper. They offered personal recollections enabling me to build upon the archival material available through the Public Record Office; they introduced me to others, most of them former wartime colleagues and subsequently personal friends; and they have maintained their cooperation throughout this entire project, coming up with ideas, advice and constructive criticism. It must be stressed, however, that Ron Curtis and John Hooper are in no way responsible for errors of fact in these pages or for opinions expressed or construed unless specifically attributed to one or other of them. I cannot thank them enough – but to try to do so, publicly, seems a starting point.

A most pleasurable spin-off when researching a book where personal accounts are essential is the enjoyment that comes from meeting new people and making fresh friends. To the following I am singularly grateful for help so willingly given and additionally, in a number of cases, for putting me in touch with others I would almost certainly have been unable to trace: Kenneth Bailey, 'Barty' Barton, 'Buck' Buckland, Clifford Cornford, Jack Emmerson, 'Ned' Fennessy, Jeff Hampson, Charles Harrold, John Jukes, Frank Metcalfe, Pat O'Hara, Len Overy, 'Roger' Reece, Harry Scott, Dave Slater, 'Slim' Somerville, John Tipton and Peter Woolland. The listing is alphabetical and I hope that each one of them will excuse me for using here the personal form of address, although the appropriate title, rank and decorations have been recorded in the source material. Sadly, Jeff Hampson, John Jukes and Roger Reece have since passed away and will be much missed; for their unique contributions I am most appreciative.

A number of organizations have been particularly helpful: the Public Record Office, whose staff I am pleased to commend alongside my formal acknowledgement that Crown copyright material is reproduced by permission of the Controller of Her Majesty's Stationery Office; the Imperial War Museum and especially the library and photograph archive staff; the RAF Museum at Hendon for locating for me a series of photographs of the first Mosquito converted for Pathfinder duties; the Ministry of Defence Air Historical Branch; the Defence Evaluation and Research Agency's Information Centre at Malvern; and the Institution of Electrical Engineers for its help concerning Alec Reeves and F.E. Jones relative to the Oboe system.

Finally I would like to place on record the debt I owe my wife and family in not grumbling too much while 'twanging away at the word processor' when I should have been doing something else, or being elsewhere 'doing my research' when my place was at home!

Michael Cumming
London 1998

Abbreviations

AA	Anti-Aircraft
A&AEE	Aeroplane and Armament Experimental Establishment
AMES	Air Ministry Experimental Station
AMRE	Air Ministry Research Establishment
ACAS	Assistant Chief of Air Staff
AFC	Air Force Cross
AFM	Air Force Medal
AOC-in-C	Air Officer Commanding-in-Chief
AP	Aiming Point
AWAS	Air Warfare Analysis Section
BAT	Blind Approach Training
BAT&DU	Blind Approach Training and Development Unit
BBC	Blind-Bombing of Cherbourg
BC	Bomber Command
BMHQ	Base Maintenance Headquarters
CBE	Commander (of the Order) of the British Empire
CH	Chain Home (Radar station)
CHL	Chain Home Low (Radar station)
CO	Commanding Officer
DFC	Distinguished Flying Cross
DFM	Distinguished Flying Medal
DSO	Distinguished Service Order
ETA	Estimated Time of Arrival
GAF	German Air Force
GC	George Cross
GEE	Air navigation radar system
G-H	Radar-based bombing system
GM	George Medal
GPO	General Post Office
GSGS	Geographical Section of the General Staff
H2S	Air-to-ground mapping radar system
HE	High Explosives
HQ	Headquarters
IWM	Imperial War Museum
LNSF	Light Night Striking Force (in Pathfinder Force)
MAP	Ministry of Aircraft Production
MTU	Mosquito Training Unit
NCO	Non-Commissioned Officer

OBE	Order of the British Empire
OBOE	Ground-controlled blind-bombing system
OC	Officer Commanding
ORB	Operations Record Book (RAF Units)
ORS	Operational Research Section (BC)
OTU	Operational Training Unit
PFF	Pathfinder Force (No. 8 Group, RAF)
PRO	Public Record Office
RCAF	Royal Canadian Air Force
RCM	Radio Countermeasures
RDF	Radar
SASO	Senior Air Staff Officer
SP	Service Police (RAF)
TI	Target Indicator
TRE	Telecommunications Research Establishment
USAAF	United States Army Air Force
VC	Victoria Cross
VCAS	Vice-Chief of Air Staff
VHF	Very High Frequency (Radio)
WIDU	Wireless Intelligence Development Unit
WOP/AG	Wireless Operator/Air Gunner
'Y'	Signals Intelligence

CHAPTER ONE

Bombing the Bombers

*'Regarding choice of site . . . we are concerned with contours and flying
conditions within 30 miles of the site, with ground contours and cliffs at the
site and with suitable sea traffic and balloon operations. We are indeed
difficult to please and there seems only to be one Bawdsey.'* A.P. Rowe, who
was successively in charge of Bawdsey Research Station, the Air
Ministry Research Establishments at Dundee and Worth Matravers and
the Telecommunications Research Establishment (TRE), TRE being
the birthplace of Oboe

It seems utter nonsense, the concept of a tiny insect carrying a powerful
wind instrument, the two uniting as a remarkable team to lay claim to a
dominant position among the triumphs of air warfare! However, when the
carrier with a bite is revealed as the de Havilland Mosquito and the war-
winning instrument inside this versatile aircraft is Oboe, it is absurd no
longer. Together, the Mosquito and Oboe were one of the success stories
of the Second World War, although the requirement for secrecy meant
that not many people have had the opportunity to appreciate their joint
value.

For Air Chief Marshal Sir Arthur Harris, Air Officer Commanding-in-
Chief, RAF Bomber Command, Oboe Mosquitoes opened on the night of
5/6 March 1943 what he called the Battle of the Ruhr; these were the
aircraft that helped to prove the system – the radar-based Oboe system of
marking and/or bombing an aiming point, irrespective of darkness, clouds,
smoke or haze, with surprise and uncanny accuracy, releasing those target
indicators and/or high explosives from operating heights as much as 6 miles
above the ground. These aircraft, spearheading over the industrial centre of
Essen that night, came from a single source, as did their pilots and
navigators. All came from No. 109 Squadron, where beam-flying had long
been its speciality. Here was a founding Pathfinder squadron – its motto
translates as 'the first of the legion' – which had already fought a previous
secret war, another beam bombers war no less, while engaged on wireless
intelligence work and pioneering radio countermeasures.

As will be seen, when No. 109 Squadron's history unfolds into the Oboe
era, the pilots and the navigators in planes equipped with this system had
their dramas and their tragedies; indeed, the single Oboe VC was a
posthumous award. That VC, as did many lesser honours earned by other

pilots and navigators for courage under fire (in one notable month, three DSOs and fifteen DFCs),[1] went to a member of No. 109.* Though the pilot-navigator teams were necessarily at the sharp end, the story of an Oboe squadron is not theirs alone, as they themselves insist: it belongs to aircrew and non-aircrew alike; it embraces the scientists who created the system and of course the men and women working at the ground stations that housed the linked equipment controlling the aircraft as distant as 250 miles away.

American bombers used Oboe too and the system was introduced into Lancasters which Pathfinder Force used to lead formations of 'heavies' in what turned out to be perhaps the most concentrated of all of Bomber Command's forms of aerial assault. On other occasions, Oboe Mosquitoes headed formations of Mosquito bombers in a less vulnerable method of daylight attack. Oboe also attracted unexpected controversy on the home front, besides the expected attention of the enemy's defences: one in three sorties are shown to have experienced some form of technical failure which prevented the aircraft releasing its markers or its bombs and by no means were all of the two out of three successful releases spot on. Furthermore, questions continue to be asked as to whether or not this unique method of finding and hitting a target was in fact used to maximum effect.

With the war in Europe coming to a close, Oboe, unique in application as a precision bombing device for so long, played a happier tune when pinpointing the dropping zone for much needed food parcels in Holland – and for containers filled with multilingual leaflets to tell prisoners of war that hostilities were drawing to an end. Oboe was a means to that end, a system conceived in a time of war for the purpose of war. It was a product based on complex principles of science that ultimately enabled even a non-pilot (at least in theory!), while concentrating on hearing a pattern of dots and dashes transmitted from one of a pair of ground stations, to keep an aircraft on its correct path to the release point. This was a precise point in the sky where a signal from the other ground station was the bomb-aimer's release cue. Aircrews might not have reacted too favourably to the idea but Oboe offered the ultimate in aerial bombardment, the opportunity for accurate automated attacks, capable of being carried out without human intervention in the target area. No more the need for the steadying hand of a pilot during the critical few minutes of the final approach to the aiming point, no more the need for a crew member to press the button which would let go the bombs.

In fundamental terms, Oboe-equipped aircraft were as if on an incredibly tight lead – strictly speaking on the end of two invisible leads – each held by one of those two ground stations and reeled out as the aircraft neared its

---

* When the RAF's only other Oboe squadron was formed (it was No. 105 Squadron, which marked with Oboe for the first time in July 1943 and initially shared an airfield with No. 109), a number of crews and aircraft were transferred from No. 109 so that the new squadron, thanks to this instant injection of sound operational experience with Oboe, would be able to make an immediate and powerful contribution to Pathfinder duties.

target. This 'invisible lead' was a pulse transmission and the Oboe system was based on the measurements at the two ground stations of the time taken by that signal to reach the aircraft and to be transmitted back. With those measurements, the distance of the aircraft from each ground station was obtained and the position of the aircraft thus known throughout the transmission period.

It will emerge that, controversy aside, the device had its outspoken critics (one wrote that he would sack the man responsible) but happily there were many more in favour of continuing to develop Oboe than there were those crying out for it to be scrapped. Basically, Oboe was an aiming system and that is, after all, a necessity in warfare; aiming at out-of-sight targets, near and far, exercised many an active brain throughout two world wars and in subsequent campaigns. Even the much-vaunted long-range cruise missiles, the product of infinite time, money and electronic know-how, showed their comparative unreliability when last used in an aggressive situation.

A half-century earlier, before the United States entered the Second World War, British scientists, aircrews and ground teams together faced and overcame the problem of consistently finding and bombing enemy targets with a degree of accuracy that hitherto seemed impossible – even when the objective was obscured by cloud, and even in darkness. The invention that made this possible was one of the Allies' most important secret weapons and was given the name Oboe because a music-loving member of the design group likened its aural tone to that of the woodwind instrument. Oboe was born within the foremost telecommunications research centre in wartime Britain and raised by parents who were, on the one side, scientists working in the field of range and direction finding and, on the other, aviation specialists concentrating on bombing techniques.

Oboe was not the only 'magic' navigational and bombing aid to come out of the research centre featured in these pages (GEE, for navigating aircraft by radar, and H2S, for mapping the ground below them by radar, were both used by substantially more crews in RAF Bomber Command than was Oboe), nor was the squadron under focus here the only one equipped with Oboe. What makes the link so important is that the aims, the people and the achievements of the centre, the Telecommunications Research Establishment (TRE), and those of No. 109 Squadron of the Royal Air Force, were intertwined in a unique affiliation that spanned five momentous years. As separate entities, each did more than many to earn a place in military history. Together, TRE and No. 109 formed a remarkable duo, with Oboe their common ground, the one unable to succeed without the other and both contributing their expertise and, sadly, their lives too, in civvies as well as in uniform.

It is a story of daydreams and night dramas; about finding and using radio beams to confound the enemy. These are the tales of pilots who were committed to following unerringly their unseen tramways in the sky and developing a technique where a handful of unarmed, high-flying Mosquito aircraft could spearhead even before the Pathfinder Force and mark the target for the hundreds of Main Force bombers lifting off from their scattered airfields in Britain in great streams, intent on pulverizing the industrial heart of Germany.

Inevitably, being designed to help solve the problem of how to make RAF Bomber Command more effective in striking against the German war machine, Oboe itself faced setbacks. There were the sceptics, there were the critics and there were the drawbacks. It was not always the means of salvation that it initially promised and its accuracy was not always as precise as the optimism of the design team and the evidence of the proving trials in the system's early days. There were surprises that plagued as well as cheered the select few who were party to the creation, introduction and use of Oboe.

Nonetheless Oboe remained the only 'blind-bombing' device of its kind available to both British and American bombers operating against targets on the Continent between the winter of 1942/3 and the end of the war in Europe in May 1945. Contemplate for a moment the disastrous and quite alarming performance of Britain's bombers trundling across Germany in the pre-Oboe period and there is no doubt that this remarkable system must have seemed a modern miracle.

Of course the British public were blissfully ignorant of the true degree of bombing success in those early days. The facts need to be recalled so that Oboe can be seen in perspective; to present the comparison is not to minimize the efforts of earlier bomber crews doing their best with the machines and the equipment then in their hands, as many as 4 in every 100 aircrew members being lost on bombing operations carried out from Britain in the last pre-Oboe year.[2]

Although the Americans subsequently concentrated on daylight bombing, with huge formations of four-engined planes, higher-flying to help protect them from anti-aircraft fire, and bristling with machine-gun positions to try to beat off the fighters, the British effort was conducted principally during the night hours. The distances involved meant that the comparatively slow-moving twin-engined planes, which were all that were available initially, would have been exposed for too long in daylight to the waiting guns of both the anti-aircraft sites and the fighter defences in the occupied countries, as well as in Germany itself.

Night raids called for the highest skills in navigation and bombing and the aircrew training programmes were geared towards these achievements. It was the captain's responsibility in each bombing crew to look after the flying and to see that everyone was doing his job properly; here again, the training programme was intended to bring out the best in each prospective captain. But there was a world of difference between the results obtained in class and those obtained when faced with the stresses and the dangers of the real thing, even though a brief period with an operational training unit would usually offer a limited opportunity for flying over enemy territory. There was a job for everyone, individually and as a team member, the composition of the crew and their roles varying according to the specific aircraft.

Each role had to be played to perfection as far as was humanly possible; the pilot in the driving seat, the navigator maintaining a constant awareness of the aircraft's position, the bomb-aimer confirming the target area and carrying out the actual attack, while everyone else on board kept an eye out for fighters. And all this time there were likely to be probing searchlights, anti-aircraft fire which would often be intense, the bombing run demanding straight and level flight, an engine failure or some other electrical or mechanical problem, the vagaries of the weather, the chance of being hit – perhaps even by gunfire from a friendly aircraft or a collision in mid-air, the risk of fire, the fear of not getting home. . . . Is it any wonder that so many crews were convinced – genuinely believed – that the target had been reached, that the bombs had gone down in the right place and that their duty had been done?

The first scientific analysis of the night-bombing performance of RAF Bomber Command crews consisted of the study of more than 4,000 photographs taken during attacks on targets in Germany during June and July 1941. The camera in the aircraft – as a function of the bomb-release procedure – took a photograph of the ground where the bombs should have exploded, this area having been illuminated for the camera by a photoflash dropped from the same plane moments after 'bombs away'. Summarized from an RAF Air Historical Branch narrative on the bombing offensive, the results showed that only one in five of the aircraft despatched arrived within 5 miles of their target, yet mostly three out of four claimed to have found their objective. As for the attacks themselves, the relationship between the evidence and the belief was still more pronounced, the truth of the matter being that only one in three aircraft whose crews claimed to have attacked was actually within 5 miles of its target.[3]

Anti-aircraft gunfire, cannon shells, machine-gun bullets – missiles such as these were all to be expected by the pioneering crews of RAF Bomber Command intent on penetrating the enemy's defences night after night, but what about the prospect of having bombs raining down upon them? Surely not. Bombs dropped from enemy bombers, carrying out a defensive operation and positioning themselves at a greater altitude with you as their target? Incredible.

It seems bizarre these days but let us go back to pre-Second World War: 'bombing the bombers' emerges as a concept that was being tackled with all seriousness by a forerunner to the establishment that was to produce Oboe. To make this fact more pertinent still, it was work taking place under the very person who would be in charge of that establishment. A.P. Rowe, Superintendent of Bawdsey Research Station, Woodbridge, Suffolk (its location until war began), retained this position throughout its growth in size and stature, throughout its changes in title and throughout its moves to various locations in different parts of Britain.

On the assumption that the enemy aircraft did not take any avoiding action, attempting their destruction by bombing the bombers was superb in theoretical terms. It was arguably more effective than sending up fighters to disperse the expected formations with their lethal loads. There was, though, one possibly insurmountable hurdle in its development, that of finding a way to make the bombs explode among the bombers: setting a fuse so precisely as to ensure detonation at exactly the height the enemy was flying was apparently an impossibility. While fuses could be set before take-off so that the moment of detonation was delayed for an appropriate period of time after release from the aircraft, the height of the target bomber formation could not possibly be known ahead of take-off. And getting at the bombs to manipulate the fuse settings while airborne was another impossibility; even the basic hurdle of accessing the bombs proved too much, despite serious investigation of the prospects with aircraft of the day such as the Henley (bombs under the pilot's seat), Battle and Heyford (within the wings), Hampden (below the main spar) and Wellesley (in nacelles on the wings).[4]

For bomb detonation alone, photoelectric cells were proposed; radio signals and a technique known as RDF were a prospect too, the latter application to be considered as a package possibility that would help the pilot find his target, aim the bomb and detonate it.* Such were the ideas being investigated at the Bawdsey Research Station where Rowe was following in the footsteps of the distinguished R.A. Watson Watt, generally regarded as the father of radar, who became its first Superintendent when Bawdsey was set up in 1936. To use Rowe's own words when he learned that the Air Ministry was adding RDF detonation of bombs in flight to his establishment's research programme on 10 December 1939, 'I have always felt most strongly that this work should go on'.[5]

A plus point about using radio and radar methods was that unless weather conditions intervened, bombing the bombers would become possible right around the clock. In darkness, searchlights could illuminate the target once the attacking bomber was close to its prey. Whatever the method, however hare-brained the proposal, this was a means of national defence that was not easy to dismiss since it was on the agenda of one of the august think-tanks of that era, the Committee for the Scientific Survey of Air Warfare.[6]

Clearly supportive of this long-time concept, which attracted criticism in the manner that Oboe would do too, Rowe kept up the pressure on trying to make bombing the bombers feasible, especially when he saw for himself the German Air Force formations crossing the water towards England. In that anxious summer of 1940, believing in the value of attacks on incoming bomber groups by one or more bombing aircraft, he even sought formal instructions on whether to launch his people into a concentrated effort to find an alternative means of bomb detonation, if the photoelectric cells

---

* It appears that for security reasons TRE used the abbreviation RDF (standing for Range and Direction Finding) prior to 'radar', which came from America (and was a shortened form of Radio Direction And Range).

method had not emerged as the solution. The answer to his request was a while coming – and it was probably not the one he expected. Told that the success of the scheme would depend on a proximity fuse under development elsewhere and that his own work was now to stop, Rowe refused to consider that there was no more to be done. He conceded that, by day, nothing could compete with visual means of bombing aircraft in flight if the target could be seen but RDF bombing would appear to come into its own in a situation where the intention was to bomb large formations by day but with the view from the defending bombing aircraft obscured by cloud.[7] It makes a fascinating study in the 'what might have been' if one ponders over this means of destroying bomber formations before they reached the British coast, as a viable alternative to the total reliance on the Battle of Britain fighters.

By now, Bawdsey Research Station had moved twice: first to the Training College, Park Place, Dundee, where, the story goes, Watson Watt, who had been at Dundee University in his earlier days, played a part in encouraging the university hierarchy to look kindly upon the suggestion that members of an important defence laboratory might need emergency accommodation in a time of war.[8] Given the fact that, when war did come, there was an added technical attraction in the presence of an RDF station at Douglas Wood, to benefit some aspects of the research work formerly carried out at Bawdsey, Dundee's welcoming mat was gratefully accepted. Ideally situated in peace but vulnerable during hostilities, Bawdsey Research Station was duly evacuated at the outbreak of war to existing buildings at Dundee, the remaining staff being distributed between Leighton Buzzard, Stanmore, Perth and Kidbrooke.

The disadvantages of relocation quickly emerged. The effect of the fast-changing weather conditions on the RDF work, a similar potential for hostile air attack and the problems caused by distance from the organization with which their work was closely linked were sufficient for a second move down south, to be approved in principle by the Air Ministry within a matter of weeks (to be precise, 6 December 1939). Naturally, moves like this are not arranged overnight and it was not until the evening of Saturday 4 May 1940 that Dundee ceased to function, that weekend being taken up with the transfer of personnel and equipment to this Air Ministry research establishment's new home in the vicinity of the charming Dorset village of Worth Matravers, some 4 miles from the seaside resort of Swanage.

The move came about through pressure from Rowe and senior members of his staff who had met as early as 13 October 1939, Rowe making it perfectly clear that while he was aware of a growing feeling that Dundee was unsuitable for RDF research work, the choice was quite simple. If he was given strong reasons for proposing an alternative location he would do what he could to have his superiors come up to see him next day for a conference to thrash out the whys and wherefores, otherwise everyone must put up with that site for the duration of the war.

Everyone could put in his two pennyworth regarding requirements. In an ideal world, it appeared, the new site would be no more than a couple of hours from Fighter Command at Stanmore, which assessed the impact of contacts achieved by the coastal radar stations, and a similar journey to the offices of the Director of Communications Development in London, the establishment's parent organization. It would not be much further away from Kidbrooke and other sites where there was a particular affinity in their research activities; minimum wind and rain (a condition which Dundee certainly could not meet); security (not necessarily close to an RDF Station and behind the Fighter Defences); near or on the coast; adequate telephone, rail and road communications; suitable living accommodation; flying facilities; and not too distant from firms building RDF equipment. The adequacy of the electrical supply could go without saying – Dundee, surprisingly, offered only a DC system!

Arguments were presented for and against the neighbourhoods of Worthing, Bournemouth and Weston-super-Mare. Within a fortnight all work ceased on preparing what would have been the new research establishment at Douglas Wood. Impatience was understandable, with bureaucracy seemingly dragging its heels sufficiently for Rowe, four weeks after Swanage had been selected 'as the best site we could find in war', to complain to his superiors that a decision appeared to have been delayed because there was no available neighbouring aerodrome when in fact 'the need for proximity can be exaggerated'. An indication of the frustrations of that period are best appreciated initially in the context of Rowe's acceptance that site selection was influenced by topographical matters such as contours and cliffs (and their effect on flying conditions within a 30 mile radius) and then in his admission in the same memo that 'we are indeed difficult to please and there seems only to be one Bawdsey'.[9]

Upwards of 200 people would be involved in this move. As well as the scientists, technicians, clerical staff and others transferred from Dundee it embraced individuals serving elsewhere, including St Athan and Stanmore.

With an initial target date of the end of March 1940 for completion, the early weeks of the year saw seven wooden buildings (six laboratories and a workshops building) en route to Swanage; there was a contract in place for further buildings of brick construction; a firm in Winchester would be putting up three 240-ft timber towers and another a smaller one, 90 ft high, the familiar hardware of such an establishment. Imagine the consternation among residents when the massive structures began taking shape. One of the locals, in a letter dated 27 February 1940 in which he offered his premises ahead of possible requisition, drew Rowe's attention to gossip being rife and ideas being broadcast 'which vary between the suggestion that the station is one for generating destructive rays, and the idea that it is simply a wireless station'.

If the science fiction suggestion was dismissed, there still remained a sinister aspect to this gentleman's letter – it came from a retired naval officer

– when he indicated that the contractors were understood to have built similar sites previously, and that on one occasion it had been bombed within a few days of completion. A more detailed version of this same story, if fiction it should prove to be, reached Rowe's desk from Watson Watt, via senior officers at the Admiralty and the Air Ministry. It relayed the information that 'one of the men on the job is telling the village that, when he was in the Shetlands, doing the same job, the German planes came down and bombed them, killing fifteen men and blowing all their half-built work, masts etc., to blazes'. Rowe, charged by his superiors with doing whatever was practicable to nail the culprit, breathed fire into the response he sent back swiftly to London: 'This is a really shocking example of foolishness.'[10]

While work proceeded on completing the site, the initial layout of what would be known as the Air Ministry Research Establishment, Worth Matravers, became evident, having already been extended in intent with a communications building, two laboratories, five huts, a first aid room and, visible way beyond the confines of the site, still more of those aerial arrays, six 20-ft CHL towers (standing for Chain Home Low, the name given to the chain of coastal radar early warning installations that picked up indications of incoming enemy aircraft, even those approaching at low level).[11]

Meanwhile, the move of the establishment's Special Duty Flight from the RAF base at St Athan in South Wales to a small private airfield (the much handier Christchurch airport) proceeded, with plans drawn up for the advance party to leave on 27 April and the road and rail parties on 29 April. The air party would depart on 2 May with its two apiece complement of Anson, Blenheim and Battle aircraft, each fitted out with whatever RDF gadgetry was in vogue at the time. As for the airfield's facilities, it became a matter of making best use of the clubhouse, mess room, wooden hut housing five Moth aircraft with their wings folded, and the small workshop. These, together with new buildings to come later, would accommodate the Special Duty Flight, Research Section and Fitting Party, the aim being to allow the work programme, conducted in conjunction with the AMRE personnel, to proceed with minimum inconvenience when Worth Matravers began operating on 6 May 1940 after the weekend move from Dundee.[12]

Given the imminence of the enemy threat to overrun France, Belgium, Holland, Luxembourg and Denmark, and the likelihood that their forces would do no more than pause before carrying on across the English Channel, it has to be acknowledged that the timing of the AMRE move was hardly perfect and its direction somewhat surprising. Events were overtaking each other, however, and Rowe's consternation on finding that he must now consider shifting the personnel and their apparatus once more, and more quickly this time, can be appreciated. The Director of Communications Development set the priorities: be ready first to evacuate papers which could be useful to the enemy, then take gear needed to carry on essential research work, and finally to smash remaining equipment – not merely to make it useless but, more importantly, so that its function was incapable of discovery.

Rowe, a man who must have hated to see any i with its dot missing or a t uncrossed, sought his superiors' policy on various contingencies. For example, what was to be done in the event of a commando-style attack aimed specifically at Worth Matravers, the sole intent being to destroy equipment and personnel? He also wanted a statement on the relative importance of personnel and equipment (the answer was that personnel *did* come first and that particular efforts should be made to safeguard key men among the scientists). He can surely be excused that rather high-blown phrase of his that 'If need be, I am sure the Establishment will defend its equipment to the last scientist'.

Rowe put forward his own ideas for continuing the work of his people rather than evacuate them to somewhere that was going to be unprepared and unsuitable. Why not, he mooted, set up a research establishment in Canada? Then, if the United States came into war, the staff might work in conjunction with them at, for example, the Bell Telephone Laboratories. Alternatively, dissolve the staff of AMRE; the air work could perhaps be done at the Royal Aircraft Establishment, basic work within the universities, and a large percentage of the staff, working under the RAF's No. 60 (Signals) Group, could assist at Kidbrooke and at the various CH and CHL stations. Clearly this would have been the last ditch attempt – 'The disintegration of this Establishment would, I am convinced, gravely affect the war of 1941 and 1942,' he wrote.

Of course the need did not arise for an enforced departure from Worth Matravers although, for the record, it can be said that steps were taken both to find someone to feed and water the 300 or so members of the scientific staff for the first two or three days if invasion came (they would have gathered at No. 2 Signals School, RAF Yatesbury) and to look for suitable accommodation to house, as and when required, a nucleus of 50 key personnel to carry out experimental work. The Royal Holloway College at Englefield Green in Surrey, the Anglo-Iranian Company at Sunbury, Middlesex, and the Distiller Company at Great Burgh, Epsom, Surrey, were all proposed and inspected for this purpose.[13]

By the winter of 1940/1, TRE, as it was now becoming known (its full title of Telecommunications Research Establishment confined to those who were in the know), was tackling an impressive range of projects which were all reviewed when the first of a series of planning conferences was held on 12 November 1940, with Rowe as chairman and J.F.W. Mercer as secretary. It was an opportunity to have everyone benefit from an overview of the Establishment's responses to its many challenges, a way of shedding a little light, where possible, on what was going on outside the confines of one's own workplace. Mercer's minutes leave no doubt as to the wealth of expertise being brought together within this one research centre: some of the mind-blowing subjects discussed at this meeting were the possibility of locating submarines using RDF or similar devices, the destruction of enemy vessels by RDF-directed gunfire or torpedo action, enhancement of the

RDF chain – which had more than proved its value as a decisive weapon during the Battle of Britain; the homing and blind landing of night-fighters, the urgent need for ensuring visual contact after a successful airborne interception (AI), general problems related to the possibility of blind shooting, and what might be construed as the more umbrella-like description of improving airborne and seaborne radio equipment. In the current context it is relevant to note that a further topic briefly discussed at that initial planning conference was the possibility of using RDF for blind-bombing, even for dropping aerial torpedoes or other lethal devices.[14]

This was November 1940, remember, and there would still be a long way to go from the concept of using range and direction-finding for the bombing-the-bomber defensive role to the adoption of those same principles for an offensive purpose, that of first getting a bomber to its objective and then facilitating the release of its load on to its target. Furthermore, both these functions would have to be achieved not only blind but with a degree of accuracy that had hitherto been beyond the bounds of capability. In broad terms, this would be the task facing a team of enthusiasts being brought together as Group 4, which had at its core little more than a handful of people with a formidable mix of skills in a variety of scientific disciplines.

A single product would emerge as a result of their endeavours, its name Oboe, though in reality there was more than one Oboe. Like so many other creations before and since, Oboe had its critics as well as its supporters – for example, those nurturing its stages of development had to contend with pressures intent on a premature launch – and times were when its use had to come under tight control for fear that the enemy might become aware of its existence and, maybe, by accident or design, appreciate its weaknesses. It is a fact, too, that even among those with the greatest need for such a promising tool, caution was ever-present, as if perhaps here was something that was maybe too good to be true. While the success of Oboe was sweet music to many ears, for some its tone was less harmonious.

Flying Down the Beam

'I have always prided myself on executing the first blind landing in thick fog in aviation history . . . apart from what happened to the pitot head of my aircraft, the only damage was to my pride!' The Reverend Group Captain 'Roger' Reece DSO, OBE, DFC, AFC, recalling an incident during his time as an instructor at Boscombe Down in the early months of the Second World War. As a beam pilot with No. 109 Squadron, he was captain of the first aircraft to bomb with early Oboe on 21 April 1941 over Cherbourg.

Throughout two world wars as well as in peacetime, one problem in particular has confronted aviators; indeed, recalling a phrase popular among RAF aircrew members during the Second World War, it has existed 'ever since Pontius was a pilot'. The problem: controlling an aircraft and maintaining safe flight in times of poor or non-existent visibility. With sight lost in total or in part in such a situation, one of the remaining human senses comes into its own – that of hearing. A pilot's ability to listen has long been the salvation when it comes to flying safely, even providing the means to bring a plane right back home and then to facilitate a landing in complete safety.

Imagine being a pilot in a basic kind of flight simulator: the familiar array of display dials jumps into life, the joystick and rudder pedals providing the means to change the height and the direction of the aircraft. In this make-believe environment you are instructed to be aware that the home airfield is close, the aircraft is at a safe height, but there is no way of looking out of the cockpit – the enclosing hood makes it seem as if you are flying in absolute darkness. Sounds help though, messages of one sort or another that you hear, conceivably of varying audible strengths of dots and dashes on either side of a flight path that merge into an equi-signal when 'spot on'. These offer the means to get you from point A to point B, to bring you back home to your own airfield, to guide you down towards the welcoming runway. Then, in a real situation, there will hopefully be a succession of powerful lights arrowing into the distance, maybe even a fog-dispersal system, to help banish the darkness sufficiently for a safe touchdown.

As long ago as the 1920s and the 1930s, airliners were using sounds as a method of international navigation and also to guide the planes on the final leg towards the runway allocated for their landing. These sounds were generated from the ground, by means of radio transmitters; the pilot would hear those signals, which would take one of any number of varying forms, and these readily recognizable sounds – perhaps the dots and dashes of Morse code – provided him with the information he needed to maintain a given course. The most widely known system, the Lorenz beam, originated in Germany. It was developed by Dr Hans Plendl, a scientist specializing in the study of radio waves. Although there have been many permutations of this form of instrument assistance, the core concept is simplicity itself. A radio station on the ground beams an invisible path towards the aircraft while the pilot, listening to that sound, manoeuvres his plane to the left or to the right so as to fly directly towards the transmitter, the optimum sound confirming the required line of flight.

In a nutshell, this was the principle used by bombers of the opposing air forces when finding their way to the target area in darkness in the Second World War. The wonders of science being what they are, a far more complex form, but still with radio pulse signalling as a basic element, came into being as the ground-controlled blind-bombing invention known as Oboe. Is it surprising, then, to find that No. 109 Squadron, whose personnel worked alongside those of TRE throughout the creation and implementation of Oboe, originated and was nurtured as a specialist unit that had been charged with developing and teaching blind flying techniques.

Under the name Blind Approach Training and Development Unit (BAT&DU) and based at RAF Station, Boscombe Down, close to Salisbury Plain in Wiltshire, it brought together at the outset two people who were vital to the successful use of radio by the RAF for range and direction finding in its various forms: Squadron Leader R.S. Blucke and Flying Officer H.E. Bufton. The former had already earned one of the top awards bestowed for distinguished service in a non-operational environment, the Air Force Cross (with a second to follow), and the latter would also receive this same honour. Pre-war, Blucke had been giving instruction in VHF blind approach at Mildenhall; the formation of BAT&DU, when war came in September 1939, put that capability on an established basis, the need for 'production line' training being quickly recognized. Bufton, who was a bomber pilot with No. 214 Squadron at the outbreak of war, received a posting to BAT&DU before the month was out; he would have a dominant and enduring connection with Oboe, beginning in those formative times and continuing right through to its operational use in Pathfinder Force.

Air Ministry Organisation Memorandum No. 385/1939 outlined the function of BAT&DU which, in that first month of its existence, received its first aircraft, its first equipment and its first flying instructors. Besides Bufton, two non-commissioned officers were posted in for flying instruction duties. Warrant Officer K. Munro, coming from SHQ Hendon, had been attached to the Air Ministry Directorate of Training in a role with the Link Trainer system used for ground-based blind-flying instruction, and Sergeant A. Reece from the School of Air Navigation. Both men would gain commissions with BAT&DU and both would experience a logged crash-landing within the year while engaged on the very work that this new unit had been formed to tackle, that of overcoming the difficulties encountered when bringing down an aircraft whose pilot is flying virtually blind. One would lose his life, the other – who came through the unit's first crash-landing unscathed – going on to hazardous flying of a sort far different from what was envisaged on the posting to BAT&DU.

Everyone was naturally keen to see the new unit functioning with the minimum delay and this was achieved, a Link Trainer having been installed in suitable accommodation in a C-type hangar, lecture room facilities provided and the first instructional flights having taken place by the end of the month. The first month's tally of a modest three flights lasting 1 hour 55 minutes, with ten pilots under beam-flying instruction, compares with the unit's peak month, August 1940, when there were 275 flights, a total of 322 hours 40 minutes flying time and 736 pilots under instruction.[1]

The incident involving Reece occurred on 5 February 1940. In recalling those pioneering days, when structured tuition for RAF pilots on bringing down an aircraft purely on instruments was in its infancy, there seems some justification for taking this opportunity to set the record straight on an episode that the BAT&DU Operations Record Book described at the time as being a 'crash-landing' at Boscombe Down in 'poor visibility'. It appears, in fact, that surprisingly this statement was far from the truth.

As Reece asserts:

I have always prided myself on executing the first blind landing in thick fog in aviation history, when referring to that particular touchdown, so it is my contention that to call what happened a 'crash' is as much an exaggeration as it is an understatement to describe the visibility at the time of the landing as being 'poor'. As I remember it, if anyone had had the misfortune to be groping about on the ground alongside the touchdown point, they would have been lucky to see even as much as ten yards ahead of them.

I had two passengers on board [pilots under instruction] and I was demonstrating how to make a blind landing, hearing in my headphones the signals from the beam that takes you towards where you are to land and then listening out for the audio signals from the outer and inner ground markers that each indicate the distance to touchdown. It was a perfect landing, only then the aircraft veered to the left – a distance of perhaps 100 yards in 1,500 yards. This was due to a combination of two factors, the fog making it impossible to see anything out of the cockpit and because the compasses that we used in those days couldn't cope with changes in an aircraft's speed and attitude – errors caused by acceleration and deceleration. Anyway, having completed the landing successfully, I continued taxiing but unfortunately into the barbed-wire fence at the far end of the field, where the pitot head, which protrudes from the nose of the aircraft and measures airspeed, hit a post. When visibility improved, I brought the aircraft back to the hangar and assessed the outcome of my 'crash-landing in poor visibility'. Apart from the pitot head, the only damage was to my pride!

Six months later though, I did have a real crash-landing, at Wyton, when I was executing a blind landing in the dark and without my airspeed indicator working. There was an aircraft parked illegally on the landing runway and I landed on top of it. My Anson was a write-off but all of us on board walked away unhurt. We had some narrow scrapes in those pioneering days and not everyone was so fortunate [see page 18].[2]

There was much to be done in the unit and little enough time to do all that was needed. As a consequence, those early months of 1940 saw new arrangements being made for the courses that BAT&DU ran for its students. Fortnightly courses of six pupils each were staggered weekly so that a new course began each week, the first week being devoted to Link Trainer instruction and preliminary blind approach flying, the second week to advanced instruction. A further flying instructor arrived, Flying Officer R.J. Sage from No. 76 Squadron, but a change in the Air Ministry's requirements, which made best use of recently developed skills within the unit, saw BAT&DU both close down and reopen in the space of just one week.

In a game of musical chairs at which the armed forces were adept, the Air Ministry posting instructions saw Blucke, Bufton, Munro and Reece departing, only to return in a matter of days when the unit came back to life on 13 June 1940 in a challenging new format, its aircraft establishment increased to eight Ansons and three Whitleys with a corresponding increase in aircrews. Within the week, Blucke, a spell at Fighter Command Headquarters behind him and now sporting the thicker middle ring of a Wing Commander, set to work reorganizing the former comparatively small blind-flying instructional unit into a much larger one which was to be engaged on highly secret flying operations – finding out all there was to know about enemy wireless signals which it was obvious going to be beamed across Britain from radio stations in countries already being occupied, to create unseen corridors the bombers could follow to and from their targets.

The quite dramatic changes affecting BAT&DU were all part of a rapid move to set up an organization under the Deputy Director of Signals 'Y' in response to a significant discovery that could affect the way that Britain's defences needed to react to the threat of aerial bombardment. What had happened was that one of the ground stations listening in routinely to enemy wireless traffic (it was at Cheadle) reported picking up German beam-type transmissions on the 31.5 megacycles frequency. It seemed highly likely that this was some form of navigational aid to Luftwaffe crews briefed to strike at targets in Britain. The first essential was to concentrate on this particular beam and then to see what others were lurking in the airwaves; there were certain to be others, perhaps using alternative frequencies and emanating from the same source, as well as other sources transmitting on still more frequencies.

Wing Commander Blucke was put in charge of these investigations with Bufton and another officer, Pilot Officer R. Gore, to assist him at Wyton, which was the airfield nominated for these early experimental flights. The equipment being placed at their disposal provided the facility to tune in to those signals: for ground observations there would be a van fitted with a Hallicrafter receiver and a diathermy jammer set on 31.5 megacycles, while for their unique role in beam detection from the air there would be a single

Anson aircraft fitted with Lorenz blind-landing apparatus, equipment which was perfectly familiar to the two senior officers because of their time spent with BAT&DU at Boscombe Down (in Blucke's case, earlier still, having run the predecessor instruction courses at Mildenhall just before the outbreak of war). In this race against time to track down those beams, which obviously could guide the incoming bombers to their target area and back home again, thus simplifying the crew's task enormously and ensuring greater success for each intended raid on Britain, the pressure was on to get Blucke's 'beam hunters' into the air right away. So, one Anson would be prepared immediately, with the promise of two more to follow the moment they could be made ready with their gadgetry.[3]

By the end of the first week in the unit's new role, all three Ansons (N9945, N9938 and L7967) had been prepared for operational flying; Sage was there, a newcomer, with old stagers Bufton – whose title would be Officer Commanding, Flying – and Munro. Reece rejoined a week later, on the same day as another newcomer, Pilot Officer P.B. Hennessy from Cottesmore. These two men would merit the distinction of becoming the first pilots to use Oboe on a bombing mission; five days apart, these separate attacks occurred long before those on Lutterade power station to which the history books have attributed this milestone.

Arriving on a temporary attachment a day ahead of Bufton, Flight Lieutenant R.K. Budge had the responsibility for installing and testing special equipment in the Anson aircraft N9945 so that it could be pressed into service right away in its new role. The requirement for such investigations having been recognized before the due processes of aircrew postings could be accomplished, it transpired that the plane was ready before its intended crew. As a consequence, for the very first flight, a pilot was provided by the Aeroplane and Armament Experimental Establishment (A&AEE) at Boscombe Down, while on hand was a member of the radio countermeasures organisation at the Air Ministry, Flight Lieutenant E.J. Alway. He had instructions to report immediately to London by telephone once the Anson was back on the ground.

There was an apt name for these investigations of the enemy's wireless signals, a name that summed up better than most the situation in which the Air Ministry found itself, with these invisible beams likely to be crisscrossing Britain and just about the only possibility of finding them quickly (short of obtaining worthwhile information from a prisoner of war knowing something about it, or, more unlikely still, getting one's hands on the equipment and/or the relevant paperwork) seemed to be to have roaming aircraft listening in in the hope of picking up those signals. The name given to this operation? 'Headache'.[4]

It is easy to appreciate the choice of this name. With blind-flying techniques, the position on the radio dial to receive a particular signal would naturally be known to those needing to use it; with an enemy transmitted signal, however, advance knowledge of its location would be a luxury beyond belief. Which was why someone like Blucke, Bufton or one of the others in this newly created unit had to be on hand to carry out such investigative flights, the pilots realizing what was required of them and working closely with a specially trained wireless operator capable of tuning in his signal-receiving equipment with sufficient dexterity that it would practically sing him a song.

It would be rewarding to learn that the haste to get the first Anson airborne, while warranted by the pressure of the moment, in fact justified itself with the results obtained in this initial crack at trying to locate first the path of the beam and then the source of its transmitter. Perhaps that would have been expecting too much. Nevertheless it did turn out to be a case of third time lucky when, on the evening of 21 June, with Bufton flying the Anson and Corporal D.J. Mackey his wireless operator, a narrow beam, 400 to 500 yards wide, made its presence known to this airborne investigative team. The beam passed a position 1 mile south of Spalding, with dots to the south and dashes to the north, on a bearing of 104 degrees – 284 degrees true. As a student of electronic warfare and author of a history of this subject asserted subsequently, 'It would be difficult to overestimate the importance of this discovery. . . . Now it seemed that the Germans could operate effectively in the dark; the targets in Britain were naked and exposed.'[5]

News of the existence of those beams (and of course any retaliatory aspirations) stayed under wraps. As far as the British public was concerned, summer 1940 was a bleak enough moment in the country's history. Places closest to them were being overrun, even the Channel Islands falling beneath the Nazi jackboots, and there was the threat of invasion becoming more and more pronounced with the knowledge that troop-carrying vessels were assembling in the Channel ports. Enemy bombers were overhead, bombs were crashing down upon industrial objectives and civilians alike; the Battle of Britain was in full swing, the tally of downed aircraft compared with defending fighters being presented as if this was a cricket match in progress beneath those clear blue skies. Nothing could be said about the lone aircraft that were roaming those same skies, by night as well as by day, searching for evidence of the invisible tramlines, BAT&DU pilots on patrol while their wireless operators supervized their equipment, twiddling knobs and listening for tell-tale sounds in their headphones. To keep in with the cricketing analogy, these crews could be likened to the outfielders waiting attentively, ever hopeful, in anticipation of a catch coming their way. Unfortunately, the odds were heavily against those in the air; not only was it problematical being in the right place to pick up the right signals, it was necessary to be there at the right time too – the beam transmissions being turned on only when required for operational purposes and during training periods.

So much was going on, in fact, during those summer months, that a number of complementary operations were introduced with BAT&DU the common factor, such was its experience, its fast-growing skills and the facilities offered by its crews, its aircraft and its equipment. There were the beams themselves to be detected, which was the opening task for Bufton and his crews, who were operating from RAF Station Wyton as well as from their Boscombe Down home base. Then, with the beams located, countermeasures were obviously the next step. Again this suggested the possibility of further airborne activities and these would fall naturally in BAT&DU's lap. There would be the need to interfere with the beams in order to remove or to diminish their value as a navigational aid; although this might well be the prerogative of ground stations set up for this purpose, aircraft would be required to test their performance. Also, there was the prospect of making use of those same beams to confuse enemy aircraft, which was something akin to turning a science fiction plot into reality, again calling for aircraft to contribute by determining the practicability of such activities.

Life in the unit had its ups and downs. July saw the arrival of Pilot Officer L.G. Bull from No. 9 Squadron, which was flying bombers, and two members of a squadron that was using aircraft of an altogether different sort – Flying Officer C.V.D. Willis and Flying Officer J.S. Kendrick, who came from No. 201 Squadron at Sullom Voe. The arrival of this pair was no doubt the source of some amusement because both were pilots from a squadron equipped with the huge four-engined Sunderland flying boat. (How were they going to cope with an airfield runway and who would be the first to commit the unforgivable and experience touchdown with the wheels still retracted?) A further new arrival the same month was Flying Officer H.J. Cundall, who would later go on to fly with both Oboe Mosquito squadrons and command the second of them, No. 105 Squadron.

Two of the Whitley bombers suffered damage during this period, an Anson was written off at Wyton and a further Anson crashed at Boscombe Down while making a blind approach landing in fog at night. Munro was the captain and pilot this time and he died in his plane, as did one of the NCOs in his crew. Two more died either in or on their way to hospital. One of the dead men was a member of an Air Ministry radio countermeasures establishment who had taken part in the very first investigations into the enemy's beams over Britain, Flight Lieutenant E.J. Alway. It was Alway who reported back to the Air Ministry after the initial flight on 19 June and it was Alway who flew as wireless operator the following day when Bufton made his début investigative flight on resuming his service with BAT&DU. There was just a single survivor of this fatal crash, Sergeant A.D.F. Allen, air gunner, who escaped with only slight injuries. Allen was awarded the George Medal for his actions during this incident, which was unfortunately followed two months later by another fatal crash when an Anson from the Wyton detachment – N9945, the first of the unit's Ansons to be equipped for beam detection – came down near Birmingham and burnt itself out with the loss of all five who were on board, the indications being that it became entangled in the defensive balloon barrage.

By now BAT&DU had moved another step nearer to becoming an operational squadron, specializing in the work in which it had been involved since the outbreak of war, the activity that is sometimes called 'riding the beam'. With effect from 30 September 1940, the Blind Approach Training and Development Unit (to accord BAT&DU its full title for the last time) received a new name – the Wireless Intelligence Development Unit (WIDU). For a time, WIDU stayed the operational responsibility of the Air Ministry's Directorate of Signals, then, on 1 November 1940, control was transferred to No. 80 (Signals) Wing. Precise a descriptive title as it surely was, WIDU would remain the unit's name only until 10 December 1940 when the final christening took place, WIDU becoming No. 109 Squadron and led briefly by Bufton until the arrival of its first commanding officer, Wing Commander W.S. Hebden from No. 80 Wing, just before the end of the year.*

The transfer of control and the choice of command was logical since No. 80 Wing, formed as recently as 7 October 1940 at Aldenham Lodge, Radlett, Herts, had packed considerable experience of radio countermeasures (RCM) into a comparatively short time. It had begun life just three months earlier as a section of the Directorate of Signals at the Air Ministry and headed by Wing Commander E.B. Addison, its primary function being to provide a countermeasure organization against German radio navigational aids.

This was a period of No. 109's life (first as BAT&DU, then as WIDU) which merits particular attention, because this was the birth of Britain's radio countermeasures activities in so far as they relate to the use of aircraft – in conjunction with other means – to wreak havoc among enemy planes flying over this country. It is a role that deserves acknowledgement outside the words of praise to be found in the formal documentation of the time.

It will be recalled that the unit was operating from Boscombe Down with a detachment at Wyton. This was the airfield from which the first experimental flights were carried out to see whether specially adapted Lorenz blind-approach equipment installed in Anson aircraft was capable of picking up evidence of enemy wireless signals being beamed across Britain from transmitters on the Continent, to help their own aircraft find and maintain required courses for navigational purposes.

'Headache', the name given to this operation run by Addison's team, involved the unit's key personnel: Blucke and Bufton were flying from Boscombe Down, Sage was running the Wyton detachment, with Kendrick and Gore working from the operation's control point, codenamed 'Radium'.

Observations making use of equipment carried aboard the unit's aircraft and located at ground stations, came up with signals on up to a dozen occasions on the 31.5 megacycles frequency prior to 10 July 1940, the width

---

* There was a No. 109 Squadron in the First World War, though its career was brief and undistinguished. It was formed in November 1917, the nucleus coming from No. 61 Training School, and disbanded in August 1918.

of that 'pathway in the sky' remarkably being less than a quarter of a mile in part. The origination point was judged to be in the area of Cleves. It was not always possible to detect either this or other beams, however, and there were times when no definite signals were obtained either by the test flights or the ground stations. Equally, ground observations indicated that there could well be a beam operating that the airborne equipment failed to substantiate, perhaps for the very good reason that, by the time the aircraft had been scrambled and attained sufficient height in a favourable geographical position, the beam had been turned off.

The distances covered by the enemy's beams were substantial. In one instance, in which an Anson was despatched from Wyton to investigate, the beam reached as far as the Orkneys; in fact a radar plot showed an unidentified aircraft in that vicinity which conjecture put as being a reconnaissance flight testing the value of the beam at long range. Another instance indicated a beam up the North Sea, probably laid on the Shetlands, which preceded an air raid on the Orkneys. The suggestion was that one or other of those two beams was used in the approach and/or on the return flight.

The beam that was thought to have originated in the area of Cleves was soon to become an old friend to the BAT&DU crews since some ten flights in mid-August 1940 produced as many as six occasions when this beam was successfully located. Evidence so gained indicated an effective range of 350 miles at 15,000 ft for navigational purposes.

New friends as well as old put in an appearance from time to time. Munro, learning that signals had been picked up on an unfamiliar frequency, carried out an investigational flight on the morning of 20 August 1940 and managed to pick up the beam some 4 miles from Abingdon, its width no greater than half a mile, and its source presumably in the neighbourhood of Husum, judging from the compass bearing. It was, 'Headache' Control noted, a 'most successful' flight.

The Cherbourg area, presumably because of its proximity to the south coast of England, appeared to be the source of more than one transmitter. Towards the end of August, Les Pieux, about 15 miles south-west of Cherbourg, emerged as the location of one transmitter operating on a frequency of 30 megacycles; by 4 September, a new beam using 66.3 megacycles was operating, again from this peninsula, and within a week a routine flight from Boscombe Down had established yet another, this time on about 68.1 megacycles.

Headache Control was lavish in its praise for Blucke who 'deserves special mention' for a 'particularly fine and painstaking flight' on 2 October 1940 to investigate 69 megacycles signals from the Cherbourg area when, it was noted, 'as a result of the very careful navigation, 11 beams were accurately determined and the bearings of 5 of these measured'.[6]

Further flights by WIDU aircraft during October 1940 drew more general praise, another of Headache Control's reports making reference to their 'excellent and accurate flying and navigational work carried out under difficult conditions'. It was all part of a complex programme to obtain definite information about the presence of particular beams, especially those given such names as Spree, Weser, Elbe, Isar and Rhine, this 'Rivers' group – emanating in the Cherbourg area – later being given an alternative name which would loom largely whenever No. 109 Squadron referred to its soon-to-come offensive action against those transmitters – 'Ruffians'.

In the course of these investigations, three main beam systems were found to be in use, Knickebein and Benito as well as 'Ruffian', their main characteristics and modes of operation soon revealing themselves under a relentless series of flights by crews from Wyton and Boscombe Down which continued through the summer, autumn and into the winter of 1940/1 without loss, damage or injury. By November 1940, Cherbourg-based Ruffian was judged so substantial a threat that more positive steps had to be taken to reduce its benefit to enemy bombers than relying solely on routine jamming to upset its use as an aid to their navigators. As these were still the early days of the RAF's bombing experiences, doubts were cast concerning the prospect of successfully hitting a target as small as a wireless transmitter installation, especially during the hours of darkness. But, maybe, after all, an opportunity just might arise, accepting that, uniquely, this particular target gave away its precise location every time that the beam was turned on!

It might be imagined that, when flying along the beam towards its transmitter, a cone of silence above it would betray the source of the signals, those tell-tale sounds no longer being picked up when directly overhead. It would be like dropping a bomb down a chimney – or would it? Unfortunately that anticipation turned out to be wishful thinking; there was a period when the signals dried up, true enough, but this cone of silence was incapable of measurement, 'ill-defined' is the term used in the relevant report from Headache Control. And in any event, bombs don't fall directly beneath their release point; in order to hit their target, bombs have to be dropped a determinable length of time before the aircraft arrives overhead. There was, however, a bonus of some sort coming out of this particular experimental flight; the radio countermeasures that had been activated against this beam proved so successful that it became impossible to continue riding the beam back to England once the aircraft had passed roughly the midway point in the Channel.[7]

Even so, bombing was considered a worthwhile proposition despite the lack of any means other than navigational skills to locate the target. A series of reports prepared by Headache Control for No. 80 Wing give an idea of some of the problems that WIDU (and subsequently No. 109 Squadron) had to face when its Whitley aircraft began, on 12 November 1940, a series of bombing attacks on the source of the Cherbourg transmissions.

On the night of 6 December, for example, with fairly accurate, heavy calibre, anti-aircraft fire directed against them, two aircraft had difficulty finding the beam anyway and, the visibility being bad, only one dropped its bombs – doing so without seeing the results. The next night, again experiencing trouble trying to follow the beam, the decision was taken to bomb the probable site by a visual fix on the coast; it was seen that the bombs fell on land but away from the intended target. On another occasion, the night of 23 December 1940, bombing on 31.5 megacycles, there was perhaps the most encouraging sign throughout this whole series of raids: the signals actually stopped in the midst of No. 109's bombing raid. This cessation occurred when their bombs exploded very near the target but, to everyone's bitter disappointment, the signals came on again later in the evening. It seemed likely that some part of the installation had been put out of action but that later it had been repaired or replaced to resume the beam.

As the year drew to a close, No. 80 Wing and of course No. 109 Squadron, the only front-line unit under its control, turned their thoughts towards ways of achieving greater accuracy when bombing these targets. Within the Telecommunications Research Establishment at Worth Matravers too, the aim of improving bombing efficiency overall was a subject very much in their minds. In the coming weeks, with those threatening radio beams continuing to radiate from the Cherbourg peninsula – those 'Ruffian' installations, so small yet so important as targets – the flying skills of No. 109 Squadron and the inventive genius of TRE, with whom No. 80 Wing was working on countermeasures techniques, would combine into a dynamic partnership unrivalled in more than four years of aerial warfare.

CHAPTER THREE

Enter the 'Broody Hen'

'A successful "Oboe" flight was made last night and I have thought it proper to take this opportunity to bring to the notice of Group Captain Addison those who have helped us in this scheme.' Wing Commander W.S. Hebden, No. 109 Squadron's first Commanding Officer, writing to HQ No. 80 (Signals) Wing on 27 April 1941 – Group Captain E.B. Addison was in command of No. 80 Wing. The letter was copied to TRE and named members of its staff who conceived the system and developed it for this début operational application

New Year 1941 ushered in a remarkable new era for No. 109 Squadron, whose crews had become initiated into bombing operations against the enemy beam-transmitting installations on the Cherbourg peninsula. It was obvious that more must be done to intensify the attacks on those beam sources; to do so would require more aircraft, the crews to fly them and above all some means to improve the bombing accuracy. All of this was made to happen in the opening days of January, spurred on no doubt by the acceptance that radio countermeasures were an indispensable part of the nation's defences and pressure from the organization that was responsible for them, No. 80 (Signals) Wing.

Visiting No. 109 on 2 January, Wing Commander C. Cadell, a member of No. 80 Wing's operations staff, provided two items of complementary welcome news: he would see to it that the long-awaited captains of aircraft, coming along through the operational training unit system, would materialize, and he let it be known that steps were in hand to ensure that none of the present flying crews would be posted away until new ones were ready to take their place. As for the aircraft for the current and replacement crews to fly, a solitary Whitley was all that remained serviceable at that moment although four new bombers, Wellingtons T2513, T2552, T2556 and T2884, were due within forty-eight hours on allotment from No. 8 Maintenance Unit at Little Rissington, Gloucestershire. More interesting still came the news that No. 80 Wing was authorizing the 'de-bombing' of the Whitley aircraft 'so that special IFF trials could be carried out'.

Here, the significance was that these trials, with modified pulsed radio equipment of the kind that friendly aircraft used to identify them from the enemy, brought together No. 109, whose crews would try out this equipment, and the Telecommunications Research Establishment (TRE) at

Worth Matravers, whose people were working on the idea of using these transponders to provide an augmented return signal from an aircraft. If there was some way to use the enemy's beam to determine precise distances from its source, this suggested a method of bombing the transmitter with considerably improved accuracy than had so far been achieved. And, if blind-bombing could be made to work at Cherbourg, it would clearly open up opportunities of infinite benefit to the RAF's struggling bomber offensive.

On 7 January 1941, when Wing Commander Hebden visited TRE with the now Squadron Leader Bufton to hear about the top-secret work taking place there, this meeting with TRE Superintendent Rowe's boffins could reasonably have been described as the union that consummated one of the most effective secret weapons of the Second World War. However, it is unlikely that either of the parties would have come particularly close to recognizing the potential of their baby at the time.

Just the previous day, so far as TRE was concerned, the bombing-the-bombers idea had finally sunk into oblivion with its parent organization, under the Director of Communications Development, becoming acquainted with the fact that with the success of Britain's fighters against enemy formations – The Few against so many – the Air Staff saw little use for bombs of that sort, unless maybe dropped from a fighter. Consequently, ruled the powers-that-be, there was no justification for designing RDF sighting apparatus.[1]

Nonetheless, using RDF to facilitate other forms of bombing – for example, ground-controlled bombing – was not only justified, it was very much a part of the TRE work programme. It was the CHL Group at TRE that had come up with the idea of combining accurate range measurement along a beam with a radio signal to indicate deviation to either side, the result seemingly offering a means of allowing an aircraft to bomb the beam source irrespective of visibility. That system was called 'Howler Chaser', though this was a name which would not last. The name change came about on account of the sound that was heard from the equipment, this modulated continuous wave that formed the note to indicate deviation from the beam. As this sound was thought to resemble something played on an oboe – and 'Oboe' was considered to have a touch of class about it – the name stuck for this particular form of range and direction-finding system in preference to 'Howler Chaser'. Credit for originating the name Oboe goes to one of the scientists concerned, Tony Bates, who became a member of TRE's Oboe group when it was formed on 4 May 1941, dedicated to developing ground-controlled blind-bombing to its full potential.[2]

The readily available Mark IIG IFF transponder that TRE was able to call upon for experiments on the signal return from an aircraft to the ground station swept frequencies on the 1½-metre wavelength band. TRE removed the automatic sweeping mechanism of the 'Cockerel' transponder and required the operator to tune manually to a particular frequency – a change in function that led to a change in name. The lively 'Cockerel', with its capability for constant sweeping of the airwaves, picking up whatever transmissions came its way, now found its activities severely limited; forced to sit on a single frequency, it was performing more as a 'broody hen'. So dubbed, this TRE adaptation of the IFF transponder called for an extremely delicate touch when the operator was adjusting to receive a particular frequency; in addition, it exhibited an aggravating tendency to slip into periods of inactivity at the most inopportune moments. Understandably, no one was exactly cock-a-hoop about the 'Broody Hen', which was not the quality of equipment likely to rule anybody's roost, but for the time being it would have to suffice.[3]

For No. 109 personnel, 'Oboe' entered their vocabulary on 21 January 1941 when Hebden, visiting Dr J. Goodier at Worth Matravers, received a briefing on the system. Unofficially at least, this was now its name. The concept was in a reasonably advanced stage and the two men were able to talk in terms of trials both on the ground, using a Link Trainer, and in an aircraft, with a very real prospect of being able to carry out the first blind-bombing of the Cherbourg beam installations once the equipment was available and the crews knew how to use it. Before the month was out, two-way traffic between the squadron at Boscombe Down and TRE at Worth Matravers increased with a conference at No. 109's base to discuss the development of Oboe and to demonstrate to the scientists the Lorenz beam system. Meanwhile the squadron adjutant, Flight Lieutenant E.T. Downing, and its signals officer, Flight Lieutenant J.N. Walker, attended briefing sessions at TRE.

A new organization had come into force within the squadron too, 'A' Flight being formed and coming under Sage, 'B' Flight formed under Bufton, and Headquarters Flight, which included Maintenance Flight, formed under Walker. As Sage was still at Wyton, Willis was in command of the 'A' Flight party at Boscombe Down.

Bombing against the Ruffian transmitters at Cherbourg resumed on 20 February 1941, with their new Wellingtons taking over from where the comparatively ancient Whitleys – the last remaining stalwarts among pre-war RAF bombers – had left off just before Christmas. Bufton, Cundall and Bull were joined by a new posting, Pilot Officer G.F. Grant, the four pilots lifting off at five-minute intervals and having to contend with bad weather which marred this début operation of the new series. Three nights later these same four men and their crews carried out a repeat performance and there were subsequent operations with a permutation of the original pilots plus another new posting, Flying Officer K.J. Somerville, who came from No. 10 Squadron where he had flown as far as Berlin on bombing missions and been awarded the Distinguished Flying Cross. In three months there were twenty-six such operations to try to knock out the beams, the majority being directed against the Ruffians, although there were also attacks on targets at Morlaix and Barfleur. It was probably the worst time of year to have to contemplate flights of this kind, where crews had to face the most demanding navigational requirements for the greater part of the mission; it was more the norm than otherwise to find ten-tenths cloud to wipe out visibility totally and severe icing to prevent the aircraft climbing to sufficient height.

During this phase, when the bombing was based on sight or judgement and there was dependence upon being able to pick up the transmissions, there was much behind-the-scenes activity taking place to see if blind-bombing could actually be achieved with the newly revealed methods. By 26 February, Willis was already carrying out tests with TRE in connection with Oboe but things had a habit of not keeping to plan all of the time. On 2 March, for example, Reece was all set to put the latest modifications to the IFF equipment through its paces but he was forced to abandon the flight owing to a breakdown in another part of the system. IFF was the electronic equipment, the other failure occurring with a system component that was less advanced in concept but equally vital – that of maintaining Morse contact between ground and aircraft at critical stages.

On 6 April, flying a Wellington Ic, R1534, which had joined the squadron direct from No. 22 Maintenance Unit only a fortnight previously, Reece made the first operational flight to test Oboe, with Barfleur as his objective. There were, though, no cries of jubilation when he touched down at twelve minutes before midnight, the 'Broody Hen' having failed to function at all and, to pile on the agony, even the wireless communications equipment was unsatisfactory. Both were tested in flight the following day and although the fault in the 'Broody Hen' was traced, the other equipment was still playing up, calling for more patient fault-finding procedures. On 10 April, the first time that as many as six Wellingtons had been assembled for operations against the transmitting stations, Bufton, Bull, Cundall, Grant and Somerville were briefed to continue the practice of visual bombing, assuming conditions allowed, while Reece, again using 'his' aircraft, R1534, its radio equipment now hopefully in working order, would use the occasion for a further Oboe test, this time over Cherbourg. The first five crews found disappointment in a complete cloud cover preventing them dropping their bombs visually while Reece suffered another setback because the communications equipment again let him down. On 15 April a morning test flight proved encouraging and another attack was scheduled, Reece to use Oboe while four more Wellingtons followed their usual bombing methods. The flight of two hours forty minutes by Reece and his crew was the best yet, all going well apart from the fact that the bomb-aimer let the side down by acting on the wrong signal.[4]

Operational flights with Oboe were scheduled for successive nights but each time the weather intervened and there had to be cancellations. Consequently it was not until 21 April that Reece was able to carry out the first combined test and bombing operation using Oboe, Hennessy doing a repeat performance on 26 April, the two Wellingtons of No. 109 riding the

Cherbourg-sited enemy beam towards the objective while the release point for the bombs was calculated by TRE at Worth Matravers using the CHL station and the signal passed to the aircraft on the W/T channel.

Whether or not the bombs hit their target was probably an academic point when considering the joint achievements of TRE and No. 109 during those early tentative probings in range and direction finding; after all, they were forced to rely on what were really the most basic bits and pieces, as evidenced by the number of times that this rudimentary rag-bag of radio ramifications failed in test situations and in the ground-controlled attack missions themselves. These operations were, incidentally, given the acronym BBC, which the quick-off-the-mark will realise stood for Blind-Bombing of Cherbourg. Alas, in the event, no serious damage appears to have been accomplished, either by blind, visual or dead-reckoning methods of bombing, and all were abandoned eventually in favour of radio jamming.[5]

Nonetheless, within No. 109 especially, this was rightly seen as a landmark occasion and Hebden, as the squadron's commanding officer, judged this to be the time to go on record with praise for those concerned at TRE in devising Oboe and in bringing it to the point where bombs had been dropped on enemy targets. In a letter dated 27 April 1941, addressed to No. 80 Wing and copied to TRE, he recalled the operational flight with Oboe the previous night and noted that the equipment and the procedure worked smoothly. It seemed, he wrote, an opportune moment to bring to No. 80 Wing's attention the names of those members of TRE who had, as far as his knowledge went, been responsible for the development of this system.

The letter went on: 'The system was conceived and worked on in its experimental stage by Doctor Taylor's Section which includes Dr Goodier, Mr Hopkinson, Mr Bates and Miss Frances. When the system was sufficiently developed for flying tests it passed into the hands of Mr Reeves, who delegated the detailed organization to Dr C.L. Smith and to Mr Hooper who was assisted by Miss Sudbury. Pilot Officer Ackermann of TRE at all times has given invaluable help.'[6]

Hebden concluded by noting his appreciation of the part played by TRE's Superintendent, A.P. Rowe, stating that without his authority and help the scheme would not have been developed. To Rowe himself, Hebden wrote, 'As you will by now have heard a successful 'Oboe' flight was made last night and I have thought it proper to take this opportunity to bring to the notice of Group Captain Addison those who have helped us in this scheme'. Addison, of course, commanded No. 80 Wing, which controlled No. 109 Squadron at that time; as a wing commander, Addison was the man who had been put in charge of the first investigations into the presence of the enemy's navigational beams over Britain in June 1940, this organization including No. 109 aircrew from the outset.

Purists may argue that the 'Oboe' of those pioneering days of blind-bombing bore little resemblance to the unique, highly sophisticated system introduced operationally by Pathfinder Force Mosquito aircraft and their two-man crews towards the end of the following year, in December 1942. It is necessary to establish a starting point for the system, however, and there is no doubt that TRE had staked a claim to the name 'Oboe' during that stage of its evolution. In June 1941, TRE's staff were instructed that in future all papers relating to the main plans on Oboe, together with drawings and other relevant documents most likely to be useful to the enemy, were to be kept within a new Most Secret file, entitled 'Oboe', and that none would be released other than on a signed receipt. No other copies were to be kept elsewhere in TRE, in personal files or wherever; those who had any such documents were to have them put in the new file at once or ensure their destruction.[7] In this determination to guard the Oboe secrets, it seemed only that the term 'under pain of death' was missed out by those charged with drawing up such clear orders for all who worked at TRE.

As for the name itself, its acceptance into aviation nomenclature began with a formal approach to the Director of Communications Development by way of a letter from Mercer, TRE's secretary, dated 18 June 1941. This stated that, within the Establishment, the suggestions for ground-controlled blind-bombing had become known under the title of 'Oboe' and made the point that 'the use of this word rather than a more descriptive title would appear politic'.[8] History shows that TRE had its way: Oboe it was then, with all concerned so enthusiastic about its possibilities, so Oboe it would stay.*

Helping to develop Oboe was far from being the singular purpose of No. 109 during the summer of 1941 and on through the autumn and winter. As No. 80 Wing had other pressing matters to tackle, with aircrews the only people able to get to grips with some of them, inevitably No. 109 – its only such capability – would necessarily be involved. Investigations into the enemy's beam transmissions continued, mostly in search of the Ruffians from Cherbourg and others from elsewhere in Continental Europe, even as far as Norway on occasions when a new series of 319 kilocycle signals was spotted coming from the Stavanger area. In addition to flights to see how effective jamming was proving, countermeasure activities required a contribution from No. 109's aircraft and crews to check the efficiency of Starfish sites. These were the decoy fires lit to attract enemy raiders, their crews assuming that the fires had been caused by bombers that had already found and successfully attacked their objective. Starfish achieved its intentions: for example, during March 1941 alone, among the seventeen occasions when these sites were lit, one near Cardiff drew more than one hundred high-explosive bombs and another, at Bristol, just under seventy-

---

* It stayed sufficiently indelible to warrant, even fifty years on, an appearance in BBC Radio's 'Round Britain' Quiz, which posed the question, What did the following make possible in the '40s: a woodwind instrument, a stinks formula and a word of encouragement to a horse? It should not take too long for readers to spot that all were forms of radar used in the Second World War.[9]

five. Perhaps the best way to determine their value as a distraction to the enemy raiders is to imagine the extent of the casualties and the damage that could have been caused if all, or even some, bombs aimed at the make-believe objective had landed as intended. The point is well illustrated by what happened on the night of 31 August/1 September 1941 when as much as sixty per cent of the effort directed against Hull was mistakenly aimed at the Starfish site, those bombs falling in fields and villages within a 2 mile radius.[10]

From early on in the year, No. 109 crews were busy testing the field strength of the various beam-jamming stations and one such flight, which benefited from being able to use a German receiver to get the real picture, exposed both the advantages and the disadvantages of the jamming practice. With a beam found to be coming from Dieppe and set on the line London–Bedford–Sheffield, the No. 109 aircraft was able to establish what it would have been like for a enemy pilot tuning in to use this beam as a navigational aid. First setting course from Boscombe Down to Bedford, it emerged that for practically the whole of the flight from Bedford to Sheffield and return, a distance of 100 miles, the jamming equipment worked so well that use of the beam was denied. Fine! This showed that the jamming process was meeting its intention. However, with nothing more scientific to fall back upon than the aircraft's compass, it proved possible to complete the Bedford–Sheffield leg and finish up only a few miles off the beam. The significance was that an enemy aircraft would be able to pick up a beam over the English Channel – at a point beyond the scope of possible jamming – and the captain, by setting a compass course, reach his objective with a degree of accuracy dependent upon his skill as a pilot. Jamming was not the be all and end all, after all![11]

In the above episode, where jamming prevented use of the beam, an enemy pilot would have been forced to use conventional navigational practices to find his way across England; what would have happened, though, if that same pilot had been following that same beam and that beam had been deflected in some way? Would the enemy pilot have trusted the beam implicitly, ignoring what his senses told him and followed the beckoning signals to the ends of the earth? An interesting point. Well, crews in No. 109 Squadron had a part to play in determining the proof of that conjecture when No. 80 Wing began sending them up on what were known as 'meacon' flights, meaconing being the function of masking a beacon and causing the intended signal to be substituted by another one – a signal on the same frequency but emanating from a different location. This method of picking up the signals beamed from sources on the Continent and using them to drive British transmitters was evolved with help from the BBC Research Establishment and the GPO Research Establishment. The result of a meacon – a 'misleading beacon' – operation? Utter confusion for any pilot following what he believed to be his own beam when really it was coming from an enemy source.

There were several meacon test flights by No. 109 during September 1941 and in all cases it was shown that enemy beacons were effectively covered over Britain; indeed, in a number of instances, the masking was found to be effective well out to sea over areas of approach frequently used by enemy aircraft. Meaconing had devastating results which not only caused consternation among enemy pilots but even seduced a number of them to land in Britain, yielding up intact aircraft, the equipment that it carried and valuable information that could be obtained from the crew under questioning, not forgetting the documents that it was too late to destroy.

The first time this happened was soon after 0500 hrs on 12 October 1941 when a Dornier Do 217E force-landed at Lydd, one of the airfields in Kent in the south-east corner of England, because the fuel was all but used up. Within No. 80 Wing it proved possible to work out how this plane came to be tricked into giving itself up, by studying the track of the aircraft and the operating schedules of the enemy beacons. The conclusion was that this aircraft, which had been performing a shipping reconnaissance role west of the Scillies, made the mistake of assuming that a meacon operating from Templecombe in Somerset was actually the beacon at Paimpol in Brittany. It seems that when he was over Templecombe, the pilot set course towards what should have been the beacon at Evreux but, presumably getting the north coast of Kent mixed up with the north coast of France, he turned south, finally descending at Lydd. On landing, the crew were under the impression that they were in France; too late, they realized their mistake only when encountering a British soldier. Thanks to this result of meaconing, Britain was able to get its hands on one of the latest examples of blind-flying technology within the Luftwaffe at that time, an E.B1.3 Knickebein and Blind Approach receiver which led the examining experts to deduce that any of thirty-four different frequencies could be quickly and accurately chosen in the air. The following month saw two more instances where navigational shortcomings caused enemy bombers to land in error in the West Country. The first was on 24 November when a Heinkel He 111 force-landed near Helston after experiencing difficulty getting reliable bearings – this crew thought they were over the Brest peninsula when actually it was the Cornish promontory. The Heinkel's belly landing was bettered on 26 November when a Junkers Ju 88, making precisely the same error in directional judgement, landed wheels-down on Chivenor aerodrome, near Barnstaple, complaining (in the manner of a workman blaming his tools!) that their radio equipment was not working properly.[12]

September had seen a marked increase in activity on all three families of frequencies that had been keeping No. 109 busy with its investigation flights – Ruffian, Benito and Knickebein – but less beneficial information had been gained than during previous periods because the signals were being radiated only for a short time. The first to yield their secrets were Knickebein beams with their half-mile or so width at about 200 miles and 20,000 ft, able to be used by all aircraft in the German air force fitted with the standard Lorenz blind-approach receiver. The Ruffians, introduced in the autumn of 1940, came as a logical extension, the higher radio frequency and better aerial system providing very much greater accuracy – a signal path of about 100 yards, with as many as nine beams (with twenty to thirty frequencies) to give No. 80 Wing even more of a nightly 'Headache'. Benito incorporated special characteristics which rendered its interpretation from ground observations alone almost impossible. It was, however, interpreted by TRE and jamming measures were recommended.[13]

Supportive work by No. 109 was not without its sadness. On 27 August, an Anson crashed in the sea at Lyme Bay, its all-NCO crew reportedly missing, believed killed, and on 5 November a problem with one of the engines in a flight over France meant the seven people aboard, including an observer from TRE, had to abandon the aircraft and take to their parachutes, reportedly to become prisoners of war although apparently one evaded capture. Having a TRE man go missing in such circumstances, someone privy to so many secrets, prompted a re-think about the wisdom of sending over enemy occupied territory any more of these specialists (who swapped 'Mr' for an RAF commissioned officer rank and their civvies for service dress). The practice, it appears, quickly ceased.[14]

Nevertheless, the work of TRE in equipping No. 109's aircraft with special radar equipment for these beam-hunting forays, together with the dedication of those members of its scientific staff who accompanied No. 109's aircrew as volunteer observers on such occasions, constitutes an aspect of the TRE – No. 109 liaison in the 1940/1 period that was not always fully appreciated.

The manner of the squadron's activities did earn accolades from time to time, one of them announced in the supplement to the *London Gazette* on 1 July 1941 being the award of a Bar to the Air Force Cross for the man who had led the unit before it gained squadron status, Wing Commander Blucke. He was no longer with No. 109, and neither was the man who had worked closest with him, Squadron Leader Bufton. Bufton had been posted to Bomber Command where, a fortnight or so later, while taking part in a raid on Cologne with No. 9 Squadron, the Wellington that he was flying failed to return and the six-man crew was posted missing.[15] It had been Bufton's first trip over Germany, the first opportunity to fly on a bombing mission without the severe restraints of riding the beam, and it now looked as if this unexpected opportunity to join a front-line squadron had signalled the abrupt conclusion to a fine career.

Amusing, informative and gratifying though it always was to hear about the success of investigative and test flying in meeting the needs of both TRE and No. 80 Wing, No. 109 Squadron was looking especially to the time when the embryo Oboe ground-controlled bombing system would become the means to achieve greater accuracy for Bomber Command generally. The crews, who had been doing their utmost to destroy the source of the Cherbourg beams, could already appreciate the potential of that system through their own experiences and in the degree of confidence shown towards it within TRE. It is unlikely though that even the best-informed individuals in No. 109 would have had any real insight into the wide-ranging schemes, bristling with their far-reaching implications, that were being put into the melting pot at Worth Matravers.

CHAPTER FOUR

Dreams and Schemes

'Any means we can find of getting our bombers accurately on to their distant targets would be of inestimable value and the effort required to produce it will almost certainly be placed in the highest category of priority.' Air Commodore O.G. Lywood, Director of Signals at Air Ministry, writing a Most Secret and Personal letter, dated 2 August 1941, which he sent to the TRE Superintendent, A.P. Rowe. Lywood indicated that if a diversion of effort towards Oboe caused other work to suffer, this would have to be accepted.

The team dedicated to concerted effort in developing the embryo Oboe ground-controlled blind-bombing system came into being at TRE at Worth Matravers on 4 May 1941. It was just one week after the milestone letter from No. 109 Squadron's CO to No. 80 Wing, copied to TRE's Superintendent, in which he put on record the fact that Oboe had now been used for the first time to bomb an enemy target; so it was, he thought, an appropriate time to single out those individuals whose contribution at TRE had made this possible.

These included the people engaged on the experimental stage and those who carried this forward to flight testing, among the names mentioned being A.H. Reeves, a telecommunications engineer given responsibility for this new team, which was known formally within TRE as Group 4 and more loosely as 'the Oboe group'. The contemporary phraseology was that this team had been formed to investigate a new system of long-range blind-bombing; that it had been agreed that in future the name 'Oboe' should denote this method of blind-bombing; also – and here is the nub of the group's objective from the outset – that Oboe should enable individual bombs to be dropped in a target area of 200 ft by 600 ft, to a range exceeding 600 miles. Over-optimistic or not, those were certainly the figures contained in a progress report produced within TRE that covered the period from 16 May to 15 June 1941 and spanned only the first six weeks of the new group's activities.[1]

In peacetime Alec Reeves had invented a novel system of telephone communication called 'pulse code modulation', something so far ahead of its time that it would have to wait for the appearance of postwar transistors to take its rightful place in digital telecommunications.* Fortunately this was

* The British patent for Alec Reeves' idea of pulse code modulation was granted in 1939. It was a transmission method designed to overcome the problem of noise, distortion and cross-talk by substituting digitally coded signals for the analogue signals that had been used previously. (Definition taken from a biographical sketch supplied to the author by the Institution of Electrical Engineers, Reeves having died on 13 October 1971, aged sixty-nine.)

a concept that he could build upon in wartime for blind-bombing possibilities, which would need an advanced means of signals communication between ground and air. It would be unkind to describe Reeves as an absent-minded professor but there is no doubt that he did cause others to wonder sometimes about his adherence to some of the more obligatory disciplines of office life. It has been noted that 'he was not the most orderly of planners' and that there had to be someone close to him at TRE 'to turn his ideas into useful hardware'.[2] Rowe, who had put him in charge of the Oboe group, would often wonder about the length of time it took Reeves to bring his thoughts back to an awareness that there were others in the office, that he was no longer alone with the ideas, the inspirations, the brainwaves, all racing around in his mind. Rowe, who admitted that sometimes he thought that no one but Reeves could have evolved Oboe, described the resulting product in the same vein: it was, he wrote, 'born and bred from daydreams'.[3]

Here, that vital someone to turn Reeve's ideas into reality would be Dr F.E. Jones, who had been recruited from postgraduate studies to work on RDF, being posted first to the Research Station at Dundee and then to work on the calibration of the CH stations in the east coast radar chain. He became the project leader in the new group, which was to include A.D. Bates, a member of the original Oboe team; A.J. Blanchard, seconded from the Post Office; D.E. Bridges, an instructor at the Yatesbury radio school; F. Harrison, electrical engineer; J.E.N. Hooper, a schoolmaster; B. Milnes, P. Redfern and E. Rollinson, who were all from Oxbridge; K.A. Russell, a Scot who joined at Dundee; Dr C.L. Smith from the Cavendish Laboratory and C.H.M. Turner from Cambridge.

A year to the day since the transfer from Dundee, Worth Matravers and its equally secure outposts now offered a self-contained workplace that provided the office accommodation, laboratory space and workshop facilities necessary to create the ideas, to experiment with them, to produce and to modify as necessary the prototype equipment for use on the ground and in the aircraft, as well as incorporating test areas to prove the components of the system ahead of flight trials. With the range of work taking place there (the Oboe group being but the latest of a number of specialist teams in this centre of excellence) the original site was soon overflowing. Leeson House, midway between Worth Matravers and Swanage where many of the TRE staff were in lodgings, became an early annexe and this was followed by first one school, Durnford House, and then by the requisitioning of another, Forres School, as the importance of the research centre grew and with it, inevitably, the size of the workforce.

While the first hesitant steps with Oboe in a bombing raid against the Cherbourg transmitters relied on a single beam, enabling No. 109's Wellingtons to follow it towards its ground station source and then obey

Worth Matravers' computed bomb-release signal, it was Reeves' intention to use two ground stations for his method of ground-controlled blind-bombing. These would take the bomber pilots unerringly to their objective, even dropping the bombs for them. The pilot would have a visual indicator to keep him on course, the needle on the instrument dial swinging to the left or to the right if he deviated; as for the bombs, no one in the aircraft need do anything because the bomb-release mechanism would be triggered from the ground.

It was all a matter of precisely measuring the distance that the aircraft was away from the ground stations. When the earliest experiments were taking place, with a single beam and the best available equipment, the theoretical discrepancy was thought to be no more than 80 yards but so far it had not been possible to validate this figure. Unbelievable as this accuracy was, with two ground stations, the intersection of their range would surely provide a more precise location point for the aircraft, and with the right answers from the right sums, based crucially on three key determining factors – ground speed, height and ballistics information – a signal could be sent from one of the ground stations which would trigger the release mechanism at the very fraction of a second needed to set down the bombs on target. Using two ground stations to determine the position of the aircraft and relying on pulse-coded modulation for inter-communication were the innovative principles of the 'new' Oboe, the Oboe precision ground-controlled blind-bombing system conceived in April/May 1941, for which Alec Reeves could be justifiably credited.

Its snags were easily appreciated: the system was not infallible and it had a range limitation due to the curvature of the earth; there would surely be inaccuracies in wind forecasting and errors in estimating how individual bombs would fall; there was the compulsion to keep the aircraft on a straight and level course for several minutes while short of the target; and, bearing in mind how British expertise had 'bent' the enemy beams, the prospect of the enemy discovering and jamming the transmissions was likely. While constructive criticism may be welcome, TRE could have done without some of the comments expressed when the principle of Oboe became known, though known only in the highest circles. An early critic was Professor A.O. Rankine, Scientific Advisor to the Ministry of Aircraft Production, who reported that the scheme was 'technically impossible'. He forecast uneconomical losses because of aircraft being unable to take evasive action in the run-up time before reaching the target. Also, he expressed the view that the limit placed on the number of bombers capable of being controlled by a pair of ground stations in the given period of time would make Oboe of little value tactically.[4]

Rankine called Oboe 'fantastic', by which assuredly he considered it to be fanciful rather than stupendous, since during the formulation of the principles of Oboe he appears to have written that if he (Rankine) had the power, he would sack the man responsible so that no longer would he waste not only his own time but that of others with these 'vain imaginings'.⁵ To be fair, that particular condemnation came at a time when Reeves was pushing the merits of one Oboe variant after another – each one all the more far-reaching in its implications – yet the basic Oboe concept had still to be proven.

The range problem facing Reeves' team was all to do with the technicalities of sending and receiving radio signals across the face of the earth. Oboe, being a line of sight system, suffered the handicap that the signals from the ground stations were unable to bend and follow the curvature of the globe. The restriction could be minimized, nonetheless, because signal range increased with altitude, aircraft therefore obtaining an advantage for the system which would extend the Oboe signal reception capability to some 150 miles at 15,000 ft. The higher the ceiling of the Oboe aircraft, the greater the distance from the ground stations that it could reach; thus, the limitation imposed on the system was that of the type of aircraft available at that particular time. It has been noted that a range of 600 miles was considered a viable prospect but this would have required an aircraft reaching 120,000 feet, which was an impossibility in the 1940s, and way beyond even the ceiling of the most ambitious experimental jets in postwar days. Instead, distant targets would have been attacked by an enhancement to the system which was envisaged right from the start – the inclusion of a 'repeater' aircraft to fly on a course between the ground stations and the target, maintaining the optical path and re-transmitting the signals. The result: it would effectively treble the range and easily put Berlin on the hit list for an Oboe bombing raid.

At that stage there was probably not much of any significance that could be done to overcome the other principal handicaps, although the Oboe group naturally reviewed them periodically. One that was addressed at the outset was the probability that the enemy would begin jamming the Oboe transmissions. Initially these signals would have to be carried on the 1½ metres wavelength, using two CHL stations dedicated to this purpose (Worth Matravers alone at first, then followed by West Prawle, near Kingsbridge, Devon). It was accepted that this was a 'jammable' frequency but these were early days and no alternatives were in prospect until the availability of a wavelength below twenty centimetres, still a way off because the technology to make this possible was not, as yet, sufficiently developed within TRE.

By early July 1941, although work had begun on equipment that would be able to make use of the later system, the longer wavelength was already available so what was now needed was to determine its practical limitations. One of No. 109's Wellingtons was used for this purpose, the 'Broody Hen' (the modified Identification of Friend or Foe airborne receiver that was used against Cherbourg), confirming that contact between the Wellington and

Worth Matravers was fine as far as 173 miles at a height of 15,000 feet but beyond that distance the signal faded abruptly. These practical results came as a welcome improvement on the forecasts based on theory. A further series of tests, the Wellington going up to 20,000 feet, indicated a likely improvement to 200 miles, a distance sufficient to bring the important French ports of Lorient and Brest within Oboe range.[6]

Knowing the exact distance of the target from each of the ground stations was at the core of the Oboe system. While the distance between ground station and target would not vary, the distance between ground station and aircraft certainly would change and it was just as necessary to know this distance, too, so as to be able to make the calculations vital to getting the aircraft to its target and to releasing its bombs. A signal pulse going out to the aircraft and being re-transmitted to the ground station was the way to produce this information, and the modulation of the pulses emanating from the ground station the means to carry the control intelligence.

Reeves' first proposal was to use two suitably placed ground stations, locked together by a landline with a variable delay. Each would transmit locked pulses to the aircraft, which would follow a hyperbolic path to the target determined by the synchronous reception of the pulses. One of the two stations, knowing the height at which the aircraft had been ordered to fly, would measure its ground speed and send the bomb-release signal at the right moment.

However, in any beam system where the angle subtended by the ground stations at the target was acute, the greater error in determining the position of the aircraft would always be along the direction parallel to the baseline between the ground stations. Hal Bufton suggested, were it possible, a system whereby the aircraft was controlled to fly in such a direction (i.e., parallel to the baseline between the ground stations) and to absorb any error by releasing a stick of bombs (and thus straddle the target).

But what perturbed Bufton more about this initial proposal of Reeves was the fact that the bomber was required to approach the target along a straight line from a fixed point in the UK. It was, he argued, as much of a dead give-away as had been the Germans' beam navigation system. Bufton spoke from experience, of course, as he and others in No. 109 had flown those very beams during the squadron's investigative work in conjunction with No. 80 Wing. With that, Reeves abandoned his landline-locked pulses concept and went back to the drawing board.[7]

It is evidence of Reeves' inspirational brilliance that he was able to avoid totally the too-revealing direct route and instead approach on an altogether different path, by having the aircraft follow the arc of a circle whose centre was just one of the ground stations, the radius of the circle being the predetermined precise distance (to the 100th part of a mile, incidentally) between one of those ground stations and the target. He still needed two ground stations but this time one would 'track' the aircraft to the target by constantly monitoring its distance from the ground station, while the other handled only 'release', computing the moment for the aircraft to drop its bombs, the plane's height and airspeed having previously been defined. Release would present challenges of its own, calling for an understanding of the principles of bombing, the effect of air drag on a falling missile and its aerodynamic variations, as well as appreciating, for instance, that in a cross-wind an aircraft pursues a crab-like movement along its track.

Despite the clear advantages that Oboe offered when compared to conventional bombing procedures, there remained one nagging disadvantage. It was one that Professor Rankine had put his finger on, the fact that a pair of ground stations controlled a single bomber and there was a ten-minute run-up time between the aircraft being locked on by the first transmitter and bomb release by the second. In fact the Oboe group was able to find a way around this problem, by proposing modifications to the ground stations to allow each pair to handle more than six times the envisaged number of aircraft – as many as forty an hour instead of six – but the work programme had its order of priority, so multi-channelling was put aside for the time being.[8]

It is likely that the low aircraft handling capability also worried another prominent government scientist, Sir Henry Tizard. He had been Secretary of the Department of Scientific and Industrial Research before the war and subsequently wrote, following a two-day visit to TRE, that Oboe 'is certainly a most ingenious method and very well worked out but I remain in doubt whether it can be used for the operation of large forces of bombers in one night'. He was also somewhat sceptical about the proposal to release the bombs automatically from the aircraft by means of a signal from the ground station; he thought that this was 'a frill', and not only that, a chance, he believed, to give the enemy a further opportunity to get the better of Oboe.[9]

In those early days, Reeves' Oboe group at TRE was keen not to be too generous too soon in the dissemination of information about its 'blind-bombing baby'. For example, Bomber Command was not told of the system, Dr F.E. Jones, the project leader, being 'not keen to bring them into the picture until the technical difficulties have been largely overcome'. He had what many would agree was just cause for wanting to keep them in the dark; he feared that Bomber Command would be 'prejudiced against Oboe, due to the lack of success of the original crude form' – the 'Oboe' that relied on the 'Broody Hen', the 'Oboe' used in the Blind-Bombing of Cherbourg operations before the Reeves group was formed. While it was the judgement of 'F.E.', apparently, that the problems still to be overcome were 'practically all technical and not operational', there was a view within Operational Research that here was a system so complex as to require the most careful planning when the time came for Bomber Command to put Oboe to operational use.[10]

With the advantage of hindsight, the first detailed schedule for Oboe trials and operations is seen to have been too optimistic. It indicated the trial bombing of targets in north-west France by the end of October, a date less than three months hence; introducing the repeater aircraft to achieve the first trials up to 600 miles away by the end of December; trial bombing of targets in the 250-mile range, using centimetre waves, also by the end of December; and the repeater aircraft for targets up to 600 miles, also with the centimetre system, by the end of April 1942. Besides proving the system, ground stations and aircraft would have to be suitably equipped – and with this in mind this same schedule called for the number of immediately available Wellington aircraft to be doubled and for an unspecified aircraft capable of reaching 35,000 ft or higher to be provided to maximize the range possibilities. And there was the anticipation of as many as twenty-four Oboe bombers to be operational within the year, the scheduled date being 30 June 1942.[11]

As did Rowe, TRE's Superintendent, Reeves and the Oboe group needed friends in high places if their plans were to gain momentum with anything like the speed they considered their work merited in that summer of 1941. Although the thrust forward did not necessarily proceed as rapidly as some would have wished, a Most Secret and Personal letter to Rowe, from Air Commodore O.G. Lywood, Director of Signals at the Air Ministry, dated 2 August 1941, gave a timely and worthwhile insight into the current thinking of the powers-that-be, not only indicating why their work was so important to the national effort, but also pointing the general direction in which the RAF's bombing offensive was likely to move in the coming months.

First Lywood confided the extreme concern of the members of the Air Staff at the high percentage of bombs that were missing the target; people were, he thought, only just now waking up to the seriousness of the situation. It would be of inestimable value to find the means to get the bombers accurately to their distant targets, the effort required would almost certainly get the highest priority even if other work had to suffer. Then, having set the scene as he saw it, the Air Commodore turned to the subject of Oboe. Reeves had already provided an outline description and just the previous day Dr Jones had been to the Air Ministry to explain both the workings of the system and its progress. Lywood, who was 'very much struck with the possibilities' of Oboe, then went on to consider the role of No. 109, which seemed to be getting on so well with the people at TRE that it would perhaps be a pity to make any changes to the current arrangements. It might be, the Air Commodore wrote, 'that the original role of the striking force flight of No. 109 as the leaders of the bombing attack by this means may now come to fruition'.

As for the way that Oboe itself should be introduced, it was his view that if the ten centimetre version was 'a very long way ahead' it would probably be worthwhile going ahead on a limited scale with the 1½-metre proposition, which could be used until the enemy began jamming it. Lywood concluded his letter to Rowe by noting that, providing the policy continued of having a small specialized force as fire raisers, leading the van of an attack, he considered that productive effort would not be great and could be more easily dealt with on a handmade basis. It is relevant, by the way, to note that with Lywood referring to the intention to have a small specialized force leading a bombing attack – the term 'pathfinder' was yet to come – this indication of quality rather than quantity would apparently demolish any further argument over the numbers of aircraft with which Oboe must cope.[12]

In the event, to ensure that Oboe would come into operational use with minimum delay, TRE must concentrate on the 1½-metre version, leaving aside any plans to have repeater facilities, and at the same time continuing with the development programme for the ten centimetre Oboe. This version would be ready, then, as the replacement when the enemy started, as was expected, their transmission-jamming countermeasures once the new signals were picked up.[13]

Policy decisions made during October 1941 set the seal on No. 109's continuing role in the evolution of Oboe. Its aircraft would carry out the experimental flying and the operational trials for the 1½-metre system and those concerned would form the nucleus of the unit which would eventually operate in Bomber Command. Events unfolding elsewhere, however, would that winter cause the Oboe team at Worth Matravers and the No. 109 aircrews and aircraft based at Boscombe Down to distract their hitherto undivided attention and instead to direct their joint efforts against two of the German Navy's most powerful warships. The fact that the battlecruisers *Scharnhorst* and *Gneisenau* had both been traced to the French port of Brest – where they were seemingly immune to the RAF's continuing attacks by conventional bombing methods – brought about pressure from the bombing policymakers and the decision to see whether Oboe might offer a solution.

With hindsight, this diversion from being able to pursue vigorously the real job in hand was as unnecessary as it was time-consuming, also, it was of questionable value, either in achieving the objective of putting both ships out of action or even in being able to benefit the Oboe thought processes. Aircrew lives were lost over and over again in this series of raids, with both the Oboe partners, TRE and No. 109, suffering personal loss in the course of the experimental stage before blind-bombing with the still unproven Oboe could commence. It was a time of changing fortunes, a time of personnel changes; it was also a time that saw No. 109's crews in action against the enemy on two fronts far apart. No. 109's expertise had singled out this squadron to make a special contribution to desert warfare in the Middle East theatre of operations.

CHAPTER FIVE

Tribulations of Trinity

'The "Broody Hen" boxes are very temperamental and are working at their extreme limit; they are typical products of an experimental laboratory. . . . Except to the TRE people themselves, they are packets of mysteries.' Group Captain E.B. Addison, Commanding Officer, No. 80 Wing, writing to Group Captain J.A. Gray at No. 3 Group HQ on 24 December 1941. The 'Broody Hen' equipment was used during Operation Trinity, when German warships sheltering in Brest Harbour were the target for an early form of ground-controlled bombing.

A change of scene, a change of purpose. This was the outcome when No. 109 Squadron received unexpected instructions during the late autumn of 1941. For some aircrew members, it meant an introduction to a different kind of work, a role in a secret operation where the troubled 8th Army in the huge desert regions of North Africa became the unit's partner in place of TRE scientists clustered in their own encampment overlooking a seaside resort on the south coast of England.

For a time, Oboe was forgotten – no test flights called to determine its potential range, no bombing missions against the source of a known enemy beam. There were no more investigative flights to locate further beams and no more flying to check on the effect of beam-jamming or on the efficiency of those Starfish decoy fires, lit to lure enemy raiders droning through the night skies over Britain.

An established specialist unit experienced in carrying out test flights and operational missions, where so much depended on the ability to understand the benefits and the problems deriving from the complexities of wireless signalling, No. 109 was given its new role in the Middle East theatre by No. 80 (Signals) Wing, the RAF radio countermeasures organization which controlled it. Those in No. 109 who would be involved would find that while the radio equipment on board their aircraft bore some similarity with their usual black boxes, this new phase was an initiation into a novel application that would bring unexpected problems and risks beyond belief. Aircrew members would be entering a so far unknown and hostile environment where every minute airborne reduced their prospects of a safe return to base.

It was the expected offensive in Libya that triggered the selection of No. 109 for this latest innovative function, its objective to try and jam communications on the 28 to 34 megacycles wave band between enemy armoured columns. The desert was a battleground that suited tanks admirably and if their facility to talk between each other on the radio could be hampered, the efficiency of the entire columns would be prejudiced. The huge extent of the terrain in which the German tanks and other armoured vehicles would be operating ruled out ground jamming so the use of aircraft was proposed for this purpose.

There was just a two-week period allowed for No. 80 Wing to have the airborne jammers produced, to get the planes and their crews out to the Middle East and to provide adequate training in what was not so much an extension of No. 109's functions to date but a totally new kind of operation. The radio equipment – standard RAF sets converted by the Marconi-Ekco company, with assistance from TRE, to act as barrage jammers over the whole band – went under the name 'Jostle', which subsequently became the codename covering the whole activity. Six Wellingtons were procured for No. 109: instead of using ones familiar to them, these needing to be a version of the Wellington with engines capable of peak performance under tropical conditions. The squadron had to design, make and fit a special aerial in addition to deciding where the jamming equipment would be installed. No one had seen the like of this aerial previously; ultimately it was akin to a section of an old bedstead, the three-inch brass tube some seven ft in length having to be let down vertically during flight through a hole made in the bottom of the fuselage, its passage eased by steel rollers made to No. 109's specifications by an ironmonger based close to the airfield.

The first three Wellingtons were prepared within eight days, the *ad hoc* trials completed to satisfaction and the crews all set to 'get their knees brown', in the parlance of the day. One of the crews was formed solely from among No. 109 personnel (Flight Lieutenant Willis, Flight Sergeants Appleby and Huntley with Sergeants Dixon, Hall and Macdonald, who flew via Harwell to leave on 15 October, well within the stipulated timespan) while the others, together with those to fly three more Wellingtons then being similarly fitted out, comprised new crews from Bomber Command.[1]

Known as No. 109 Squadron Detachment, Middle East, the whole party was under the command of Squadron Leader W.B.S. Simpson, a member of the operational staff in No. 80 Wing. All six Wellingtons were in place by the end of October, ready to start operating, but as the need did not arise as soon as had been anticipated there were now a few bonus days that could be devoted to further training for the uninitiated crews and for more extensive trials with the equipment. This welcome breathing space provided a useful opportunity for crews both to gain experience in the use of the jamming equipment and to measure the scope of its effect. In some respects the delay in swinging into action could be regarded as an aggravation; Operation Jostle had been born amid an intense atmosphere of almost indecent haste, the phrases being passed around the Air Ministry, Group Headquarters and Middle East Command referring to its importance as a means of 'seriously disorganizing' enemy communications, the 'extreme effort' required to have the first three Wellingtons prepared for their role and the 'maximum priority' to be given to despatching them out to Egypt.[2]

On 14 November, three of the Wellingtons moved to one of the forward airfields, followed two days later by the remaining three, the detachment's desert stint spanning the five-week period from 18 November to Christmas Eve at its ultimate base, known as LG75. There was a promising start when the first two sorties took place over the Sidi Omar area on 20 November, with the jammers operative for 2¼ hours and prisoners reporting that those efforts had caused a breakdown of tank-to-tank communications. Next day the mood changed when, putting up twice the number of sorties and causing eight hours of jamming in the Fort Capuzzo area, one of the Wellingtons failed to return – an aircraft with Colonel R.P.G. Denman, the top War Office specialist in radio countermeasures, among the seven people on board – the other aircraft managing to return home despite being badly damaged in combat with three 3 Macchi 200 fighters. Its pilot was the only one coming from No. 109 itself, Flight Lieutenant Willis, a flying boat captain at the outbreak of war; the bravery of everyone in the crew was recognized that day with his immediate award of a Distinguished Flying Cross. The three fighters pounced only fifteen minutes after jamming had begun on this third sortie of Operation Jostle; one of those fighters was shot down but the Wellington was severely damaged, its rear turret useless and the wireless operator wounded. It had to limp away to seek safety in a small patch of cloud, the crew relieved that there was no further attention from the enemy. The Wellington, Z8948, completed the major portion of the trip home in a cloudless sky but the damage inflicted was so pronounced that it could no longer take any part in these operations.

Impacting further on the parlous state of this handful of specially equipped Wellingtons was the fact that an enemy air attack on one of No. 109's desert landing grounds left two aircraft on stand-by badly damaged by bombs. Then, more disturbing still, in a further series of sorties over the El Adem area which continued for 10¼ hours, one Wellington had to be posted missing and another was badly damaged in combat with as many as nine Macchi 200s, this pilot shrugging all that aside and continuing the jamming patrol for a further hour.[3]

A total of twenty-two sorties were flown throughout Operation Jostle, Sergeant Spencer completing six, Sergeant Russell five, Pilot Officer Williams four, and Willis and his all-No. 109 crew, two: Sergeant Nicholson failed to return from his third sortie and Pilot Officer Hughes went missing on his second sortie. And to give the aircraft a roll of honour too, Wellingtons Z8907 and X9986 completed six sorties apiece, Z8944, four, and Z8948 just the one where, with Willis the captain and pilot, it was damaged beyond repair; X9988 disappeared on its third sortie and Z8905 was shot down on its second sortie. None of them escaped damage, whether from anti-aircraft fire, fighters or in an air raid. The surviving aircraft were released by the 8th Army on 23 December 1941, the intention being to make them available for wireless investigation from Kabrit pending the formation of a Special Signals Squadron at Ismailia.

Back home, Simpson, as the officer in command of this special Wellington detachment, gave a graphic report on their experiences; there was not a single sortie which did not encounter anti-aircraft fire from both heavy and medium batteries, whose accuracy or good fortune was such that one of the planes was hit by an opening burst.

'The operations placed a great strain on the flying crews owing to their unexpectedly prolonged nature. Although some sorties proved uneventful, the strain of flying alone far out over the enemy lines, continuously scanning the horizon for fighters for two or three hours on a cloudless day was very great,' he reported. Some crews showed definite signs of tiredness, he went on, but all 'continued to carry out their duties with a magnificent spirit'.[4]

In theory, the desert exercise should have been successful because subsequent tests with the enemy's own tank transmitting and receiving equipment showed conclusively that, despite the ideal conditions under which the experiment was carried out, communication could be completely jammed by an airborne 'Jostle' over areas extending to 12, 25 and 50 miles radius with distances of ½, 1 and 2 miles respectively between transmitter and receiver. Under war conditions, of course, reception would be rendered increasingly difficult by the movement of the vehicle and the clamour of battle.[5]

The sequel to No. 109's desert dramas came as much as a year later, though a meeting held on 24 July 1942, to examine the Army's requirements for jamming equipment, did hear that evidence as to the effectiveness or otherwise of airborne jamming by the Wellingtons during November/December 1941 was 'scanty and inconclusive'. It was mentioned that some of the aircraft were still in service, though being used as ordinary bombers, and the meeting agreed to have them held in readiness pending any call from the 8th Army. Ultimately, in response to direct questioning to try to find out the military viewpoint, 8th Army let it be known to the Air Ministry that 'the question of jamming enemy tank communications has been considered' and the decision reached that 'they do not require it in any operation in the immediate future'. Although no reason was given, it can be speculated that there was concern about the risk of tit-for-tat action by the enemy but more likely is the recognition that intercepting radio messages can be a most valuable means of obtaining intelligence material, and successful jamming would make that source dry up. Anyway, it seemed that no one wanted to be seen to 'Jostle' for first place in any queue to use a product with a record as yet unproven on the battlefield.

In the closing weeks of 1941, while Operation Jostle was taking place beneath the generally cloudless blue skies of North Africa, with No. 109's aircraft endeavouring to cause disruption to enemy communications in the desert, an aerial campaign of a different sort was commencing in Europe. Its objective this time was to destroy two of Germany's biggest warships, the *Scharnhorst* and the *Gneisenau*, relying on No. 109's air crews to perform a further series of secret missions, this time under the name of Operation Trinity.

Again, No. 80 Wing was the medium through which the squadron would receive its instructions, the purpose of the exercise having been determined by the Air Ministry during the last week of October 1941, the intention being to use ground-controlled bombing of the two ships in dry dock at Brest. The precise method proposed was what might well be described as a halfway stage between the initial 'Oboe' used against the Cherbourg transmitters and the 'Oboe' that was now proceeding towards the first experimental flights. The 'real' Oboe, the system that the Pathfinders of RAF Bomber Command (the Americans too) would eventually apply to their ever-mounting offensive, required more time and this was lacking at this most demanding, this most critical period of the war. Those two battlecruisers, now immobile yet ever a threat to the convoys bringing vital supplies to Britain, offered a unique opportunity to be wiped out at a single stroke so long as the French port remained their shelter.

As early as 23 July 1941, three Stirlings of No. 15 Squadron and another three from No. 7 Squadron were taking part in bombing attacks on the *Scharnhorst* alone, which had by then been located at La Pallice; the next day, at Brest, it was the turn of the *Gneisenau* to become the target for more RAF crews in daylight, joined this time by formations of American Fortresses. Those raids would be maintained, when circumstances allowed, during the months of August, September, October and November, at first including Stirlings from Nos 7 and 15 Squadrons, bombing in the conventional manner, and then with these two squadrons from No. 3 Group taking a more positive role in the quest for an improved form of bombing.

Reminiscent of the attacks on Cherbourg, Operation Trinity envisaged the bombers following a single beam aimed at the port of Brest, with its source in Cornwall, with a second series of pulse signals which would have a dual purpose: distance measurement and bomb-release information. Responsibility for the technical operational control of the operation was vested in No. 80 Wing, which also had to provide, operate and control the beam transmission equipment, while TRE was given responsibility for operating and maintaining the transmission equipment necessary for range and release – the communications link, in fact, with the third component of this particular 'trinity', the aircraft carrying out the bombing. Although the distance between each transmitter and the target was in excess of 120 miles, accuracy was forecast as being of the order of plus or minus 200 yards, with bombs dropped from as much as 18,000 ft. The bonus was that in this ground-controlled form of aerial attack, cloud and/or smokescreening would have absolutely nil effect on precision.

Group Captain E.B. Addison, who was in command of No. 80 Wing, made no promises. When the time came to explain the principles during a conference at Bomber Command Headquarters on 6 November, Addison laid stress on the fact that the ranging equipment was purely experimental and therefore liable to failures.[6] In the air, ranging and communication would be obtained with the modified IFF sets used on Cherbourg – the 'Broody Hens' – while Hallicrafter S27 receivers would again be used for riding the beam; the beam would be transmitted from Helston, the range measurement, speed and bomb-release signal coming from West Prawle. It will be recalled that the range/communication equipment was a modification of the IFF (Identification of Friend or Foe) gear, its aerial attached to the fuselage just below the rear turret, while the receivers enabling the pilots to track to the target were the sort familiar to aircrew when undergoing training in blind-approach landing.

By the evening of 6 November, the equipment to transmit the track beam – a narrow Lorenz-type 'Baillie beam', produced within No. 80 Wing – had been positioned at Helston and a first short trial transmission made and one of No. 109's Wellingtons was detached to RAF Station Predannock to carry out flight tests along the Baillie beam. At 125 miles its signals came through loud and clear, though falling off rapidly after 180 miles. Within the week, twelve Stirlings had been fitted out at Wyton and Oakington and it was time for a trial operation. In all, eighteen experimental flights took place in a 22-day timespan; it turned out that weather conditions were impossible on sixteen days so all eighteen tests were actually completed during a period of six flying days.[7]

A minor incident began a chain of events that had a profound effect on those participating in Operation Trinity: a Stirling belonging to No. 7 Squadron overshot while landing at Boscombe Down. One of the planes taking part in Trinity, it had made an abortive test flight on 19 November and had to make a forced-landing at St Eval. However, when resuming its journey on the following day, the Stirling broke its tail wheel ploughing through a hedge in the overshoot at Boscombe Down, necessitating its crew – together with others from No. 109 and TRE – having to be ferried back to the squadron's base at Oakington in two of No. 109's Wellingtons. Unfortunately, while circling in readiness to land, one of them crashed a mile and a half from the airfield with the loss of all nine persons in this aircraft, T2552. The crew of six were all members of No. 109 and with them were three passengers – two were with No. 7 Squadron and the other a civilian from TRE. It was an incalculable loss because among the dead were Flying Officer Hennessy, the No. 109 pilot whose successful Oboe operation on 26 April had prompted Hebden's congratulatory letter next morning to No. 80 Wing, and G.G. Samson, the scientist in charge of the TRE team at Oakington. Samson and Hennessy had been responsible respectively for 'Broody Hen' and beam trials up to the time of this tragic flying accident. Additionally the crash took the lives of Pilot Officer R.M. Lewin GC, Flight Sergeant Bates and Sergeants Carnforth, Mackey and Snape, all from No. 109, while No. 7 Squadron lost Sergeants Archer and

Grant.* Referring specifically to the deaths of Hennessy and Samson, a report in No. 80 Wing conceded that 'a great deal of valuable information was therefore lost', while TRE reported that the accident 'considerably hampered' the Trinity programme. A 'considerable fund of information' had been lost and this 'had to be obtained anew'; it had also meant having to organise a fresh crew to take the work forward to fruition.[8]

Further test flights yielded further benefit. One trial run, on 23 November, produced an error of plus or minus 100 yards at 180 miles on the Baillie beam but communications over the 'Broody Hen' proved impossible in the Stirling, due, it was thought, to interference from the RDF School at Yatesbury. Subsequently, arrangements were made to have transmissions from that source turned off while the Trinity trials were in progress, a test run with a Wellington carrying a TRE specialist, familiar with the equipment, having proved successful. After bad weather had brought a four-day interruption, another problem emerged with communications over the 'Broody Hen' signalling equipment, this time the supposition again being correct, that the Stirlings had a 'dead area' on the starboard quarter, the 'Broody Hen' aerials being adjusted as a consequence of this discovery.

With the fear that the target warships could be preparing to move from the docks, No. 80 Wing decided that tests of accuracy must now be abandoned and the programme continued purely with procedure tests in an effort to train the 'Broody Hen' operators, none of whom had yet had a fully successful run.[9]

A new month brought a new spirit of optimism when, on 1 December, two Stirlings carried out the first fully successful runs for the 'Broody Hens'. Three days of bad weather then intervened but on 5 December two more successful runs were made. By now, the TRE scientist in charge of these tests had given the encouraging information that 'we can reasonably hope for a range fix over the target of less than the plus/minus 200 yards anticipated'. [10]

It will not have escaped notice that Stirling bombers, rather than No. 109's Wellingtons with their much-reduced bomb load, figured in those experiments; it would therefore follow that Stirlings would carry on to the operational climax of Trinity and bomb the battlecruisers. It did not mean, however, that No. 109 would be losing out to other squadrons – far from it. The plan was to continue the earlier arrangements where each aircraft

---

* It seems not to have been generally known that Lewin, an operational bomber pilot before he came to No. 109, held the George Cross, the highest civilian bravery award. A sergeant pilot at the time, he was captain of an aircraft which crashed and caught fire when taking off on a night bombing mission from Malta on 3 November 1940. Although hurt and well aware that the bombs and the petrol on board formed a lethal combination about to explode, he part-dragged, part-carried his injured second pilot for some 40 yards to a hole in the ground where he lay on him as the bombs went off.

carried, additional to the normal crew, a No. 109 pilot and two No. 109 wireless operators, each of these pilots being experienced in beam-flying and their radio specialists the men who would have charge of the 'black boxes' – the link with ground control throughout – on which so much would depend.

A meeting between No. 80 Wing and TRE representatives had long since confirmed the procedure to be followed in the run-up to the target, the final two minutes being critical to the success of the bombing mission. The 'Broody Hen' operator and the bomb-aimer would have a warning signal from West Prawle, two minutes before the moment for bomb release, this alert comprising twelve dots, at which point the pilot must prepare to keep to the course dictated by the beam from Helston. The final warning would take the form of a one second pause in the transmission from West Prawle; at this point, it was proposed, the 'Broody Hen' operator would light a red lamp situated in front of the bomb release operator – a 'fail safe' visual indication in case of equipment failure. Following the one-second pause, there would be a further transmission from West Prawle, this time lasting between ten and thirty seconds approximately, depending upon the speed of the aircraft. Cessation of West Prawle's signal would mark the exact release point.[11]

It was a procedure that placed particular responsibilities on those flying the aircraft and those concerned with handling the wireless equipment and the bomb-release mechanism. With two pilots on board – the captain and first pilot always from either No. 7 or No. 15 Squadron, the beam pilot or second pilot always from No. 109 – each must know who was in control at which point during the flight. The intention was for the captain to relinquish control to the beam pilot when the aircraft was at a height of no less than 6,000 ft and the ground signal was being received; he would ensure that the bomb doors were open and pass visual messages to the beam pilot as to receipt of last warning and release signals. Then, with 'bombs gone', he would take over the aircraft at his own discretion. For his part, having changed places with the captain, the beam pilot would plug in the Hallicrafter and pick up the beam; on receipt of the two minute warning he would maintain correct height, course and speed with extreme care, then, with 'bombs gone', or later, depending on the captain, he would relinquish control to the captain at the appropriate moment. The special operator would receive the two minute warning, which he would pass on to the captain on the intercom, he would then stand by for the bombing signal, which would be his prompt to illuminate the red lamp as a visible alert within the cockpit. Once the 'Broody Hen' had been tuned in, it was never again to be touched unless requested by the navigator, who would take up the bomb-aimer's position where he would plug in to the 'Broody Hen', using this (or the red lamp if he failed to hear the release signal), to tell him precisely when he must let go the bombs.[12]

The first raid took place on 7 December after a period of enforced inactivity, the fog giving way to ideal flying weather, and there were five

Stirlings taking part. Three reported that the track beam from Helston was satisfactory while the other two found it difficult to follow. As for the West Prawle transmission, four reported interference so heavy that all the signals were unintelligible. Only one aircraft – its captain, Squadron Leader D.J.H. Lay DFC from No. 7 Squadron – received the signals successfully from both ground stations but the aggravation here was that this Stirling was unable to open its bomb doors. Beam pilot Squadron Leader Sage, with No. 109 wireless operators Flight Sergeant McFarlane and Sergeant Jack, conceded disappointment in the extreme: the mission 'abandoned owing to technical hitch' with two 2,000-lb bombs jettisoned and the other three of equal size brought back to base for 'recycling' ready for a subsequent raid. As for their colleagues, in one instance all the signals were heard by the special operator but not by the navigator – and he was the crew member responsible for dropping the bombs. He found the bomb-release signal masked by interference and not reliable, so his bombs were not released on signal. A third chose to bomb visually with the benefit of the Baillie beam to keep the aircraft on track, the remaining pair resorting to what was described as the 'normal manner'.[13]

It was not, therefore, a promising start to the series, with the message going forward to higher authority that there had been an eighty per cent failure rate already with the 'Broody Hen' equipment which was meant to monitor the aircraft's range and signal the moment of bomb release. In mitigation, however, there was the possibility that the interference came from a recognizable source; as a precaution, steps were taken to turn off all pulse transmissions over 200 megacycles in the south-west of England while Trinity ran its course.[14] Reporting to the Director of Signals at the Air Ministry, No. 80 Wing conceded that the five aircraft taking in this début operation were not successful. The track beam was good and apparently accurately laid, also the navigational and operational procedure on the part of the aircrews was very good. For 'the main cause of failure', No. 80 Wing blamed the inability to receive 'Broody Hen' signals at full range.[15]

Alongside No. 7 Squadron crews, Sage carried out five more flights in the Trinity series of operations; Flight Lieutenant Somerville completed a further four flights; and with No. 15 Squadron, another of No. 109's pilots, Sergeant J. Cartwright (a Pilot Officer with effect from 1 December 1941), flew on the first and six other nights within the nine-night spread of Trinity. A minimum of three Stirlings operated on each of those nine occasions, which were 7, 11, 12, 15, 16, 23 and 27 December and 2 and 3 January. The number of aircraft carrying out the attacks peaked at six on the night of 12 December when, besides the previously named trio from No. 109, Flight Lieutenant Grant and Flying Officer Reece (who flew on all but the first night of Trinity) were the beam pilots with crews of No. 7 Squadron and Flight Lieutenant E.P.M. Fernbank was performing the same function with a crew from No. 15 Squadron. That night the navigators in four of the aircraft reported satisfactory reception enabling bomb release according to the signals, though in one case the bombs did not drop. On three of those nights (15 and 23 December as well as 2 January), either one or two of the aircraft riding the beam were accompanied by non-Trinity satellite bombers formatting upon them, the idea being for these supplementary aircraft to attack in 'follow-my-leader' fashion and thus make extended use of the ground-controlled bombing facility.

With bombing having taken place on six nights when the weather conditions permitted, Christmas Day was taken as a natural break with operations suspended from 23.59 hrs on 24 December to 00.01 hrs on 26 December, though Bomber Command had stand-by crews on various airfields in case there were signs of the warships trying to make a dash for it. The resumption of Trinity, however, saw the resolve of the German defences further strengthening; this determination made its presence known in a box barrage of anti-aircraft fire so intense and so accurate that the bomber crews' tenacity in maintaining the final attack up to the target will be regarded as being all the more remarkable, all the more praiseworthy. In an endeavour to ease this burden, by changing the line of approach towards their objective, it was decided to move the Baillie beam transmitter from Helston in Cornwall to Bolthead in Devon, the effect of this switch being to vary the bombers' approach by as much as thirty degrees. It was not possible, though, to do anything about changing the range and bomb-release signalling system, the 'Broody Hens', that required tuning in so carefully to pick up West Prawle's transmissions, which weakened with distance; the suspected unreliability of this system, especially over such an extreme range, now being confirmed. TRE had long since taken this fact on board and there were teams busy modifying alternative equipment, an air-to-sea radar system (which would be called 'Peacock') eventually superseding the IFF-based 'Broody Hen'.[16]

The dangers and the dramas of Trinity have been recalled by the then Flying Officer Reece:

Those were unusual times, especially for the pilots of Nos 7 and 15 Squadrons, who had to hand over their aircraft to unknown pilots and sit there while – to quote them – 'all hell broke out' and they were being flown straight and level at constant height, speed and direction. As beam pilots, on the other hand, we were used to flying in that manner – and from my point of view I didn't want to know what was going on outside. I just sat as low as possible, concentrating on flying the beam.

It was an ordeal, particularly for the captains in Nos 7 and 15 Squadrons and those who flew with them as complete crews. The requirements of Trinity transformed the kind of bombing operation to which they had grown accustomed into what would now be described as an altogether different ballgame. After the second night, the Germans were waiting for us and I seem to remember that every aircraft suffered some minor damage from anti-aircraft fire. We became used to the flak coming up to greet us over Brest, though 'Jock' Kyle, who was with me on all eight ops, took the biscuit for a capacity to ignore it. He was completely unflappable. Once a shell fragment passed literally between the two of us and Jock just kept on doing what he was meant to be doing with his wireless equipment.

Afterwards, when I asked him if he hadn't been scared, he said only that he wouldn't worry 'until one of the wee petrol pipes' was hit.

Enemy attention was expected during Trinity but what wasn't expected was to find our own guns opening up on us. That happened to us on two separate occasions before Trinity began, when we were carrying out ranging tests with West Prawle, using the Baillie beam, and from time to time this necessitated flights in the direction of Cherbourg. Once, having been flying up and down the South Coast for about an hour and a half, in and out of cloud, I suddenly saw a Hurricane coming head-on with what looked like four pretty little twinkling lights on each wing. It was, of course, very unfriendly fire from his machine-guns – apparently we had been reported to his control as being an enemy aircraft approaching from Cherbourg. On the other occasion anti-aircraft shells began bursting a couple of hundred yards behind us and on landing there was a telephone call from the Senior Naval Officer's staff at Portsmouth to enquire about the accuracy of their gunfire![17]

Leaving aside six failures in Operation Trinity that were caused by interference, the three times that West Prawle was unable to contact the expected aircraft and the two when the bombs would not release, there were three times when an aircraft could not find the tracking beam and three when the range/release signal faded; two instances of engine failure, two when the anti-aircraft fire forced them back, one instance of the plane icing up so severely that it had to return, one where the West Prawle signal was picked up too late and one where West Prawle was at fault with an incorrect procedure. Overall, then, solely from the point of view of the way that the system itself behaved, just eleven sorties were successfully operated – in mathematical terms, a 31.4 per cent success rate for the thirty-five occasions that a Stirling left its airfield for a Trinity bombing mission.

A twelve-page TRE report on the operation includes the telling statement that while all the 'Broody Hens' were tested before and after each of those thirty-five flights and none was found to be unserviceable, adjustments to this equipment were extremely critical and the non-uniformity of these adjustments caused the failures experienced during Trinity. If, in the first place, TRE had known the length of time available for the operation, they would have suggested the use of 'Peacocks' from the start – these, the report indicated, had the advantage of much higher power and better sensitivity, as well as being capable of simpler adjustment.[18]

As for the achievements of Trinity, even postwar reports are imprecise: in one, the *Scharnhorst* and the *Gneisenau* are both stated to have received six direct hits, the overall accuracy appearing to be of the order of a quarter of a mile at 150 miles range, while in the other, the performance best claimed was that one bomb fell between the target battlecruiser and the quay. However there is a third report that possibly is the definitive conclusion: it appears to hinge on intelligence sources which yielded information ten months after Operation Trinity to indicate that 'some excellent results had been achieved'. These referred to one direct hit, one bomb exploding between the wall of the dock and the side of the ship and repeated damage done to dock installations.[19]

With regard to the continuing development of Oboe, the plus side of Trinity was that the bomber crews had demonstrated, time and time again, both their ability and their determination to stick to the required track for the several minutes dedication to course, height and speed that was critical with ground-controlled bombing, ignoring whatever the enemy was throwing at them. The minus side of the operation was less obvious; it was the immeasurable extent of the time and effort lost to the Oboe programme. This was the subject of comment in various quarters, even to the point when the Director of Signals at the Air Ministry, Air Commodore Lywood, wrote a Minute addressed to the Deputy Chief of Air Staff, through the Director of Bomber Operations, stressing that, 'as you know, both the Ministry of Aircraft Production and ourselves are much concerned at the delay that has occurred on the development of the Oboe scheme owing to the diversion of research and technical personnel to the Trinity operation'.[20]

For the sake of the record, the obvious sequel to address is to recall what happened to the *Scharnhorst* and the *Gneisenau*, whose presence in Brest and apparent invulnerability to conventional bombing was the spur to the introduction of ground-controlled bombing. It was a decision made, perhaps, more in a mood of desperation than anticipation. It meant, of course, having to adapt a method that had already proved unconvincing in operational use because the system that was really required was still far from ready, even for test purposes. The warships escaped, leaving Brest for the English Channel when weather conditions on 12 February 1942 nullified the urgent efforts of the combined air and sea forces when looking for them. To the chagrin of all concerned, the escape route funnelling to a few miles wide in the Strait of Dover, the *Scharnhorst* and the *Gneisenau* (with the *Prinz Eugen* too) made their way to their home waters.

There is a final sequel, however, which helps put into perspective the viewpoint of higher authorities concerning the wisdom of trying the Oboe equipment in the only form then available, for what was in essence an experimental application. The time had come, Air Marshal R.H.M.S. Saundby considered, when the crews of whichever squadron in Bomber Command was providing the aircraft for ground-controlled bombing should be able to operate the special equipment without the need for No. 109's involvement. He sought Air Ministry approval to transfer equipment and testing apparatus from Oakington to Wyton and to provide instruction for the aircrews – to train pilots in 'the art of flying on the beam edge' and wireless operators in handling the Hallicrafter receiver and the 'Broody Hen' apparatus. At that time, Trinity was in fact still in progress – Saundby's request was made on 30 December 1941 and there was no end date for Trinity to cease. Made aware of this Bomber Command HQ viewpoint, Air Commodore Lywood indicated on 2 January 1942 that No. 80 Wing had been instructed to make the arrangements outlined by Saundby, whose proposal was prompted because No. 7 Squadron was to be withdrawn from operational flying on 9 January for re-equipping with GEE, the radar-based navigational aid developed by TRE. It would leave No. 15 Squadron alone to carry the Trinity burden for as long as this operation went on.

The significance of Saundby's proposal to train squadron personnel in the Trinity type of bombing is best appreciated in the comments expressed at a lower rung in the RAF hierarchy. These were made by Group Captain Addison, Commanding Officer, No. 80 (Signals) Wing, when writing to Group Captain J.A. Gray at Headquarters, No. 3 Group, which controlled Nos 7 and 15 Squadrons. Addison said he had been giving 'a lot of thought' to Saundby's proposal that a start should be made on contemplating the training of pilots in the art of beam-flying 'if this Trinity business is to go on much longer'.

He laid on the line the fact that the beam edge must be followed very accurately, otherwise there could be errors of direction of up to a mile from the target; that the beam receivers, belonging to No. 109 Squadron, were normally employed for wireless investigation purposes; and that this equipment was both scarce and difficult to obtain. Then, in a remarkable confessional, as if one group captain was unburdening his soul to the other, he went on to describe the 'Broody Hen' hardware as being very temperamental and working at its extreme limit; the sets had been 'specially knocked together for this operation by TRE and are typical products of an experimental laboratory. Except to the TRE people themselves they are packets of mysteries'. Continuing in this same vein of expression, Addison referred to the 'precarious working' of this part of the system, adding that the TRE-operated ground station at West Prawle was 'a mysterious experimental installation which only they understand'.[21]

So, those 'Broody Hens' were 'temperamental', they were 'typical products of an experimental laboratory' and they were 'packets of mysteries'. Harsh comments or not, a reflection of the truth or not, an expression of a widely held view or not, operational experience went on to show that purely from the performance of the technical equipment there was no more than a one-in-three success rate with the Trinity series of ground-controlled bombing operations. As for the future, the much more sophisticated Oboe, even a Mark I version, seemed still to be months down the line, the initial scheduled date for trial bombing of targets in north-west France by the end of October 1941 already having passed.

Mercifully, the situation was not as bleak as it might have appeared. The 'Broody Hen' would cluck-cluck no more, its exasperated operators no longer having to fret over its idiosyncrasies: there was another bird coming along. The 'Peacock' range-and-release communications equipment would hopefully ruffle fewer feathers. Also, direct-line tracking to the target was to give way to a less vulnerable, more accurate form of tracking along the arc of a circle drawn around the flight-controlling ground station, this arc passing over the target. There was renewed optimism in the Oboe development group at TRE, now that members could get back to their 'proper' work, with Trinity at an end. And there were moves afoot within No. 109 Squadron towards securing their place as pathfinders-for-the-pathfinders – the 'first of the legion', to use its future motto – when the pressure mounted in the Allies' bombing offensive against the German war machine.

CHAPTER SIX

Mosquito Makes its Mark

*'A pilot of average skill and with a sound knowledge of beam technique and
of instrument flying should have little difficulty in being successful with
Oboe. However . . . to be fair to the system it would be necessary to select
pilots carefully.'* Wing Commander C.C. McMullen, who was
Commanding Officer of No. 109 Squadron at the time when Oboe's
black boxes were fitted into the first Mosquito, DK300, a Mosquito
transferred from a daylight bombing squadron, on its arrival at RAF
Stradishall in July 1942.

The names of the first cities that suggested themselves as potential targets
for ground-controlled bombing with the 'real' Oboe in 1942 rolled off the
tongue like an index of key locations in an atlas that focused on Nazi
domination of the German nation: Berlin, capital and largest city;
Nürnberg, where huge rallies were addressed by Hitler himself; and
Munich, cradle of the movement that had long revered him as its Führer.

The way that Reeves and his group at TRE were progressing, despite the
Operation Trinity diversion, these distant industrial centres were all feasible
objectives – if the Air Ministry so decided. Those three cities and others
were probabilities because, as early as 30 December 1941, the
specifications were in place for what amounted to an entire Oboe family.
There was Oboe Mark I, necessarily relying on the 1½-metre wavelength,
with the optional extra of repeater aircraft to boost its range from some 250
miles to around 600 miles. There was Mark II, using instead a wavelength
of the order of ten centimetres to retain the range capability yet reduce
substantially the possibility of enemy jamming, again with the repeater
facility. There was Mark III, which would enable the line of approach over
the target to be varied from one aircraft to another within limits of about
plus or minus 45 degrees, and there was Mark IV, a combination of the
Oboe system with the Mark XIV bomb sight, the aircraft being able to
'jink' within wide limits, even at the moment of bomb release, and the
repeater aircraft no longer forced to maintain a predetermined route. Now
it would be able to go cruising around within what was described as 'a
certain fairly wide area'.[1]

So that no one was in any doubt over the potential range capabilities of
Oboe, A.P. Rowe, Superintendent of TRE, had a map drawn which covered
the continent of Europe to include Germany's northern cities, eastwards to

Dresden and into Czechoslovakia, then down through France towards its frontier with Spain, indicating some of the principal cities relative to the system's 600 mile arc of range possibility. So convinced was Rowe that Berlin was destined to become Oboe's initial target, that he had already nominated the positions for the two ground stations which would control such an operation, naturally requiring the help of repeater aircraft to re-transmit the signals and so boost the operating range to around 600 miles. Also, he had proposed that the fastest means of securing their availability was to allocate existing radar stations for this purpose. In a memo on 1 February 1942 to the Director of Communications Development, he wrote, 'I should like to point out again, that if the Berlin area is to be covered first, the two sites concerned are the Sunderland and Dunkirk regions.'[2] Although Worth Matravers and West Prawle were by now at TRE's disposal, their geographical situation on the south coast and in the West Country respectively made them unsuitable because of their distance and direction from Berlin.

While the virtues of successive versions of Oboe were there to be extolled whenever the occasion arose, the present practicalities were possibly regarded as being less important; notwithstanding, the progress by mid-February was significant. The ground stations at West Prawle and Worth Matravers were now complete; two Wellingtons now carried the 'real' Oboe repeater and pulse communication systems; two of the special high-flying Wellingtons with a pressure cabin were due for delivery; and several runs had taken place over a camera obscura to determine range accuracy, the first results showing an average error of plus or minus 34 yards on readings with a maximum error of 180 yards.[3]

Even before Trinity, No. 109's role had been cast. A special flight would carry out the experiments for what was destined to be known as Oboe Mark I; this same flight would take this work forward to and through the operational trials, then go on to form the nucleus of the unit which would eventually operate in Bomber Command. The way that things were going, even those whose more lowly position in the pecking order kept them in the dark like mushrooms were able to make inspired guesses. During and post-Trinity, for example, there were a succession of organizational changes and personnel announcements, some of them directly associated with the squadron's burgeoning responsibilities, while others paid tribute to significant personal achievements or marked a fresh step up a career ladder.

The 1942 New Year Honours List included the Air Force Cross awarded to Flight Lieutenant Cundall, who took part in the early investigation flights and the attacks on Cherbourg beam transmission stations. The Air Force Medal was awarded to Sergeant D.J. Mackey, whose contribution to No. 109's distinctions in wireless waves work began even earlier with that historic flight as Bufton's wireless operator when their efforts confirmed the presence of the first enemy beam picked up over Britain.* Within three months there were further distinctions for No. 109 aircrew when Flight Lieutenant Grant and Flying Officer Reece were awarded the Distinguished Flying Cross and Sergeant J.W. Kyle the Distinguished Flying Medal; the two pilots and the wireless operator all earned their awards for operational flights during Trinity.

The squadron now had a new commanding officer, Wing Commander C.C. McMullen, succeeding Wing Commander Hebden on his posting as instructor to the RAF Staff College, Gerrards Cross, the effective date for this change in command being 5 December 1941. Squadron Leader Bufton, who had been second only to Hebden in seniority before leaving No. 109 in mid-August that year, returned to the squadron towards the end of January; although posted missing during a raid on Cologne with No. 9 Squadron, it emerged that Bufton and the five others in his crew had parachuted from their Wellington south of Valenciennes in northern France. Bufton – finding himself separated from the rest when he landed – ultimately made his way home via Paris, Marseilles, Barcelona, Madrid and Gibraltar (see page 80).

Under McMullen, No. 109 underwent a protracted metamorphosis that spanned the first half of 1942, commencing with its various discrete activities being split – the Wireless Investigation Flight remaining at Boscombe Down, the Wireless Reconnaissance Flight (less those on detachment at Wyton) moving to Upper Heyford, while the Headquarters and Wireless Development Flights went to Tempsford. Further organizational changes followed the transfer of the parent group, No. 26 (Signals) Group, out of Technical Training Command and into Bomber Command (on 10 February 1942), which then saw both Boscombe Down and Tempsford vacated (23 March 1942 and 6 April 1942 respectively) in favour of one of the principal airfields in No. 3 Group, Stradishall, home of one of the front-line bomber units, No. 214 Squadron. A meeting on 29 June 1942 between Air Commodore Lywood, Director of Signals, and 'Bomber' Harris, who was by now AOC-in-C Bomber Command, determined the final changes necessary to achieve the formation of an Oboe squadron with minimum delay. Now comprising what had been known as the Headquarters and Oboe Flight, a 'Y' Investigation Flight and a Radio Countermeasures Flight, No. 109 would be reorganized as a two-flight squadron dedicated to Oboe – one flight to carry out operations, the other for training purposes. As No. 109 Squadron, it would be brought under the operational control of Bomber Command, the components responsible respectively for signals investigation development flights and for radio countermeasures reconnaissance flights being hived off to continue whatever functions were required of them at other airfields and under separate control.[4]

---

*Denis Mackey's AFM was a posthumous award. Tragically, he was one of the six members of No. 109 Squadron who lost their lives in the air crash during the preparations for Operation Trinity the previous November (see page 46).

A matter of days after TRE's Superintendent pressed his case for ground stations specific to the choice of Berlin as the opening target, Air Commodore D.H. de Burgh, Director of Telecommunications, laid down for TRE's controlling organization the path that those developing Oboe must follow. There was no mincing words: these were the Air Staff requirements. In essence there were two demands. The end of April was to be regarded as the time limit to complete the bombing experiments testing the accuracy of the system and great urgency had to be devoted to the continuing investigation and development of the 1½-metre version – 'as it is not until we get greater range from Oboe than is possible without repeaters that it will be really useful'. The view of the Director of Telecommunications himself was that the principles for using repeater aircraft were unproven. And with regard to Oboe on ten centimetres, the line here was that more concrete evidence was needed before Air Staff would consider it. In fact TRE's Oboe group was well aware of the high priority placed on the 1½-metre system; the effort on the ten centimetres system had been 'much reduced due to personnel limitations' but this work was going forward 'as well as these limitations will permit'.[5]

Having booked facilities at a bombing range in the sea off Stormy Down, South Wales, Oboe-directed bombs had been dropped only on two occasions by the due date of end of April; two more days were still needed to complete the first series of tests and a further two days to bring the second series to an end. For these experiments, Worth Matravers was the ground station responsible for transmitting the signals to keep the No. 109 Wellington pilots on track and West Prawle was the one sending the bomb-release signal, the two points producing an angle of forty-nine degrees over the target; the target being ninety-seven miles distant from the tracking station and eighty-seven miles distant from the releasing station. The fifty practice bombs dropped in the course of those six days constituted the first trials that had been performed to test the accuracy and consistency of the 'real' Oboe, the system now generally known as Oboe Mark I.

In the words of J.E.N. Hooper, the Oboe group scientist at TRE in charge of those trials, the accuracy attained was comparable, if not better, than that obtained with accurate visual bombing, and he went further by stating that if these had been 4,000-lb bombs rather than the tiny practice missiles, a large proportion could have been considered direct hits. In an expression of well-deserved praise that he put into his report, Hooper said that the speed with which the bombing trials had been completed, together with the success achieved, was due to a large extent to the patience, skill and zeal of No. 109's pilots. It is not surprising, however, that a note of caution was also introduced into this report. Hooper judged it prudent to emphasize that an insufficient number of results was available to ensure a reliable estimate of the accuracy of the system.

In time, 'Cat' would become the term given to the tracking station and 'Mouse' that of the releasing station. Chronologically, circulation of

Hooper's report on those first bombing trials may be regarded as the definitive moment when 'Mouse' came into general awareness, though its purpose at that stage was specifically to describe a discrete item of hardware and certainly not to attach any form of title to the ground station itself. The equipment so named was that used for measuring the ground speed of the aircraft (the apparatus was described in a TRE memorandum by F.E. Jones, entitled 'The Electric Mouse', reference D.1634/FEJ). As a note accompanying the bombing trials results explained, not only did the 'Mouse' measure the ground speed but, when set up correctly with regard to trail and time of fall of the bomb, it determined the instant of release and automatically interrupted the transmission accordingly.[6]

It should be recognized that while this 'Mouse' was a single piece within the entire Oboe system, and that the method of operating this one basic component has been summarized here in no more than thirty or so words, the successive actions of dreaming up, putting on paper, creating, building, modifying as necessary and then proving Oboe as a working entirety demanded countless hours of dedicated effort, centred on the most advanced scientific expertise drawn from among contrasting people, whose loyalty was unswerving to their far-sighted team leader and to the unique research establishment that was their workplace. A product of daydreams, maybe, but Oboe would not have existed without others to help untangle the complex web with which the myriad shreds of fantasy were woven.

What was to be done with Oboe? Would Berlin be its first target? It is an intriguing fact that a small group of people was assembled on 18 June 1942 for what was agreed as being an 'informal discussion' on using Oboe operationally to destroy a specified target in a single attack; and it may leave those who were not present wondering exactly why ('to avoid any misunderstanding') the title given to the notes of this meeting was subsequently changed both to refer now to 'a possible operational use of Oboe' and to delete the name of the target, which was, by the way, the Gelsenkirchen oil plant.

Under Sir Henry Tizard's chairmanship, the fourteen people present included Rowe and Reeves, Watson Watt, Dr L.B.C. Cunningham from the Air Warfare Analysis Section, Dr B.J. Dickins and G.A. Roberts from Bomber Command Headquarters, Wing Commander D.H. Johnson from the War Cabinet Offices, and Wing Commander R.E.G. Brittain representing the Director of Telecommunications at the Air Ministry. It was recalled that the early trials with Oboe at Stormy Down had produced very promising results and it seemed probable that this method of blind-bombing at ranges up to about 250 miles (there being no mention of repeaters on this occasion) would turn out to be more accurate than the best daylight results so far obtained against protected targets.

There was general agreement that the operation under discussion was perfectly feasible and justified full-scale trials over Britain, which would simulate a raid taking place over the enemy country. It is not too difficult to guess the mood of that meeting since there were suggestions that Fighter Command should be invited to try to intercept the first of the twelve-plus aircraft required for the exercise (one with Oboe, the rest formatting on it), and there might even be searchlights employed to make the experiment all the more lifelike. Someone had certainly done their sums in preparing the paperwork presented at the meeting: it was reckoned that the planned twenty-one Lancasters with their 10,000 pounds of high explosives apiece would alone reduce output at this oil plant by close on 90 per cent, the effect of the remaining three Lancasters, packed tight with incendiaries instead of HEs, to be looked upon as a bonus.[7]

A theoretical proposition, an exercise based on conjecture or an honest simulation intended to test and to sharpen the thinking of the dozen or so people closest to the decision-making when the time would at last come to put Oboe into practice? A mix of all three alternatives is probably nearest the truth. Be that as it may, there was no rehearsal as envisaged; the focus tightened on the 1½-metre system – albeit with less emphasis on repeater aircraft to push Oboe to new range limitations – and the bombing trials entered a new phase. At TRE, though, there were other matters to be absorbed into the pattern of life at Worth Matravers.

For a start, the threat of a German invasion remained, so much so that as late as the spring of that year, 1942, people working at TRE were still indicating an anxiety about the role expected of them if the enemy were to arrive. In the event of an invading force gaining a foothold, there was the ultimate choice facing those in any of the sites, either to evacuate or to stay put and offer some form of defence. There was the thought that Britain's own guns might be turned on this highly secret research establishment in order to safeguard its treasures. Perhaps there would be no other course open to the authorities in such dire circumstances; while staff could make an effort to burn their documents, individually destroying apparatus was impracticable so a thorough shelling seemed to be the answer.[8]

In reality there was a more simple expedient: solve the problem by moving the whole shooting match to a less vulnerable location. Apart from comparative newcomers to TRE, this would be like turning back the clock, bearing in mind the transfers first from Bawdsey to Dundee and then from Dundee to Worth Matravers. Such a move was certainly in prospect, as Rowe had already intimated to TRE's security officer, D. May. There was no need for long-term planning, Rowe indicated, because he thought there was no doubt whatever about having to leave Swanage within a few weeks. He probably knew then, towards the end of April, that this was more than a prospective transfer.

In the space of forty-eight hours, the Worth Matravers complex was bombed twice: in the early evening of 6 April, three bombs fell (two did not explode) and there was minor damage to technical equipment, while in the early afternoon of 8 April a second incident put the ground station off the air for thirty-five minutes and caused some casualties among the defence personnel. Air attacks alone would probably have been insufficient to force a move, in the event the reason being the possibility of a ground assault as a reprisal for the British commando raid which had taken place on a German radar station at Bruneval towards the end of February.[9]

The evacuation actually began on Friday 1 May, though it took three weeks to complete, an estimated 250 lorry loads of equipment, plus 120 trailer vehicles, being needed for the cross-country road journey via Salisbury, Swindon, Cheltenham and Tewkesbury to their new home, Malvern College for Boys, the college itself having gone to Harrow.

By now there was still more information available about the performance of Oboe Mark I, with test bombing showing that from 10,000 feet, a Wellington was able to drop 50 per cent of its 11½-lb practice bombs within an ellipse measuring about 400 yards by 200 yards, the probable error therefore being a distance of plus or minus 200 yards on the major axis and plus or minus 100 yards on the minor axis. Subsequently there were tests to determine the range of the system, a Lancaster flying at 22,000 ft obtaining a range of 260 miles, a distance from the ground station that compared favourably with the theoretical performance. So, with the two sets of critical performance statistics now available (although TRE and No. 109 could obviously continue their tests), this was the moment for the ultimate decisions: when and where to go first with Oboe, how best to use the system and with what airborne and ground-based technical facilities?

A recommendation from the Operational Research Section at Bomber Command Headquarters, as early as 14 June 1942, covered all but the 'when'. Oboe Mark I should be put forward as 'an extremely urgent operational requirement' to help locate targets in the Ruhr, the industrial heart of Germany, and two ground stations should be set up for that purpose, the 'highest priority' to be given to fitting six suitable aircraft with Oboe. The role for a single Oboe aircraft: to drop flares accurately over the target at zero hour, immediately turning about to make a second run as soon as possible after the first. The concept of dropping flares rather than bombs was one that seems to have begun with Dr Dickins at Bomber Command Headquarters because Rowe, the TRE Superintendent, in a note to Sir Henry Tizard, wrote that he 'wanted him to know of a brainwave Dickins has had regarding an early operation'. It was Rowe's understanding that RAF bombers had great difficulty in finding Essen so Oboe might be used 'at once' to drop flares with an accuracy of half a mile or so without the crew requiring much training. Elaborating on the concept, Rowe's note proposed that others following the Oboe aircraft could bomb the flares and drop more flares. After fifteen or twenty minutes, another Oboe aircraft could drop more flares and so on. Rowe, who was clearly not inclined to miss an opportunity to press for the means to achieve what TRE intended with Oboe, drew Sir Henry's attention to the fact that 'the aircraft which could do the Oboe work at once, if it is flyable, is the Wellington VI'. At 32,000 ft, this pressurized cabin version would meet the range requirements for Essen and, as Rowe put it when concluding his note. 'AA guns would not matter, nor probably would fighters.'[10]

There was more to bombing Essen, or anywhere else with Oboe for that matter, than having someone with sufficient authority to get his hands on an aircraft that was capable of reaching a height sufficient to obtain the required range, yet allow the crew to operate effectively in such a rarefied atmosphere. The pressure cabin Wellington, the Mark VI, appeared to be the most suitable so this was the aircraft promised to No. 109.

Halfway through the year, with Air Marshal 'Bert' Harris now in charge of Bomber Command, a number of discrete activities were taking place that would take the squadron still closer to the point when it could start making a significant contribution to the RAF's bombing effort with Oboe. Those activities included the selection and completion of the first pair of ground stations to track the Oboe aircraft and signal the moment of release; there was the decision to create a 'pathfinding' force to lead bombers to their target (Path Finder Force, hence PFF, was more usually written 'Pathfinder Force' in later years); and there was the unexpected availability of the de Havilland Mosquito multi-purpose 'Wooden Wonder' aircraft, so called because of its wooden rather than metal airframe.

The remarkably versatile Mosquito was without doubt the long-awaited answer to No. 109's prayers, a magic carpet, if you will, on which to carry the squadron forward to greater achievements. Where the Wellington was an aircraft dedicated to a bombing role alone, its load-carrying capability dictating speed and manoeuvrability, the smaller, lighter Mosquito was a bomber with a fighter-like performance. Although the plane's bomb load would be less, it would be able to fly higher, further and faster than the current version of the Wellington. The advantages were considerable: the 'Mossie' would not only optimize Oboe's capabilities, it would also reduce the crew size (from a minimum of five to just the pilot and a navigator/bomb-aimer) and much improve their chances against anti-aircraft fire and enemy fighters.

Events moved swiftly at the Air Ministry, at Bomber Command HQ, at Stradishall, where No. 109 was now based, and at Horsham St Faith, home to a squadron that was already operating with Mosquitoes, No. 105 Squadron, the first to receive these innovative aircraft and as yet still the only one flying them. This début use of the Mosquito was for daylight bombing, in which those crews excelled.*

On the afternoon of 19 July a cipher message from Bomber Command, BC/S.25547/Org,[11] set in motion the authorization enabling No. 109 to obtain one of No. 105's precious Mosquitoes at a particularly critical time –

---

* No. 105 Squadron received its first Mosquito on 15 November 1941 at Swanton Morley, delivered personally by Geoffrey de Havilland. The first operational flights were on 31 May 1942, by which time No. 105 was at Horsham St Faith, with the task of carrying out bombing and photographic sorties over Cologne in the immediate aftermath of the Thousand Bomber Raid.

the period when the Wellington VI was still on its way to No. 109 and when there were decisions to be made about new Oboe trials that Bomber Command required McMullen to begin.

In time Hal Bufton, who ranked as No. 2 in the squadron during that period, would divulge that a week before the final decision to begin installation of the Wellington VI on a production basis, McMullen 'got hold of a Mosquito and installed all four Oboe bits into it just in time for the conference, which accordingly rejected the Wellington in favour of the Mosquito'.[12] In fact Bomber Command HQ had put all the 'nuts and bolts' in place by instructing Nos 2 and 3 Groups to make the necessary arrangements for this single aircraft to be 'detached on temporary loan' between the two squadrons, No. 109's role being, in the clipped wording of that cipher message, 'to complete trial installation full equipment for Oboe operations', with assistance in fitting obtainable from No. 26 Group 'if required'.

So it was that a Mosquito Mark IV with the serial number DK300 duly arrived at Stradishall. Just a few days previously on 11 July 1942, with five other aircraft from No. 105 Squadron, it had carried out a low-level bombing attack on the submarine slips at Flensburg (Pilot Officer R.G. Ralston and Pilot Officer S. Clayton were the crew). It was a mission so low level that one of those Mosquitoes crashed in the target area and another actually struck a house on the way, bombing early and somehow managing to get back to base.[13]

Just about the time that DK300 was having the Oboe equipment installed, McMullen, as No. 109's CO, learned of Bomber Harris's immediate intentions for his squadron in a letter from Group Captain W.E. Theak, Chief Signals Officer, on behalf of the Senior Air Staff Officer at Bomber Command Headquarters. There was to be an operational Oboe squadron within Pathfinder Force, that there were going to be trials so as to develop an Oboe operational technique, and that No. 109 Squadron had been selected for the purpose. It was now No. 109's function to determine the time limits for the first Oboe-equipped aircraft to reach a given target, the time intervals needed to bring further Oboe aircraft over the target with a single pair of ground stations in use and the range of Oboe coverage with aircraft flying at various heights and in a mix of meteorological conditions. The trials would be performed with two aircraft equipped with Oboe and six non-Oboe aircraft in a follow-up role, McMullen to use the experience so gained to form the basis for his ideas on putting the Oboe system into operational use as a target-marking technique within Bomber Command.[14]

The first flights in the Mosquito delighted those in No. 109 who were privileged to take it up and the first Oboe trials showed right away that this was the type of aircraft that promised the best results so far. At the ground station, the signals response from the Mosquito was 'complete saturation at 145 miles . . . and surpasses anything obtained from the Wellington at 80–100 miles'.[15] This was not yet the end of the Wellington as a potential

Oboe-carrying pathfinder, however. Not only was the series of tests that Bomber Command required the squadron to conduct carried out with the squadron's Wellington Ic aircraft, the long-delayed but higher-flying Wellington VI did eventually become a part of the squadron's complement and this version too had a part to play in Oboe flight testing. However, on 6 August 1942, when No. 109 was absorbed into Pathfinder Force and the squadron moved from Stradishall to Wyton, it was the original Wellington, the Mark Ic, that formed the operational nucleus of this new striking unit.★

It was at Stradishall that Sergeant F.M. Griggs, pilot, and Sergeant A.P. O'Hara, navigator, joined No. 109, shortly after taking part in a bombing raid from that same airfield in which both earned an immediate Distinguished Flying Medal for bravery (see page 78). And it was there that the pair flew in both the Wellington – the Mark Ic and ultimately the 'Six' – and, for the first time, in the Mosquito, an aircraft in which Griggs and O'Hara soon rose to great heights.

Pat O'Hara recalls:

In those early days I remember carrying out a height test with 'Monty' Thelwell when we reached 30,000 ft. It was a no-nonsense trip, doing everything by the book, probably because on that particular day Don Bennett, the Pathfinder Force Commander, happened to be with No. 109. On that occasion 'Monty' and I were up for just an hour. It was altogether different a week or so later though, when, with Frankie Griggs, in the same aircraft [a Mark IV, DK321], I was up for 2 hours 20 minutes on another height test and this time we kept on going up and up and up, soon passing 30,000 ft.

Frankie said something to me about letting us see how high we could really go in the Mosquito. He was coaxing every foot out of it. All I could do while we climbed higher and higher still was to sit there, alongside him, watching the altimeter needle keep creeping up, 100 ft, another 100 ft and so on, until the inevitable happened. The engine stuttered and we just fell out of the sky. By then we were at 42,000 ft and going into a spin. I could tell that Frankie was having great trouble getting us out of it – and at one point I reckon he must have had to get a leg round the stick to exert sufficient pressure to bring us back on an even keel. It was a wonderful aircraft, the Mosquito.[16]

It surely was a delight to fly because on a subsequent occasion during training, that same pair, Griggs and O'Hara, all but committed the sin of taking one of No. 109's Mosquitoes over enemy held territory some six weeks before the first operational sorties. This was the outcome of experiencing a 75-knot tail wind during a cross-country practice flight from Wyton. One leg was to maintain a course along the south coast from Poole

---

★ The Wellington VI had but a brief stay with No. 109 Squadron. Meetings of the RDF Chain Executive Committee 'B' Oboe, which Sir Robert Renwick chaired, heard on 4 November 1942 that the trial installation [of Oboe] in the Wellington VI had been completed and the aircraft cleared, and on 7 January 1943 that No. 109 Squadron establishment had been amended and Mosquito aircraft substituted for Wellingtons. The question of further trials with Wellington VIs 'did not therefore arise'.[17]

to Herne Bay but, as the navigator subsequently explained, 'I hadn't realized where the wind was taking us until the French port of Calais came into view'. With that, Griggs carried out the aerial manoeuvre that was next best to an about-turn on the parade ground and pursued a homewards course to cross the coast at Mablethorpe.

Encouraged by the news that preliminary tests of bombing with Oboe were sufficiently successful as to give every hope that it would be an accurate means of achieving blind-bombing, McMullen (with whom, incidentally, Pat O'Hara made one of the early training flights in No. 109's first Mosquito, DK300), gave a personal assessment as to the level of skill that would be required of potential Oboe pilots. It was McMullen's view that, 'A pilot of average skill and with a sound knowledge of beam technique and of instrument flying should have little difficulty in being successful with Oboe. However, it must be appreciated that it is not a task that is suitable for all pilots of the average squadron and that to be fair to the system it would be necessary to select pilots carefully.'[18]

In readiness for No. 109's intended role as a spearheading, target-marking force over the Ruhr, the prime objective during the forthcoming winter offensive in 1942/3, much had been done to set in place the sites, the equipment and the personnel for what were designated 9000 Series (later, Type 9000) ground stations, which were paired and given individual numbers according to the originally intended purpose, odd numbers as bombing stations, evens as tracking stations. Worth Matravers became 9011 and West Prawle 9012, Trimingham was to be 9021 and Walmer 9022, while Trimingham House was allocated as 9031 and Swingate 9032. The proposed establishment for each of them was one flight sergeant radio mechanic, one corporal radio mechanic, two aircraftmen radio mechanics and four aircraftmen radio operators, with Bomber Command attaching an officer to each station to act as controller.[19]

Reeves himself, perhaps understandably because Oboe was his creation, proposed the geographical locations to place the first pair of ground stations. He did so at a meeting in Whitehall on 14 July 1942, under the chairmanship of Sir Robert Renwick, with representatives from various Air Ministry departments and including Squadron Leader E. Fennessy from No. 60 Group Headquarters, the group which would become responsible for the construction, maintenance and operation of the ground stations.

Pre-war, Fennessy had been on the staff of the Air Ministry Research Station at Bawdsey, planning the telecommunication system for the rapidly growing chain of CH stations (coastal radar stations) and the development of electronic devices for the effective use of the radar information from the CH stations by Fighter Command. In July 1939 he proposed that, in the event of war, a Base Maintenance HQ (BMHQ) be formed, as a section of the Research Station, to be responsible for the continuing construction and maintenance of the CH stations upon the outbreak of war. He set up that unit at Leighton Buzzard when war came, the civilian-staffed BMHQ becoming an RAF formation, No. 60 Radar Group, Fighter Command. Fennessy joined the RAF and was responsible for the building and upgrading of the CH system around the whole of the British Isles until late 1941 when he was given the duties of planning and building the rapidly growing system of GEE, G-H and Oboe stations for use by the British and American bomber forces.[20]

At the Whitehall meeting chaired by Sir Robert Renwick, Reeves proposed that there should be a station on the Norfolk coast and a station on the Kent coast, paired with each other, and that this pair of one northern and one southern station be duplicated. He explained that the nearer the angle of intersection of lines drawn from the northern and southern stations to the target was to 90 degrees, the greater was the degree of accuracy to be obtained; a 30 degree angle, the maximum obtainable for the particular target in view, would nevertheless give sufficient accuracy. If the sites selected gave an angle of 23 degrees, there would be an 18 per cent loss in accuracy.[21]

Two radar sites, one at Walmer, near Dover in Kent, and the other at Trimingham, near Cromer in Norfolk, were obtained from the army for conversion into a pair of ground stations, a duplicate pair to occupy a second site at Trimingham and one at Swingate. This latter site was, like Walmer (which was paired with the first Trimingham station), also in the Dover area. The endeavour was to have the first pair 'on the air' by 23 August 1942.[22]

Finding experienced and specially selected aircrew officers to take responsibility for the operational control of each station was to prove a more difficult task than was first envisaged. Some twenty-one commissioned and non-commissioned officers from bomber units duly presented themselves for interview on 13 August 1942 – all WOP/AGs (wireless operator/air gunners) in line with what Bomber Command considered the most likely category to slot into the new position. Bomber Operations, Directorate of Telecommunications and No. 60 Group representatives formed the panel to choose from among those twenty-one people, each of whom had a one-in-three chance of being picked to take on the function of controller and therefore have day-to-day charge of a ground station. Chaired by Group Captain Theak from Bomber Command HQ, the panel reached the unanimous conclusion at the halfway stage, that to carry on would be a waste of everyone's time. None of the candidates had the experience, basic knowledge or qualifications that the panel regarded as essential background for training in the use of Oboe equipment. With only one exception, it appeared, those who had been interviewed 'knew nothing of elementary navigation, of the theory of bombing, of RDF or cathode ray apparatus'. WOP/AGs were not the right candidates, the panel considered, and in their view 'the only personnel with the necessary background to enable them to start Oboe work at once were observers or pilots with navigation training'. A recommendation was put to Bomber Harris that six good air observers experienced in GEE, who had finished or nearly finished their operational tour, should be allotted to the Oboe ground station controller's job. With reservation, Harris agreed – 'You can have,' he told his SASO, 'any observers or pilots who have completed two tours or are medically unfit for operational flying'.[23]

Although much of the early Oboe equipment was made in the TRE workshops, there had to come a time when production versions would become the responsibility of British manufacturing companies. Security was always liable to be a problem; during transportation, in fact, Oboe system components were under armed guard. In the air, tests were restricted to Britain so that there was no risk of equipment falling into enemy hands before the system could be introduced operationally. At the ground stations, where there remained the chance of enemy invasion or infiltration, a means of easy destruction had been devised 'just in case' – TRE had named the calibrator, double strobe and navigator panels on the ground receiver which were to be destroyed in the event of an enemy landing, with certain members of the ground station staff being given the necessary instructions.[24]

Training in the air continued with the original sets that had been built during the development and trial stages. Constant use gave rise to signs of strain and there was concern over the increasing difficulties posed in maintaining this equipment in serviceable condition. Bomber Command took up the cudgels and urged the Director of Telecommunications at the Air Ministry to see what could be done to have TRE ensure that there was an 'adequate supply' of airborne equipment available to No. 109. TRE responded with one more set, which meant that the squadron now had four sets in total; every effort was to be made to send further sets as soon as possible.[25]

With Pathfinder Force now in being – No. 109 was a founder member alongside one squadron apiece from the other groups in Bomber Command – and everyone involved in Oboe now looking forward to an early application against an enemy target, this was not the time to have to concede that there was a paucity of sets for the squadron's aircraft. TRE already had enough on its plate, so much so that it could well have done without the serious and quite unexpected technical problem that occurred at about the same time. The pressure was on to get all the Oboe ground and airborne equipment installed and serviceable by a given date in October 1942 but what happened then was the 'Peacock' transponder began to arc when the aircraft reached about 21,000 ft. It took time, expertise and above all patience – much of this time being spent in a pressure chamber to simulate the environment at altitude – before the cause could be established and the difficulties overcome. It was a problem that just had to be beaten because Oboe needed adequate height to obtain the required range; a 'Peacock' that could not function sufficiently high in the sky would have grounded the entire blind-bombing system. At Bomber Command HQ, Dr Dickins, in charge of the Operational Research Section, learning that a successful test had demonstrated that all was now well, wrote to Rowe at TRE to say that 'We are all bucked at this and sincerely hope that the apparatus will prove itself to be reliable and that operations will be able to start soon'.[26]

Unfortunately, now that this particular challenge had been met and overcome, another was looming. It transpired that while aircraft and ground stations were exercising in readiness for operations to begin, someone was repeatedly interfering with the crucial signal transmissions which were the pulses to and from the heart of the Oboe system.[27]

CHAPTER SEVEN

Spirit of the Pioneers

*'The observers on the Stormy Down range couldn't believe that bombs could
be dropped with such precision from an aircraft they could not see – on a
target invisible to its crew. As for the rest of us – those who were from TRE
and No. 109 – we were not at all surprised; it was what we intended, it was
what we expected!'* TRE scientist J.E.N. Hooper, a member of the Oboe
group from its formation, recalling the first bombing trials with Oboe,
which took place during April/May 1942 on a sea range off Margam
Sands, South Wales.

It is intriguing to find that classic pathfinding techniques were being
performed by one particular squadron in Bomber Command as much as
two years and more before Pathfinder Force was born. One of the senior
pilots in No. 109 Squadron knew all about those innovative methods of
target marking over the Ruhr; he was familiar with them because he had
carried out his first tour of operational flying while with those early
pathfinders back in the summer of 1940.

Then a Pilot Officer, K.J. Somerville was a member of No. 10 Squadron
whose commanding officer at the time was Wing Commander S.O. Bufton,
elder brother of the then Flight Lieutenant H.E. Bufton. Syd Bufton, when
promoted to take a bomber operations role at the Air Ministry, would press
hard for wider recognition of the merits of pathfinding, and Hal Bufton
would be with No. 109 Squadron when, on 6 August 1942, this pioneering
Oboe squadron moved to Wyton at the birth of Pathfinder Force.

Somerville – he was always known as 'Slim' in the RAF – served his
apprenticeship as a navigator and as a second pilot in Sergeant 'Mac'
MacCoubrey's crew, flying Whitley bombers to carry out an assortment of
roles which began with a reconnaissance of canals and targets in the Ruhr
Valley on 6 April 1940 – 'Too dark to see any traffic on roads, railways or
rivers' – and ended by bombing the harbour and shipping at Ostend on the
night of 8/9 September 1940, the intention being 'to cause maximum
damage and dislocation' to Hitler's plans to invade Britain.[1]

Though abortive on occasions, those early flights were not without their
moments of drama. For instance, one mission directed against airfields in
Norway was a failure twice over: it had been necessary to change from one
aircraft to another at the last minute because the original one was
unserviceable and then, due to generator trouble with the replacement

aircraft, it meant having to return without completing the mission. Subsequently, and ironically because the target was again the same group of airfields, there was a rare recall as late as the Norwegian coastline when it was learned that the aircraft had taken off with the safety pins still in the long-delay bombs.

The night of 2/3 June is one that stands out more than most where Somerville and others in No. 10 Squadron were concerned. The target was the Homberg oil plant near Duisburg and it was here that the crew of one of the squadron's aircraft acted as what was called the 'identifying aircraft' for the remainder of the operating crews. The function of this particular aircraft was to illuminate the target continuously with flares while the remainder of the crews attacked. Severe anti-aircraft fire was encountered over the target area during the flare drop and this aircraft was hit several times by splinters. In one burst of gunfire the rear gunner was so severely wounded that the pilot chose to make a premature landing at another airfield to give the injured man a better chance of survival.[2]

During that pathfinder-led raid, visibility prevented MacCoubrey's crew from seeing the results of their own bombing but later, against the same target, direct hits were claimed. Other attacks elsewhere in Germany were frustrating to say the least. Detailed to attack an aircraft factory at Bremen, it proved impossible to make a positive identification so the decision was taken to go for the secondary target, which was the marshalling yard at Osnabrück. In fact this, too, proved elusive that night so there was a further change in plans, this time an airfield at Borkum being chosen as the alternative target. Despite a barrage of heavy anti-aircraft gunfire, two sticks of bombs were dropped on this airfield with a four-minute gap between them. It was a case of third time lucky for this crew and it avoided them having to bring back their bombs, as had happened on a previous occasion, and would occur again soon when, spending twenty-five minutes over the target, their aircraft was never once out of the clouds. Oh-for-Oboe, Somerville would doubtless have said if he could have had an inkling of what was in store when later he was flying with No. 109 and he had become party to the secrets of this ground-controlled blind-bombing system.

When July came, Slim was himself captain and pilot, the time with MacCoubrey having brought sufficient experience to be able to take a crew of his own on bombing missions, an early one being a trip to Turin lasting 9 hours 55 minutes. A series of aborted missions served only to drive home the fact that in those early days, the summer of 1940, it was trouble enough locating the target area only to find that the objective was obscured either by cloud or industrial haze.

A first tour of thirty-five ops behind him and the recipient of a well-earned DFC awarded on 23 November 1940, just forty-eight hours ahead of his posting to No. 109, Slim Somerville arrived when this embryo squadron was at Boscombe Down and still known as the Wireless Intelligence Development Unit (WIDU). Wing Commander S.O. Bufton (whose award of the DFC was in the *London Gazette* on the same day as Somerville's) was yet to move to the Air Ministry,[3] while his brother, Squadron Leader H.E. Bufton, waited to see who No. 80 Wing would be sending to take over the reins of No. 109. Then, pathfinding tactics were little more than the tender seeds of an idea in search of determined men to coax it towards fruition – men, in fact, like the Buftons.

For Somerville and those he would be joining at No. 109, ahead were those flights down the beam towards Cherbourg in ever-hopeful bids to bomb the transmitter; even further on was Operation Trinity with the irascible 'Broody Hens'. As for Oboe Mark I, the 'real' Oboe, as yet this indispensable tool for more effective bombing lay dormant among the team of scientists who were being assembled at what was now the Telecommunications Research Establishment (TRE) at Worth Matravers.

One of the scientists who joined TRE in October 1940 was a physics graduate and former schoolteacher, J.E.N. Hooper, whose six-month spell doing de-gaussing work with the Admiralty had come to an end. The proposal now was to move him to where the work would be to do with radio. Hooper made the honest admission that he 'didn't know a lot about radio', to which the interviewer responded, 'Just the man – off you go!' The first day at TRE saw him put into the library to read a manual about the CH (Chain Home) system that detected incoming enemy aircraft – 'It was nearly Greek to me, with "squegging" oscillators and other unfamiliar terms.' However, he visited several groups of specialists, the purpose being to let the section heads decide where he could make the most useful contribution. This turned out to be in the GCI section whose work on ground-controlled interception equipment enabled RAF night-fighters to be directed on to the tails of enemy bombers.

When the rest of that group moved elsewhere with the first mobile GCI station, he remained to cooperate with members of Goodier's section, who introduced a crystal-controlled calibrator enabling aircraft ranges to be measured with precision and consistency. It was the kind of work that could only be tackled with the support of dedicated and skilled aircrew, which meant Hooper became a frequent visitor to Boscombe Down, the airfield where Bufton and others were based while carrying out their beam investigation flights. So those same crews contributed to further researches too, flying along predetermined paths and signalling when immediately above specified landmarks, such as the end of a pier or a railway junction, to validate this measurement system.

It wasn't long before Hal Bufton came knocking on TRE's door to see what assistance the scientists could offer in his efforts to destroy the beam sources at Cherbourg. The result: TRE's involvement in the BBC – Blind-Bombing of Cherbourg – and Trinity operations in which John Hooper was respectively ground station controller and TRE liaison officer at No. 80 Wing's headquarters in Radlett.

A member of the Oboe group from its formation, he remembers Reeves as the thinker and Jones as the doer, Reeves being a man of ideas who could express them on paper and Jones a contrasting person who would, for example, never flinch at 'climbing an aerial tower with a soldering iron to fix some trouble at a CH station'. When their work had progressed to the Oboe bombing trials, Hooper was in charge; he was ground controller at Worth Matravers, which was linked by landline to the control room at the sea range off Margam Sands, whose female observers watched for each exploding bomb and recorded its position by triangulation. 'At first, the Air Ministry would not allow the navigator to release a bomb unless he could see the bombing range,' Hooper recalls, 'but when the results proved the accuracy of the system, they gave us permission to bomb if necessary from above the clouds. Then, when the girls saw the bomb-bursts still appearing in the right place, they were absolutely amazed; they became more and more excited with each release. They couldn't believe that bombs could be dropped with such precision from an aircraft that they could not see – on a target that was invisible to the crew. As for the rest of us – those from TRE and from No. 109 – we were not at all surprised; it was what we intended, it was what we expected!'[4]

When the Mosquito arrived at No. 109 – 'Bufton's brother Syd at the Air Ministry arranged this, I feel sure,' says Hooper – the problem of finding an aircraft to give sufficient height to use Oboe against targets in the Ruhr was over. At that time the Wellington VI was the only plane in prospect, 'our only hope'; it was anticipated that the Six would do the job, though it was none too popular with No. 109's aircrew members because, there being a pressurized cabin, escape in an emergency would not be easy. However, unlike the Wellington, which had gun turrets at the front and back for defensive purposes, the Mosquito was unarmed. 'Oh dear!' – or words to that effect – summarised the astonishment of No. 109 fliers on hearing that piece of news. Fortunately there was the compensatory virtue of remarkable speed, it could outfly any enemy aircraft of that era.

Height posed difficulties for the Oboe equipment, John Hooper remembers, and there was a problem with high-voltage arc-ing in the signal transmission part of the aircraft's transponder. Bertie Blanchard entered a pressure chamber with this equipment on one occasion, intent on finding first the cause and then the solution. As the simulated altitude increased, the arc-ing began, and Blanchard, in the rarefied atmosphere, neared a state of unconsciousness where the unavoidable collapse over high-voltage equipment would probably have killed him. Fortunately, prompt action from others involved in this experiment was able to prevent this happening so he emerged with the answer, which called for a careful repositioning of certain components within an already severely congested casing.

In the view of some people at TRE, killing Germans was the object of Oboe, certainly the intention was not to lose the lives of their own scientists. John acknowledges that the purpose of Oboe was clearly understood by all concerned in its creation, that it was being developed purely and simply to provide an answer to a problem: that the RAF was unable to carry out its bombing programme effectively until some means were found to get the crews to their target and their bombs on the aiming point. He recollects, 'We were less concerned with the outcome of our work; we were producing a precision instrument, that was the way we used to look at it. After all, you could argue that probably more civilian lives were being lost in Germany by inaccurate bombing than would be lost if Oboe gave Bomber Command the means to bomb more selectively and with greater confidence.'

A week or two after the main contingent – a fortuitous delay which fitted his domestic arrangements – John Hooper moved from Worth Matravers to TRE's new home at Malvern in June 1942. It was at Malvern that the initial intake of six Oboe ground station controllers – a former Blenheim bomber pilot from No. 82 Squadron, Squadron Leader F. Metcalfe, among them – learned for the first time that there was such a device as Oboe.*

Until then, the use of this word in the context of air warfare would have meant nothing and, to be fair, the first morning's classroom explanation of the working essentials of Oboe probably meant nothing either. As Frank Metcalfe recalls, 'It was all bananas to us. There we were, all bomber aircrew who were no longer flying for one reason or another – tour completion, recovery from wounds, etc. – and we were being bombarded with a barrage of scientific terms that were beyond us. We had no inkling of what this posting to TRE held in store; no one had told us what we were going to be doing – nobody *could* tell us. Still, thanks to the boffins being such understanding fellows, we all soon began to get the hang of it.'[5]

A front-line pilot well into his first tour, Frank had spent many weeks in hospital as a result of injuries sustained while taking part in a sortie on Armistice Day 1940, which epitomized the problems that confronted Bomber Command then and for a long time afterwards – the very problems that Oboe now promised to overcome. It was a night attack, daylight bombing having been abandoned because of the murderous losses; the three men were lost, clueless to the whereabouts of their intended target, so in desperation bombed an anti-aircraft position. They were hit, the plane was crippled and so much time gone that there was not enough petrol to cross the English coast. The Blenheim ditched, the radio operator/air gunner was killed and the two others seriously injured in the impact with the water. Metcalfe and his navigator scrambled out, bobbing up and down in their Mae West lifejackets in what turned out later to be a minefield. A destroyer, HMS *Vega*, came to their help, only to be seriously damaged herself by one of those very mines, causing the vessel to be towed into Harwich with its crew and the rescued pair still aboard.

Recovering in hospital and subsequently as an instructor and on flying control duties, Frank contemplated the 'appalling picture' that was emerging

---

* To avoid unnecessary disclosure of the name, RAF documentation posting personnel for training at Malvern used the term 'airborne musical instrument' instead.

of the RAF's night bombing efforts in the early 1940s, with a minor percentage of hits because the crews lacked the tools to find and to hit the target. Then, taking his place as a member of that first controllers class at TRE that autumn of 1942, it appeared that there was now something called Oboe which people there were saying would bring about a dramatic change in Bomber Command's fortunes.

When the training in the classroom was over, and with hands-on experience of the Oboe system, Metcalfe moved from Malvern to Trimingham where two independent ground stations on this single site in Norfolk were paired with two separate stations in Kent, Hawkshill Down (previously known as Walmer) and Swingate. As Oboe placed joint responsibility on the crew in the aircraft and those in the ground stations for a successful conclusion to each sortie, it seemed obvious that the people in the air and the people in the ground must quickly be able to appreciate each other's problems.

Frank Metcalfe remembers:

I wanted us to have the right spirit, to understand how we could help one another to get the most out of this new device, so I spent a lot of time at Wyton getting to know the pilots and the navigators who would be carrying out the early Oboe missions. As the controllers were all ex-aircrew, it was so much easier for us to mix with the Oboe squadron aircrew. We spoke the same language, which gave us an instant advantage, we drank together, we played poker together and we came to understand one another in a unique manner that I was convinced would work wonders when the time came for the first ops. On the ground station, handling the equipment that was going to get the aircraft to its target and give the signal to release, we would know who was flying that plane but there would be no verbal communication whatever between them and us. Oboe dictated their actions – we could not override the system or the decisions of the crew – but by watching their every move we were in a unique position to help them in their learning process with this incredible new bombing tool.

I knew that by developing this tremendous bond that was growing between us, we were going to be in a situation where we could all benefit. We would know when a pilot was wobbling while running up to the target – we could monitor that movement by means of distance markers on our cathode ray tube. And we would know if the navigator had released the bombs or the markers early or late because his action instantly ceased the signals transmitted between us. This way, we could measure the time difference between the intended and the actual moment of release. So, in a crude manner, with that information it would be possible to estimate – to guesstimate really – the point of impact in distance and direction from the aiming point.

When I was mixing with No. 109 at Wyton in those early days, I had no doubt whatever that the close personal relationship that was being fostered between those in the air and those on the ground would be invaluable in enabling all of us to get the best out of Oboe. There was a fair amount of leg-pulling, of course, but this was all a part of getting to know one another better. It paid off; I am certain that it did. For instance, when we knew that those in the air had been unable to do a proper job because of an equipment failure on the ground, we would defend our pilots for all we were worth. And when the flight commander or even the squadron commander rang with a query, he knew that he could always rely on us for the answer.

Inevitably there were equipment failures in the air too, additional to whatever the circumstances were that may have caused a pilot to deviate from the track that the Oboe system had determined for that particular flight or resulting in a navigator releasing (or failing to release) at the moment that the system required for a successful operation. So far as the aircrew were concerned, Oboe either worked or it didn't work, either you heard the 'noises in your ear' to get you to the target and to release whatever you were carrying, or you didn't; it would be someone else's job to discover the whys and wherefores, and to get the set working again. For some of the No. 109 and TRE people who were on the squadron when the Mosquito came on the scene in the summer of 1942, people like Corporal L.W. Overy, one of the 'sparks', the initial challenge was not to establish what was wrong with the Oboe hardware but whether everything would even fit into a Mosquito, which was so much smaller than the Wellington.

There were aerials to be positioned and there were the black boxes with their countless yards of wiring of different sorts and sizes which were peculiar to Oboe. These had to be linked in to the more routine components which enabled the Mosquito to fulfil its objective as a weapon of war, for example all the complex mechanisms that came into play when the navigator pressed the bomb-release button. Everyone knew that all the stops must be pulled out to be able to confirm that the Mosquito was the right choice. McMullen, the squadron commander, who had no doubts that this was the best aircraft around at that time, made sure that his own enthusiasm swept through the squadron, engulfing all those around him in a massive tidal wave of exuberance and unbridled confidence.[6]

Len Overy saw that first Mosquito (DK300) arriving at Stradishall. Detached on temporary loan from No. 105 Squadron, a daylight bombing squadron at Horsham St Faith, it looked brand new but, as soon became evident, this was one that had seen operational service. 'It had been shot up, that much I did discover,' Len says, 'but much later I read an article by its No. 105 navigator. It seems that the aircraft had to make a belly landing because the hydraulics had been damaged by flak, which made it impossible to operate the flaps and to lower the undercarriage. We reckoned we must have been given one of No. 105's cast-offs! Anyway, if this was the case, we were able to even the score in due course when a number of No. 109's Mosquitoes were transferred to No. 105.'

The aircraft had to be repainted all over in matt black, because No. 109 would be flying operationally only at night; even the transparent plastic nose was given a coating in the interests of security on the ground and to avoid the possibility of reflection if caught in the beam of a searchlight. As for the Oboe installation, supervised by Flight Lieutenant J.N. Walker, No. 109's signals officer, and Flying Officer J.M.D. Symons, the engineering officer, this required a fitting team comprising wireless mechanics, electricians and the airframe trades – the latter were mostly cabinetmakers and carpenters because this was largely a wooden aircraft. Len's involvement was principally concerned with related electrical circuits associated with the the bomb-selector switches and the bomb distributor, which was redesigned to handle the smaller number of bombs (or the new target indicators in bomb casings) that an Oboe-Mosquito would be carrying. Also, the individual units at the heart of the Oboe system itself had to be fitted and wired up, most of them going into the nose, which first had to be cleared before anyone could contemplate a decision about the location of the new equipment. There were circuits to be drawn and tested; there were components to be modified on the workbench; there were holes to be cut and areas to be strengthened; and there was the interrelationship of one specialist's expertise with another to be exercised to achieve the maximum benefit to the team's total endeavours.

Len Overy recalls:

> We were working 24 and even 36 hours with no real break but there were no gripes because there was always this extreme anxiety about getting the job done without a moment to lose. All of us were caught up with the excitement of what was going on in No. 109 at that time. We knew the improvements that Oboe was expected to bring to our bombing of Germany. And we knew that the sooner this and the subsequent Mosquitoes were able to be equipped with Oboe, the sooner the crews could get on with their training in readiness for operations. What did aggravate us was the fact that we were putting in all these hours and then being forced to do guard duty too. So we would finish a shift and then be called out to patrol the airfield perimeter or to guard the aircraft. Obviously security was necessary – none of us questioned that fact – but it seemed to us that our own most vital work would suffer. I do know that when the Pathfinder Force commander, Air Commodore Bennett, learned what was going on – apparently someone was up before him on a charge for raising some sort of an objection – he put an immediate stop to this practice.

No. 109's Mosquitoes were kept from prying eyes, even from others on the airfield. They were never allowed in view for longer than was absolutely necessary and as soon as one of them landed, it was whisked away to its hangar and the doors were closed. Len recalls No. 83 Squadron, flying Lancasters, arriving at Wyton from Scampton at about the same time as No. 109; 'obviously great interest was shown in this comparatively tiny aircraft, the "Mossie" already being something of a legend, but enquiries were not welcomed'.

Squadron aircrew were generally quick to acknowledge the debt owed to their squadron colleagues on the ground who worked long and hard to ensure that the bombers were correctly serviced and efficiently maintained to get them to and from the target. If the airframe, engines, wireless equipment, armament and all the other bits and pieces of a front-line operational aircraft were in good shape – and this would be the case when you could put your trust in the ground crew – then the aircrew could get on with their individual and team roles in the hazardous hours ahead. The weather, the anti-aircraft guns and the fighters posed problems enough on top of finding the way to the target area, picking out the objective, releasing the bombs and getting back home, hopefully with aircraft and crew all in one piece.

Sergeant A.P. O'Hara, who joined No. 109 Squadron a day or two before Pathfinder Force came into being in early August 1942, had every reason to commend the diligence of the ground team responsible for his four-engined heavy bomber when, twenty minutes before midnight on 27 June that year, he took off from Stradishall as observer in one of the nine Stirlings from No. 214 Squadron detailed to attack a target in Bremen in northern Germany. This tenth op in a Stirling added a further perspective to this crew's operational experience because eight flares were being carried as well as some three tons of incendiaries. It was a pre-Pathfinder Force role for them, the purpose both to concentrate their minds on accurate target identification and to light the way for other bombers.

This was an operation, as it turned out, that underlined the importance and the vulnerability of one particular member of the crew, the rear gunner, the 'tail-end Charlie' as he was often described. For the majority of the flight he would have to occupy a remote position, isolated from the rest of the crew except for sporadic radio contact, sitting behind his machine-guns for hour upon hour. It was his job to keep at bay any fighters which might choose to attack from a direction that the enemy seemed to regard as offering the best prospect of destroying the bomber with the least personal risk. Only that night, two of No. 214 Squadron's nine Stirlings aborted the mission because the rear gun turret would not function; one experienced a failure in the engine pump working the turret and the other lost use of the turret because of damage from anti-aircraft gunfire.[7]

In both instances, it appeared, the decision to return early was because the aircraft found itself without the benefit of its critical rear defensive position. In the case of Pat O'Hara's aircraft, sadly there was clear recognition of the fact that the rear gunner was especially in peril whenever a crew found itself exposed to enemy action – as did this crew on the way back from Bremen. They had bombed from 16,000 ft, dropping their 8 30-lb flares and 1,625 4-lb incendiaries in bright moonlight.

Because the Stirling lost the use of one of its starboard engines over the target area when sustaining much damage from anti-aircraft fire, it was decided to return from Bremen using the shortest journey, a route by way of Holland where enemy airfields occupied by night-fighters posed a further threat for homeward-bound bombers. It was therefore a time for continued vigilance for all on board: Sergeant F.M. Griggs (pilot), Sergeant T.N.C. Prosser (flight engineer), Sergeant W. Wildey (wireless operator), Flight Sergeant J.I.C. Waddicar (mid-upper gunner), Sergeant R. Watson (front gunner) and Sergeant H.A.W. Sewell (rear gunner), with Sergeant O'Hara (observer). While still in the early stages of the return journey, however, two enemy fighters did attack, the bomber sustaining further damage and the wireless operator being wounded in the arm, though one of their opponents suffered a mauling at the hands of the mid-upper gunner whose long and vicious burst sent it spinning towards the ground where it exploded on impact.

With the homeward track set via the Zuider Zee, Rotterdam and the North Sea, renewed trouble struck unexpectedly when searchlights began to display more than a passing curiosity. As a consequence of a combination of evasive manoeuvres to get out of their way, and the imbalance that resulted from the loss of one-quarter of its engine power, the Stirling began to spin and lose height rapidly. Pat O'Hara recalls that the pilot had his feet on the dashboard in a desperate effort to achieve control, the plane diving to around 1,500 feet before equilibrium was restored.

To use Pat's words:

Things now began to get a bit hectic and being as low as we were, with dawn breaking, we could clearly see three Messerschmitts taking off from an airfield at Alkmaar, obviously intent on coming for us. Two closed in and the front gunner, who had been tending the injured wireless operator, experienced difficulty trying to get back into his turret, which had jammed. He was half in, half out, so I jumped down and pushed him inside, hanging on to his legs to keep him steady while he fired his guns. Anyway, he got his Messerschmitt, it was sheer luck, of course, what really happened was that Jerry ran into our bullets! The gunner who had already knocked out one of the opening pair of enemy night-fighters took a crack at the one still left from this fresh pair, opening up at close range with the result that it promptly dived away and exploded before hitting the water. Of the trio of Messerschmitts that we had seen taking off from Alkmaar, one still remained but when he did put in an appearance, a few minutes later, the return fire from our mid-upper gunner was sufficient for him to break off the engagement.

During this time, Frankie Griggs had been throwing the Stirling around the sky as if it was a Spitfire. Outside, it was becoming lighter now, which was fortunate because we were over the water and flying so low that it was a miracle we stayed airborne – at one point our tail struck the water and we bounced up again. We were well clear of the Messerschmitts so I made my way through the aircraft to see what had happened to our rear gunner; we had lost all our means of wireless communication and were out of touch with him since being hit by the first of the fighters. Only then did we realize that he was gone – hit in that opening combination of cannon and machine-guns and probably unaware, until it was too late, that there were any fighters in our vicinity. Sadly he was dead, a bullet through the heart, poor lad.

By this time it was problematical whether or not the rest of us were going to get home alive, the aircraft being in the state that it was, being left with little or no fuel to feed the three remaining engines, a gaping hole in the side of the fuselage and goodness knows what other damage. Over the airfield a second engine cut, the starboard outer this time, which meant that Frankie would have to get us down in a situation where the two engines still running were both on the same wing. We braced ourselves for the inevitable crash-landing. Frankie made it though; many a time he had shown himself to be an ace landing a Stirling but this time he was going to have to make the touchdown of his life. There was really no choice; he made a no-nonsense approach, going straight for the perimeter track and clipping a hedge in the process. Thanks purely to him, none of us were even scratched. Those of us who were able scrambled out of the astrodome in record time, deciding not to hang around in case the Stirling was about to catch fire, though I doubt if, by now, there was any petrol left to ignite! The ambulance people managed to get the wireless operator clear of the aircraft.[8]

All six survivors were awarded an immediate Distinguished Flying Medal which was recorded within the month, the awards being announced in the *London*

Gazette on 21 July 1942.* O'Hara went on a week's leave and Griggs had a spell in hospital but the pair did one more op together, Wilhelmshaven, before Griggs' departure on detachment to Upavon, with promotion to Flight Sergeant, split the team. Soon, though, he would be reunited with O'Hara at Wyton, the pair going on to fly together as pilot and navigator respectively in two-seat Mosquitoes when No. 109 began bombing with Oboe later in the year.

Two raids on Duisburg and one each on Hamburg and Saarbrucken concluded Pat's time with No. 214 Squadron, an interview at the instigation of No. 109's CO, Wing Commander McMullen, leading to Pat joining his squadron on 31 July 1942 for Special Duties. During August, new crews were arriving, as were the first Mosquitoes, so Pat had a word with the CO about contacting Frankie Griggs with a view to getting him on the squadron. This was agreed, the posting was arranged and the two pals from No. 214 were together again in early September, by which time both men had been given the news that they were to be awarded a commission.

Since the beginning of 1942, when Squadron Leader Bufton re-joined No. 109, the squadron had moved from Boscombe Down to Stradishall and now to Wyton. Within two months it had lost two of its aircraft on special duty flights; first to go was Flying Officer G.J. Maygothling and members of his crew, then Flight Sergeant Eddy's, while a third aircraft on similar wireless investigation work, with Flight Lieutenant Fernbank its pilot, unusually came up against a German fighter, an Me 110, which it engaged and was able to claim as damaged in the skirmish.[9]

As one of the senior officers in the squadron, and a member of a bomber squadron before the war, Hal Bufton knew better than most the anguish that envelops people in such a tight community when an aircraft and its crew fail to return to their home airfield within the expected time. Indeed, besides understanding what being missing meant to families and friends, he was also well aware personally of this trauma from the viewpoint of someone who had become long overdue while carrying out an operational sortie over enemy territory. For Bufton himself had been posted 'Missing in air operations'.

After spells as a pilot, making beam investigation flights and carrying out radio countermeasures operations which included bombing the transmitters on the Cherbourg peninsula, Bufton was posted to Bomber Command in August 1941. Then, as captain and pilot of a Wellington belonging to No. 9 Squadron at Honington, Bufton took off at 2233 hrs on the 26th of that month for what turned out to be a one-way flight to Cologne. The eight Wellingtons from this squadron were airborne at one-minute intervals, joining other aircraft from the

---

* The citation quoted in I.T. Tavender's book, *The Distinguished Flying Medal, A Record of Ccourage, 1918–82*, states that Griggs displayed 'fine airmanship' in getting his severely damaged aircraft safely back to base, and it pays tribute to the 'unflinching courage, great fortitude and splendid team work' of the other five recipients of this award, 'in foiling the attacks of five enemy fighters, three of which were shot down'.

same airfield and also from Feltwell which together comprised the No. 3 Group contribution to Bomber Command's operations that night.

The four squadrons from No. 3 Group had specific objectives in the Cologne area for their primary target and Bufton – he was a Squadron Leader flying with an all-NCO crew (Sergeants J.T. Stickles, W.F. Crampton, S. Murray, R.P. Wright and K.B. Read) – reported having bombed at 0122 hrs. The home airfield had no inkling that anything was wrong until an SOS over the radio at 0207 hrs stated that the aircraft had engine trouble; this was followed by further radio messages until 0312 hrs, then nothing more was heard because the signal faded.[10]

For Bufton, the problems had begun before the Wellington even arrived over Cologne. As he explained later, engine trouble developed just before reaching the objective. The bombs were unloaded and a course was set for home. Shortly afterwards there was more trouble with the engines but this time it was much worse when one caught fire and the other seized up. Now over the Catillon area of northern France, some 15 miles south-east of Le Cateau, there was no alternative but to abandon the aircraft and take to the parachutes. All six crew members reached the ground safely, Bufton, Crampton and Read being more fortunate than Stickles, Murray and Wright who were apparently arrested together by the Germans in less than twenty-four hours.[11]

Bufton, intending to try to collect his crew, walked until daybreak without seeing any of them. That day French families gave him shelter, food, clothing and a map; at one point, after having to hide briefly on a farm because the Germans were conducting a search, he was joined mid-morning unexpectedly by Crampton. Helped again and again by the French, the two men travelled by bike and by car from one location to another until news of their whereabouts could be passed to a group dedicated to passing Allied airmen and others along a well-trodden escape route towards a neutral country. In the early stages, Bufton and Crampton spent two days at La Madeleine, near Lille, where Read joined them, then the trio were able to join forces with four more aircrew members and six soldiers to continue their travels under the care of the escape organization.

This was a journey that took the group by train first to Paris and then on to Tours. There then followed a river crossing on a boat, mile after mile on foot, a car ride and ultimately a further long stretch on a train through Toulouse and down to the southern port of Marseilles. There, RAF and Army members were split; Bufton and the others stayed temporarily in Marseilles while the soldiers were taken to Nîmes. The final stage was the familiar combination of travelling by rail, car and on foot, via the foothills of the Pyrenees and on to Barcelona in neutral Spain, where the group reported to the British Consul. Preparations were soon in hand to get everyone back to Britain through Madrid, Gibraltar and the Welsh port of Milford Haven, which was reached on 20 December 1941, sixteen weeks and four days since taking off on that one-way flight to Cologne.[12]

With the Christmas break over, Bufton's new posting came through – and it was the news that he had been waiting for and wanting to hear. He was going back on flying duties, back to No. 109 Squadron.

CHAPTER EIGHT

Choosing the Targets

Reference telephone conversation Commander-in-Chief and Assistant Chief of Air Staff (Operations). 'You may begin operations with Oboe, repeat Oboe, as soon as you are satisfied of its technical efficiency.' Cipher message to Bomber Command HQ from the Air Ministry, Whitehall, AX 311, classified Most Secret, Important, Serial No. Y1650, dated 7 December 1942. It was in this way that the Air Ministry authorized the first operational use of a ground-controlled blind-bombing system that promised hitherto unattainable precision.

There was no doubt about it, Bomber Command's winter offensive of 1942/3 would see more and heavier aircraft in action, carrying more and heavier bombs to attack Germany's industrial heartland where, thanks to new bombing aids, crews would have a better chance than ever before to find and hit their target. With the nights beginning to lengthen, the more detailed preparations were being made for a promising new phase in the air war, an era in which the developing techniques in pathfinding would be concentrated in the hands of selected squadrons, a practice that certainly had its critics – Bomber Harris himself among them. These élite units would comprise specifically trained crews, flying aircraft carrying the special equipment that was being created for this dedicated task. There would be several squadrons performing such a role, and there would be various kinds of bombing aids to benefit their crews, but there was one partnership of product and people which was especially in focus that autumn of 1942. For all those in the know, eyes were on Oboe, a system which was still to be proven, and on No. 109, the squadron that was working alongside the Oboe team at TRE to take the bombing trials to the next level.

With Oboe scheduled for introduction against the enemy before the end of the year, No. 109 Squadron was by now beset with problems which impacted on the aircrew training programme. Not only did the squadron still lack sufficient airborne sets to give its pilots and navigators the necessary experience on Oboe but, worse because there seemed to be no ready solution, some form of interference to the ground-to-air/air-to-ground wireless signals compelled the system to be shut down for hour after hour, day after day, at this most critical time. While Oboe was based on the transmission of wireless signals, it used an advanced form of radio-wave technology. This meant that potential trouble could come from two sides: on the one, wireless signals are susceptible to interference so this was a risk always to be expected, quite apart from any attempt at deliberate jamming; on the other, the more sophisticated the equipment, the higher the risk of something going wrong with it.

Now that Pathfinder Force had been formed and No. 109 was one of its founder squadrons, Wing Commander McMullen, No. 109's commanding officer, could address complaints to the force commander, Air Commodore D.C.T. Bennett, a man who had always shown that if action was needed, action would generally be swift to materialize. In his early dealings, McMullen was as direct in his criticism about the shortage of Oboe equipment as he was about the need for more aircraft for aircrew training. At a time when there were not enough Wellingtons to go around the operational units in Bomber Command, McMullen successfully pressed vigorously for his own squadron's complement to be increased. He argued that the three Wellingtons available to him (supplemented by a single Lancaster) may 'just cope' with the task of producing a total of six trained crews by mid-October. On the matter of the equipment shortage, where he called for measures to ensure an adequate supply of airborne Oboe sets from TRE, McMullen noted that while TRE had in fact provided a further set – which took the total to four – the performance of this latest set had been 'anything but satisfactory'. To get that one set to function correctly required Bertie Blanchard, one of the most experienced scientists in the Oboe team at TRE, to forsake his work at Malvern and go instead to Wyton for two or three days.[1]

Interference on the Oboe frequency was manifest as early as August, raising the inevitable query as to whether or not the enemy had somehow managed to pick up the signals and found a means of jamming them. Bomber Command wanted 'immediate action' to determine the source of the interference; if it turned out to be friendly in origin, action 'forthwith' was sought to suppress it. The Air Ministry acknowledged that this was a serious matter and promised to let Bomber Command know immediately the results of their investigations. In the meantime, No. 109, whose aircrew training with Oboe had been brought to an unwelcome halt, took matters into its own hands.

Conducted in conjunction with the Cossor Experimental Station at Matching Green, Essex, the squadron embarked on a series of tests which showed that the 'severe interference' on a component of the Oboe system known as the 'ARI 5148' came in fact from radar gun-laying equipment that the Army was using as a critical part of the anti-aircraft defences in eastern and southern England. If McMullen was in any way pleased that No. 109's own investigation 'in desperation' had identified the cause of the problem (the squadron had been, he said, 'extremely lucky' to do so without specialized equipment) he was far from happy about the manner in which others had reacted to this interference. In a letter to Bomber Command Headquarters, which he addressed for the attention of Group Captain

Theak, Chief Signals Officer (later to become Air Officer Commanding, No. 60 Group), he let it be known that the squadron had information which indicated that little had been done to clear up the trouble. It seemed, he wrote, that either there was 'a disregard of orders' or the task was not considered to be a matter of urgency.

The source now traced, Oboe transmissions were able to resume, the Army having accepted that their gun sites should stop using this equipment during specified hours, unless – and it was made clear that this would override that agreement – hostile or unidentified aircraft were in the vicinity. This first incident with jamming was not, however, the last. In the coming weeks and months there would be other occasions where friendly sources were found to be the culprit, Bomber Command's own navigational and other airborne aids among them. Although 'K' Oboe was introduced to counter such effects, by doubling-up the signals between ground and air, Oboe was never completely clear of interference caused by the operation of other people's radar-based devices. When this happened, it was necessary to track down the source and this was inevitably a haphazard search based on minimal information. In an ideal world there might have been some central authority charged with the responsibility for allocating and monitoring wireless frequencies, in a time of war – though McMullen certainly saw the need for such a move – it could be no more than wishful thinking. His concern was understandable; during that initial spell of interference, in the months of August and September 1942, the number of flying hours available to pilots training on Oboe was, according to McMullen, limited 'to a greater extent than is acceptable when the aim is to commence operations in the near future'.[2]

At that time, everyone involved in the Oboe programme was working to a schedule that called for six aircraft to have the system fitted by 3 October and a further four to be similarly prepared a week later. This was also the date for the ground stations to be ready and there was a tentative date for operations to start, just one month later on 8 November. Those were optimistic times, of course, and the pressure was so great that sometimes the desire to achieve was greater than the ability to attain.

When Pathfinder Force came into being, Oboe was of course as yet unavailable. Then came that 'tentative date' of 8 November to start operations with it, a forecast which turned out to be too ambitious. At a meeting at Wyton on 18 November, which Bennett attended with his senior Oboe controller, Flight Lieutenant B.W. Finn, and representatives from TRE, the Air Ministry and Bomber Command, the requirements and the practicalities of meeting them were reviewed so that an updated schedule could be agreed by these principal parties. The end result was minuted as a programme 'which would be adhered to', with immediate calibration flights, an operational trial with PFF backers-up at Cardigan Bay three days hence, aircrew training to be completed by 9 December and the first operation now scheduled for 12 December.[3]

Despite worthy aspirations and honest intentions, for this was a programme effectively set in stone, those dates also would not be met – the programme that 'would be adhered to' began crumbling before the concrete carrying the key dates had set. That old bugbear, interference with the Oboe signals, returned with a vengeance. Advising the other parties of the necessity for a delay of 'about one week' – an imprecise judgement because it wasn't yet known when the difficulties would be overcome – Pathfinder Force referred to 'severe interference' already having upset the schedule. It meant, therefore, a target date no earlier than 19 December for the first Oboe operation.[4]

A key part of the Oboe programme which was the responsibility of neither Pathfinder Force nor TRE was that of targeting, although both organizations would have to make an input with respect to their practicability. A prospective target that was borderline in range from the ground stations would have the effect of over-extending the Oboe system, while one that was too fiercely defended would overtax the aircrew. In the initial operations there was no sense in placing an unnecessary strain on Oboe itself or in needlessly risking the lives of the men whose flying and navigating skills would make or break this new blind-bombing tool. For ease of attack in the first operational application of Oboe, Aachen was proposed and among half a dozen other possibilities which were put forward to Bomber Command by the Director of Bomber Operations at Air Ministry, Air Commodore J.W. Baker, the one that was judged to be 'the most difficult' was Essen, the specific objective there being the Krupps works. It is doubtful whether any bomber crew with experience of taking a crack at Krupps would have disputed that assessment. The other aiming points suggested for practical consideration were in Cologne, Düsseldorf, Duisburg, Eindhoven (two of the Philips factories) and the synthetic petroleum plant at Gelsenkirchen.[5]

This was a time of 'good news and bad news, which do you want first', No. 109's squadron commander learning that there was a prospect of having to give up valuable training opportunities if, as seemed would be the case when the squadron began bombing, he would lose the use of the ground stations at Worth Matravers and West Prawle. He argued that if those on the east coast were to be confined to operational use, then Worth Matravers and West Prawle must be retained; if the east coast stations became available for training, however, Worth Matravers and West Prawle could be released. McMullen made a fervent plea for sufficient training facilities, the point being that there was much more to riding a beam than might be imagined. He reckoned that, once a pilot had mastered the technique of holding a narrow beam, a couple of hours practice a week was necessary to maintain consistent accuracy. Even if a pilot completed as many as five Oboe operations in a week, he would spend only about forty minutes on the beam, hence the need to have facilities both for trained crews and for those undergoing training.[6]

Procedural points that were put into the melting pot around this time included proposing and agreeing bombing and tracking signals, the details of which were not always sufficiently precise to suit the mix of individuals concerned with making such decisions. Not unexpectedly, TRE's scientists insisted on dotting the i's and crossing the t's for clarity in circumstances where indecision or misunderstanding would prejudice the mission. Differing viewpoints emerged in other terminology, for example with 'Cat' and 'Mouse', which eventually began to appear in documents as well as in less formal applications. It was Dr Cunningham from the Air Warfare Analysis Section, it appears, who completed this pairing by proposing 'Cat' as the name for the ground station responsible for keeping the aircraft along the arc towards the target ('Mouse' being the name already given to the 'reversible clock' mechanical timing device which determined the moment of release). As late as mid-November, however, Bennett was urging that 'in order to avoid confusion' the station providing what he described as 'the beam' should be called the 'tracking station' and the one 'which watches the aircraft to determine the release point' should be called the 'releasing station'. These names were, he suggested, 'more clear and less susceptible to mistakes' than those previously suggested. He was probably right but Bomber Command seems not to have taken up his proposal.[7]

Bomber Command Headquarters, meanwhile, let it be known to him that, once No. 109 began bombing with Oboe, there was a policy for the squadron to follow when weather conditions put a halt to 'normal' bombing against Germany yet did not hamper the use of the home airfields. The Oboe squadron would carry out 'light-scale blind-bombing attacks against important industrial plants in Germany'. The targets chosen for what would become known as nuisance raids were all steel works: August Thyssen-Hütte in Duisburg, Bochumer Verein in Bochum, Vereinigte Stahlwerke in Ruhrort, Meiderich in Duisburg and Friederich Alfred Hütte in Rheinhausen. The selection was made because of their function – these were all continuous process plants – and because of their 'relationship and key importance' in the steel industry. By keeping up the pressure on those steelworks, No. 109 would be waging a mini-campaign of its own against the Germans by hopefully causing a substantial drop in steel production.[8]

Nuisance raiding had wider implications: it took its toll on the general population by disturbing their sleep, on the defences over a big area by unnecessarily placing them on a state of immediate alert and on industry at large by upsetting production schedules.

Although the date for the first Oboe operation had been postponed more than once already, the way was now clear to proceed just as soon as everything slotted into place. This meant No. 109 having enough Oboe-equipped aircraft ready, their crews sufficiently competent, and paired ground stations functioning satisfactorily. The Air Ministry gave its blessing to the system coming into use in a Most Secret cipher message on 7 December, referring to a telephone conversation between Bomber

Command's C-in-C and the Assistant Chief of Air Staff (Ops) and authorized the commencement of Oboe operations 'as soon as you are satisfied of its technical efficiency'.[9]

It was a timely moment to bring on stage something that was surely going to benefit further the mounting night-bomber offensive against Germany. Pathfinder Force was already operating, though the first operation was judged to be a failure (it was against Flensburg on 18/19 August 1942) and subsequently some crews committed the 'undesirable practice' of releasing their markers without being certain of the target.[10] Nevertheless there was optimism in the conduct of the air war and there was confidence in the progress generally of the global war. In the desert of North Africa, the Battle of Alamein had been won; the Axis forces were in full retreat westwards. The Russians were on the offensive on their bleak and bitter central front. And in the Far East, in the Solomons, the Japanese suffered severely in a three-day sea battle that cost them two battleships, eight cruisers and many smaller vessels. In Europe, in the air, though American bombers had commenced daylight raids, heavier round-the-clock attacks by the USAAF and the RAF would await the turn of the year.

For Oboe, though, its time was here at last, the moment to test the system in action, the moment to test the men and machines of No. 109, and the moment to test the personnel – RAF and TRE, service and civilian, male and female – who now stood ready at the ground stations.

Where would this first blow fall – the bombs dropping at night and probably from above the clouds, yet hopefully landing directly on the chosen objective? It is doubtful that anyone could possibly have made a correct guess about the target location for Oboe's operational début. It was not going to be Berlin, which TRE Superintendent Rowe had proposed in the system's early days, nor would it be Gelsenkirchen, which the think-tank had contemplated during that round-table conference involving the principal parties concerned with the development and application of Oboe. Most assuredly it would not be Essen with its prime target, the massive all-important Krupps industrial conglomeration. Surprisingly, this first Oboe target would not even be anywhere at all in Germany.

CHAPTER NINE

The Lesson of Essen

'Essen has been a headache for Bomber Command for a very long time. With its heavy defences, searchlights, smoke screen and natural industrial haze it has proved a difficult target to hit with the old methods. By the proper use of Type 9000 Stations to mark the target, we have almost completely written it off.' Air Commodore D.C.T. Bennett, Pathfinder Force Commander, in a message of appreciation, on 10 March 1943, to Oboe ground station personnel via Air Vice-Marshal R.S. Aitken, AOC, No. 60 Group.

Although bombing-range trials had by now confirmed Oboe's accuracy, justifying the scientists' expectations and boding well for the mounting bomber offensive in that 1942/3 winter, No. 109 Squadron in the air and TRE and No. 60 Group on the ground must now meet the greater challenge of proving the system under operational conditions. Depending on the choice of target and the element of good fortune in respect of the enemy's defences, Oboe-equipped Mosquitoes of No. 109 would be presumed capable of repeating those results – results which were of course obtained with the unbridled advantage of structured visual observations on the ground.

In stark contrast, dropping bombs on either Germany itself or on a German-occupied country posed two significant problems: the first was to get the aircraft to the target unscathed, using signals from one of a pair of ground stations, and the second was to establish the impact point of the bombs released on the signals from the other paired station. The closer the target to home, the less risky would be the flight and if the target happened to be in friendly territory, so much the better when it came to finding where the Oboe-controlled bombs had fallen, to supplement the intended subsequent aerial photography. These were the factors, then, which influenced the selection of the target for the crews of the six Mosquitoes detailed for the Oboe début sorties on the night of 20 December 1942.

Targets in Germany having been ruled out – Berlin would have been too far, Essen and Gelsenkirchen too well-defended – the Low Countries offered the shortest and hopefully the least troublesome trip, coupled perhaps with the possibility of getting feedback from a resistance organization. As for the aerial evidence anticipated from one of the RAF units specializing in photo-reconnaissance, establishing the position of bomb impact beyond any doubt would demand a virgin target, otherwise pinpointing Oboe bombs among conventional bombing would be like . . . well, like looking for a particular hole in a slice of Gruyère cheese. The need for knowing exactly where each bomb had landed was certainly not attributable to vanity, or even mere curiosity, it was a necessity, absolutely vital for the Oboe programme. Pinpointing the fall of each and every one of those bombs was not only the means to confirm the accuracy of the system, it was the means of determining any systematic error – a sequence of bombs dropping short or overshooting the aiming point, or maybe to one side or the other, and to what extent, distance and direction, precisely; then adjustments could be made to recompense for any such variation. So a virgin target was a requisite for those concerned with this critical stage of introducing Oboe as a bombing technique, Pathfinder Force and Bomber Command who controlled the airborne activities, TRE and No. 60 Group who controlled the ground stations.

At Wyton, where No. 109 was now based, the initial target was at last disclosed: a power station at a small town, Lutterade, close to the Dutch–German border. At Hawkshill Down and Trimingham, the No. 60 Group ground stations where TRE civilians would control respectively the tracking and release signals, the target remained undisclosed, other than under cover of a codename, 'Lucia'.

First to take off at 1755 hrs was Squadron Leader Hal Bufton, whose navigator was Flight Lieutenant E.L. Ifould, the flight across the water and over enemy occupied territory causing no more problems than if this had been a training exercise. At the pre-determined height of 26,000 ft, with both members of this crew having heard and acted upon the signals from their respective ground stations as if still on a practice, Ifould pressed his bomb-release button when the 'Mouse' equipment showed the time to be 1925 hrs, 15 seconds. Come 1926 hrs and the first Oboe-controlled bombs were exploding on an enemy target.*

Bufton was complimented by Trimingham, which marked the occasion for posterity by logging these words: 'The signal strength was good as was the flying'. The next crew – Flight Lieutenant Somerville with Flying Officer M.S. Maas – had the misfortune to suffer the first Oboe failure in an operational sortie. It seems that overheating occurred on Maas's set, the Corona rings became unsoldered and the screen on the modulator came off. Bombing with the Oboe system required precise reactions to precise aural signals, so no Oboe signals, no Oboe bombs, the consequence being that Somerville and Maas bombed their last resort target: Duisburg.

---

* Ballistics information then available shows that it would have taken 42.7 seconds for a bomb to reach the ground. As will become clear, the reliability of bomb-fall statistics was questionable, imperfections in the metal casing and storage conditions were not alone in exerting an influence on the rate of descent.

With the six Mosquitoes scheduled for take-off at thirty-minute intervals, Pilot Officer Griggs with Pilot Officer O'Hara were number three into the target waiting area. Again there was an equipment failure, O'Hara's set apparently experiencing an unserviceable condenser, so this plane delivered its bombs to Duisburg too. At the halfway stage, therefore, the score stood at one Oboe success and two Oboe failures.

The fourth and fifth crews, respectively Flying Officer C.F. Campbell with Flight Lieutenant J. Turnbull, and Flying Officer E.H. O'Neill with Flying Officer J.E.B. Jefferson, fared better, the equipment behaving as did the leading crew's. Turnbull dropped his bombs at 2055 hrs, 15 seconds and Jefferson at 2128 hrs, 30 seconds, ensuring that there would be a minimum fifty per cent success rate for this first demonstration of the RAF's revolutionary and secretive form of bombing. Unfortunately, Flying Officer J. Thelwell with Flying Officer G.D.S. Koester, who were last on the scene, held on to their bombs for reasons that were different from the two earlier Oboe failures. According to Trimingham the receiving equipment was picking up heavy interference to the signals and this caused 'a rough note which had no meaning to the pilot'. This sixth aircraft also dropped its three 500-lb MC bombs on Duisburg, the three Mosquitoes which aborted over Lutterade adding their two tons worth to the amount deposited by some 200-plus heavies that same night on Duisburg.[1]

Exactly what happened to the Oboe bombs deposited at Lutterade that night remains unclear, conflicting reports doing nothing to help the historical records for what was after all a landmark occasion for Bomber Command, being the début performance of the long-awaited answer to the long-lasting problem of how to improve bombing accuracy. One of those reports indicates that the bombs released first, by Ifould, were calculated to have fallen about 200 yards from the aiming point, these being the closest to the target (the coke ovens in the power station); another, which was published postwar and quotes a local report, puts all nine bombs (three apiece from the three attacking aircraft) as having missed by as much as 2,000 metres.[2]

It will be recalled, however, that the intention was to use aerial photography to position the impact points of all the bombs dropped on Lutterade. Surely, then, there would be no such dispute. Unfortunately, Lutterade was not the virgin target that had been anticipated; Lucia had fallen from grace, in effect gang-raped by other British aircrews before No. 109's came on the scene! There had been no intention to bomb Lutterade ahead of the Oboe début – that was perfectly clear – but, when the post-Oboe photographs duly emerged from the printing process, it was obvious that somebody had carpet-bombed the area far more severely than would have been possible with just the Mosquitoes. The craters seen on those photos transpired to be from bombs that had been dropped in error, intended for Aachen in a bad-weather raid. The result was misfortune for the community and aggravation for everyone waiting to test the accuracy of

Oboe. This left no alternative but to find somewhere else to bomb, within those same parameters of distance and comparative safety for the aircrews, coupled with the possibility of someone on the ground being able to verify where the bombs landed.

The area selected for the second calibration raid was Florennes in Belgium, where there was a major military complex containing an airfield, night-fighter control centre, cadet school and specifically a large, isolated country house which would serve as an aiming point. The date was a memorable one: New Year's Day 1943. So, with an early morning take-off, three Mosquitoes were about to disturb the rest of those who were sleeping off the effects of the previous night's parties, the purpose being to drop bombs by Oboe and have their positions confirmed by observations made on the ground, rather like those on the bombing ranges during the Oboe trials. What wasn't generally known was the surprising fact that No. 109's target had been disclosed, in advance, to people on the Continent.

Flying Officer Thelwell with Flying Officer Koester, who aborted Lutterade because of interference to the signals, had better luck this time at Florennes; they tracked successfully to the target and on the ground station's signals, released from 28,000 ft at 0619 hrs. Some twenty-one minutes later, a crew carrying out their first operational sortie with Oboe, Flight Lieutenant P.A. Kleboe with Flight Lieutenant R. Findlater, released their bombs from a similar height. However the third crew, Flying Officer O'Neill with Flying Officer Jefferson, who had been successful at Lutterade, this time experienced equipment problems aboard their Mosquito. So the final score on this second calibration raid was two successes against one failure.[3]

Thanks to an initiative by Dr R.V. Jones in Air Intelligence, who had obtained agreement to letting the Belgian resistance know that this raid was going to take place, within forty-eight hours TRE's boffins had information enabling them to correlate the impact points with the track and release data in the Oboe system. Distances between where the bombs were intended to fall and their actual drop point were apparently paced for accuracy before the Belgians were content to pass to London the results of this remarkable on-the-spot calibration. Statistics aside, important though these were going to be to the scientists at Malvern and at the ground stations, the aspect of the Belgian observation team's findings that brought immediate satisfaction was the report that one bomb had fallen directly on to a building used to control night-fighter operations.[4]

A subsequent report refers to a wind speed in excess of 100 m.p.h. and bumpy conditions making accurate bombing runs extremely difficult – bear in mind that during this critical period the pilots must maintain speed and height while hugging the track for perhaps as long as ten minutes before tension could ease with the moment of release. However, based on a study of photographic evidence obtained from the air, the results showed that 'the accuracy of Oboe at Florennes is of the right order'; this was the view of Bomber Command's Operational Research Section (ORS), which judged that there was an average error of about 700 yards for the two 'bad' runs attributable to the effects of the poor weather.[5]

In the meantime, with no reason to doubt the value of Oboe despite the inability to validate its performance at Lutterade, No. 109's crews had carried out a number of nuisance raids on targets in Germany. These gained operational experience for pilots, navigators and ground controllers and compensated for time lost because of continued interference to signals during the periods set aside for training. The first such sortie was carried out by O'Neill with Jefferson, whose target was Hamborn, and the second by Thelwell with Koester, against Rheinhausen. In the half-hour before these two aircraft took off from Wyton, two other crews had been forced to turn back before even crossing the coast. Campbell and Turnbull found that the wheels of their Mosquito would not retract, while Somerville and Maas had an unserviceable compass. These were consequences that served well in illustrating that even if Oboe was up to scratch every time, other factors were nevertheless likely to upset best-laid plans. The tally that night was therefore two successes for the system, 100 per cent, but two aircraft failures.

The following night, the same four crews were again in action and joined by Bufton with Ifould, whose target was a first-time crack at Essen with Thelwell and Koester, no opposition being encountered despite the known severity of the defences. O'Neill with Jefferson bombed Hamborn again – it was their target also the previous night – and Campbell with Turnbull, this time avoiding any problem with their aircraft, dropped Oboe bombs on Rheinhausen for the second night in succession. The one Oboe failure in five prevented Somerville with Maas from carrying out their planned raid on Ruhrort so their bombs were directed against an alternative target in Duisburg.

Christmas Eve saw a further attack on Essen, by Campbell with Turnbull, and an Oboe failure for Bufton and Ifould. However, there was a revealing sequel to the attack carried out by the third crew to become airborne in the space of ten minutes, Somerville and Maas, who were now into their fourth sortie and still looking for a first successful Oboe bombing. At 1940 hrs, Maas perpetrated the first Oboe failure 'due to the human element', the words of Pathfinder Force Commander Bennett in a report to Bomber Command Headquarters which covered the sorties up to 31 December. Maas delayed pressing the release button for about three seconds (which would have produced an error of about 600 yards) and was probably responsible for damaging not the intended steelworks target but a German cemetery. This piece of information came from a statement on a German radio programme which reported that British aircraft had 'broken the peace of Christmas night and attacked Western German territory'; it added that 'several graves in a remote cemetery were destroyed by bombs'. Bomber Command's ORS team looked again at the aerial photographs and came to the conclusion that the first of Maas's three bombs 'might well have fallen in the cemetery but no crater can be discerned'.[6]

It seemed not unreasonable to take the Germans own version at face value, the consequence being that with the scientists' earlier awareness of the release delay, they could use the unsolicited gift of this unexpected knowledge about the distance and direction of those bombs from the aiming point in order to build up further data on Oboe's performance against targets on the Continent. Like archaeologists sifting for fragments, here was something coming to the surface that would no doubt make an invaluable contribution to the end result. The scientists thrived on intelligence of this sort, another instance about that same time being word coming from the Air Warfare Analaysis Section (AWAS) – one of their responsibilities was to provide essential precision data to Oboe users – to say that further researches into the correlation between the French and German survey systems had shown that there was an error of 300 yards on previous calculations for all German targets. The effect of this discovery was that in the Oboe raids so far on Essen, Hamborn, Rheinhausen and Ruhrort, No. 109 Squadron's bombs had been aimed 300 yards west of the desired aiming point with a similar misplacement of its flares when sky-marking Düsseldorf and Essen.[7]

The AWAS team was headed by Dr L.B.C. Cunningham, a Fellow of the Royal Society of Edinburgh. Immediately they became acquainted with the intricacies of Oboe, AWAS resolved that with a ground-controlled blind-bombing system promising such precision, any input which they themselves might be asked to provide must in no way be allowed to degrade that accuracy. This would have been unthinkable in any event because, by now, AWAS had built a reputation for meticulous work – an achievement in which Cunningham could take the bulk of the credit. Widely known as 'The Prof', because of his time spent in the RAF's education service in the pre-war years, Cunningham had latterly been at the Air Armaments School at Eastchurch where most of the senior armaments officers serving at the outbreak of war had passed through his hands. Then, posted to the Royal Aircraft Establishment at Farnborough, he gathered a small group of people around him to help complete a study that he was doing into the theory of air combat.

Early on in the war, 'Prof' Cunningham's group became known as the Air Warfare Analysis Section (AWAS). It had been formed under the aegis of the Deputy Director of Scientific Research in the Ministry of Aircraft Production, the capabilities of this handful of serious young men being turned towards performing a variety of tasks on behalf of branches of the Air Staff, particularly in the areas of Operational Requirements and Air Tactics, and later in support of the radar branches as these were formed. This work led to a first involvement with TRE, when GEE was undergoing accuracy trials at West Freugh which AWAS analysed. For one of the AWAS team, E.C. Cornford, it became his role to manage the production of the mathematical data required for the creation of the first charts for users of this radar-based navigational system. Consequently, when early Oboe came on the scene, it was perhaps not too surprising that AWAS was the organization whose help was sought in connection with Operation Trinity. Clifford Cornford completed the sums for target range and established the azimuth setting for the beam which the Stirlings of Nos 7 and 15 Squadrons – their crews supplemented by pilots and wireless operators from No. 109 Squadron – followed to attack the German warships in port at Brest.

Later on came the 'real' Oboe, which of course called for high precision and the requirement to know the distance between each of the two ground stations and the target – precise to one-hundredth of a mile. When bombing trials in the UK gave way to operational sorties and it became necessary to generate distance data to targets on the Continent, Cliff realized that the incompatibility that existed between the map systems of the various countries created a potentially serious handicap. A visit to the Directorate of Military Surveys produced the suggestion that perhaps GSGS at Cheltenham could help – GSGS being the Geographical Section of the General Staff. Cliff takes up the story:[8]

> I was introduced to an extraordinarily helpful individual, Dr Calderwood, who seemed to know all that there was to know about the survey systems of western Europe. He explained that, between the various countries, there was a lack of conformity about the very basics of their survey systems: for instance, the unit of measurement employed for the base line, the longitude difference between their prime meridian and the Greenwich meridian, and even the shapes and sizes of the spheroids to which their surveys were related.
>
> It was clear that we had to establish conformity if we were to measure target distances with the accuracy that was required for Oboe. For a starting point, what was needed was territory occurring where two systems abutted – a visual survey link was available across the Strait of Dover – to establish the displacement across this juxtaposition. It emerged that in fact there was a displacement of the order of 150 or 200 yards in the coordinates given to the same recognizable landmark. It was a discrepancy such as to be not ignorable, since the greater the distance between the points to be measured, the greater would be the displacement.
>
> Given the responsibility for target distance measurements, AWAS could not afford to risk degrading Oboe. Appreciating the situation, Dr Calderwood came up with a number of ideas which he thought would solve the problem and I put them into practice.*

There were just three more bombing sorties before the end of the year, two against Ruhrort (Campbell with Turnbull and Thelwell with Koester) and one against Essen (O'Neill with Jefferson), all from the customary height of

---

* Suffice to say that the process adopted in determining the British coordinates to be assigned to targets in other survey systems was a complex one, involving the calculation of a grid of corrections covering the German, French and other target areas to be applied to the latitude and longitude of targets taken from the best large-scale maps available, to bring them into conformity with the British survey. Thereafter the required Oboe target ranges were calculated just as though both the Oboe ground station and target were part of the British survey system. The value of the AWAS contribution cannot be overstated since without it the data supplied to the RAF and USAAF Oboe users would have been incorrect, and the aiming points systematically displaced by an amount sufficient to cause serious degradation of the Oboe system's inherent accuracy.

28,000 ft. To see the old year out, however, Oboe Mosquitoes introduced target-marking for the first time when Bufton, flying as usual with Ifould, with whom he had Oboe-bombed Lutterade in that début operation, successfully dropped flares over Düsseldorf to pinpoint the target for a small force of heavy bombers. Here, because weather conditions obscured the region, Oboe-marking was used to signify a hole in the clouds through which to bomb, rather than ground-marking which became the preferred form. As distinct from solo bombing with Oboe, target-marking was deemed necessary to require the services of a reserve aircraft. When the Mosquitoes were operating on their own as nuisance raiders, it was immaterial if an aircraft missed its slot for whatever reason and went on to bomb an alternative target. Where other aircraft would be following on, relying on the Oboe Mosquitoes to indicate the spot to bomb, it was imperative to have a stand-in in case of a problem, equipment failure or some other inability, causing the primary Mosquito-marker to miss its place.

As indicated, the markers which Ifould released that night were not candles to burn on the ground but parachute flares to ignite above the clouds – the term was 'sky-marking' – and what the heavy bombers would be doing was heading for that illuminated point in the sky and aiming upon it. It was far from foolproof, for example the wind would carry the flares and the extent of this drift was impossible to calculate. By taking advantage of Oboe's potential accuracy, sky-marking gave a means to bomb through cloud and here was a chance to test its effectiveness. Eight Lancasters of No. 83 Squadron were detailed for that Düsseldorf raid, that night of 31 December 1942, each carrying a 4,000-lb bomb and close on 1,000 incendiaries. All but one bombed as instructed, the other releasing on a reciprocal heading 4 miles south of the sky-markers, and one Lancaster failed to return. Doubts have been expressed over the value of this trial from the standpoint of 'bombs on targets', since subsequent photographic reconnaissance revealed no new damage in Düsseldorf, 'but the responsibility or otherwise of Oboe for this failure was not, of course, apparent'.[9]

Up to the New Year's Day calibration raid on Florennes, during which time No. 109's Oboe Mosquitoes were detailed for twenty-three sorties, Oboe equipment failed on only five occasions. During the first fortnight of 1943, which saw a second pair of ground stations brought into operational use (Trimingham II and Swingate), Essen was their target on six nights and Duisburg on one night, a further twenty-nine sorties which brought the total number of completions to fifty (this ignores the two on 22 December which were aborted because of aircraft failures). By now the Bufton (pilot) and Ifould (navigator) partnership headed the league table with nine sorties completed and Campbell/Turnbull just one behind, at eight; three crews had flown seven sorties apiece, Griggs/O'Hara, O'Neill/Jefferson and Kleboe/Findlater, while Thelwell/ Koester had completed six, as had Somerville whose half-dozen sorties to date comprised five with his usual navigator, Maas, and one with Flight Lieutenant A.C. Douglass. Of those fifty sorties, thirty could be described as successful because the intended Oboe-controlled release of bombs or markers took place,* and fourteen sorties could be regarded as unsuccessful because some form of failure with the Oboe equipment prevented the planned release. As for the remaining six sorties, these were all instances where the aircraft was flying as reserve and it was not necessary to make use of the Oboe system. Excepting this last half-dozen sorties, with thirty releases and fourteen failures, Oboe had achieved an almost seventy per cent success rate, it was a mathematical sixty-eighty per cent, during the first fifty occasions in which a No. 109 Oboe Mosquito had operated over enemy or enemy held territory, this period covering 20 December 1942 to 13 January 1943.[10]

With No. 109 active for six nights over Essen in this first fortnight of 1943, Oboe was now starting to be used for the main purpose for which it was designed – given its range limitations from the ground stations in England – and this was to attack targets in the Ruhr, principally the important and huge Krupps works in Essen. In these raids, sky-marking was carried out each time for a small force of aircraft from bomber squadrons, the number of Mosquitoes employed in a single night being no more than four and the heavies varying from just under twenty to as many as seventy. The routine was for the primary Mosquito to drop warning and marking flares of different colours and for a stand-in aircraft always to be available – on the night of 4/5 January, against Essen, the decision was to send '2-plus-2', though in the event neither of the reserves was required. On another occasion, when unfortunately there was such a requirement, by then it was too late for the stand-by Mosquito to function, the timetable for an Oboe operation being critical, with each aircraft having to be in the waiting area within a given period and, when called forward, to be correctly positioned in terms of height, direction and distance from the target. Acting as if on a taxi rank was something that stretched the skills of crews in training and sometimes troubled even those who were more experienced and operationally seasoned.

In those early days of Oboe bombing and marking over Germany, it had been found possible to make and to put on record what was probably no more than an inspired guess at the quality of an Oboe release. For example, in successive operations when marking Essen, the estimated impact point was 'dead accurate' on the first night and 1,200 yards away, at 160 degrees from the aiming point, on the second. Whatever the reason for such a variation, honour was fortunately restored four nights later with the judgement that on this occasion – and the job again was to mark Essen – the estimation was that the TIs were 'spot on' – not just once but twice![11]

---

* Here, 'markers' meant flares, the first target indicators (TIs) were not used until 27 January 1943, when those dropped by Griggs/O'Hara from 28,000 ft to pinpoint for an attack on Düsseldorf were 'seen to burst on the aiming point', according to No. 109's Operations Record Book.

Even from more than 5 miles up, Oboe Mosquito crews operating over the Ruhr were able to take a somewhat detached view of much of the action, untroubled by the renowned anti-aircraft defences because the flak was directed not at them but towards the heavies at much lower altitudes. Still, there was a panorama of drama below them: flares entering cloud over the target; fires that burned with an orange glow in the target area; the flashes from the 4,000-lb 'blockbusters' that could be seen even through the clouds; once a 'red flare shot out'; the 'considerable amount of bombing that appeared to be well concentrated'; and, on another occasion, huge fires – 'definitely not dummies' – that remained visible for 40 miles.[12]

After solo bombing, ignored by flak and generally releasing nothing more lethal than a single salvo of comparatively small bombs which burst unseen far beneath the clouds, these Ruhr raids in the first fortnight of 1943 were (for those not already familiar with it) an early insight into what the crews of bomber squadrons had to face in their nocturnal wanderings around the shell-torn skies above Germany. Perhaps unseen by the Mosquito crews was the fate that befell others in those attacks on Essen and the one on Duisburg. Out of a total of 280 heavy bombers for whom No. 109 was lighting the way on seven nights, only one night went by without at least one of the heavies from Nos 1 and 5 Groups going missing, the thirteen which failed to return representing a loss approaching five per cent.

Who faced the greater risks, those flying the two-man Mosquitoes or the Wellingtons, Halifaxes and Lancasters with up to seven in each crew? One yardstick that could have been applied related to the losses of aircraft and crews on bomber operations over the Continent where, to date, fifty Oboe sorties had been completed without loss. At that stage of the war, with Main Force suffering losses in the region of four per cent, two Mosquitoes could well have been lost. Shortly, someone would make a ruling on comparative risks and it was Bennett, the Pathfinder Force Commander, who did so in a memo that he sent to Harris, the AOC-in-C of Bomber Command. The subject of the memo was the length of the operational tour of aircrew personnel engaged on night Oboe operations. It was Bennett's judgement that currently the fatigue on an Oboe operation was less than that of an ordinary night bombing raid by heavy or medium aircraft, and that 'under present circumstances' the element of risk was lower. He went on to quantify that comparison by proposing that an operational tour of night Oboe ops should be regarded as forty sorties instead of the usual thirty. In a sense 'balancing the books', Bennett suggested retaining the familiar thirty-sortie tour for his Oboe Mosquito pilots and navigators and counting each night Oboe operation as three-quarters of a sortie.[13]

For the first fifty sorties, No. 109 had to rely on just seven pilots and seven navigators, though others were completing their training. Before the end of January, however, a further three crews were flying operationally: Squadron Leader F.A. Green with Flight Lieutenant Douglass, joined by Flying Officer A.W. Raybould with Flying Officer H.A. Scott, bombing

Aachen on 15 January (this was the first Oboe raid on Aachen) and Flight Lieutenant L.J. Ackland with Flight Sergeant F.S. Strouts, on 30 January, also bombing Aachen. This latter occasion was a night that saw Oboe raids directed against targets in four different German cities: Cologne, Bochum and Essen as well as Aachen.

During this period, observations among staff manning the ground stations were proving useful, in their different ways, both to the aircrews at No. 109 and to the scientists at TRE. At Hawkshill Down, for instance, information became available about the manner in which the pilots were coping with beam-flying. The comment 'Was in centre of beam at bombing signal' was encouraging, a score of ten out of ten perhaps?, whereas 'Appeared to have difficulty in flying the beam, but improved towards the end of run' clearly indicated that there was room for improvement, just a six out of ten maybe, with a visit to the headmaster if this pilot didn't pull his socks up! For the scientists, it would have been helpful to learn that, for a short period, there was mutual interference when two aircraft switched on at the same time. Less welcome news, although vital feedback nonetheless, came with reports of jamming on the station's frequency on four evenings in January (but not when operations were in progress), jamming which the station attributed to enemy sources. The anti-jamming measures were tested for the first time on this system and were found 'effective on all types so far experienced'. The following month jamming did occur once during operations, while the station was performing as the 'Cat', and another time there was 'heavy interference at times' while operating as the 'Mouse'.[14]

Trimingham ground stations, there were two in use at that time, produced an anomaly that for a while confounded both the station personnel and the scientists at TRE. There had been two separate Oboe attacks on Cologne, the first on the night of 22/3 January, the other on the night of 2/3 February, and both times the tracking failed on 228 megacycles. It was said this was because the signals being received at Trimingham II were too weak, whereas Trimingham I on 220 megacycles was satisfactory. Bomber Command ORS, which brought this to the attention of TRE and reckoned that Trimingham I had about 15 miles more range than Trimingham II, invited an investigation with a view to improving the performance of the weaker station.[15] It could be assumed that this comparison had not come to light previously because earlier targets were nearer home. Cologne was 273 miles from Trimingham, however, and this was the greatest distance which had yet been attempted operationally.

TRE's response was that their people already knew that there was a difference in performance between Trimingham I and II and that comparative tests were being carried out. The sites of the two stations could well account for this variation, however a pre-amplifer had been produced and would be installed shortly. The scientists seemed adamant that this was not the way round this problem, nonetheless they chose not to go into print, at that point in time, as to what was surely the root cause, which was that Bomber Command was pushing Oboe to the limits of its range.[16]

Range was a thorny problem anyway. Bennett was looking for calculations to be made that would add industrial centres in such towns as Dortmund, Elberfeld, Remscheid, Munchen-Gladbach, Solingen, Leverkusen, Witten and Duren to the potential list of Oboe nuisance raid targets and the Air Ministry was seeking the latest views of TRE's scientists on balloon-carrying aerials and airborne repeater equipment to boost the range of the signals between the ground stations and distant aircraft. At Bomber Command, Harris was rather more specific: Air Vice-Marshal Saundby, on his behalf, sought Air Ministry authority to allocate an aircraft and to use 'the one available set' of repeater gear on the Mark I wavelength to bring Emden particularly, as well as Münster, within the Oboe coverage. Bennett had already done his homework on airborne repeater methods. As nothing had been done with balloons to raise the repeater gear – and to develop such a means would apparently take two or three months – he pointed out that it would be possible immediately to reach Emden with the 500 lbs of repeater gear carried in a suitable bomber, naturally ensuring that this aircraft was capable of defending itself.[17]

In early February, a section of TRE's former home at Worth Matravers was being turned into an Oboe ground station, two CHL-type technical blocks and a brick-built hut on 'A' Site being adapted for use as the operational and office buildings for a Type 9000 installation, with two CHL-type transmitters and one Type 9000 receiver. At 0001 hrs on 10 February, with technical officer Flying Officer B.O. Smith and controller Flight Lieutenant T.M. Jones RCAF, in charge, this latest station was in a fully operational state. The following evening the first trial flight was carried out and 'a good maximum range of 360 miles with 9/1 signal/noise ratio was obtained'. Further trial flights followed, including bombing runs at Stormy Down, and by the end of the month Worth Matravers was ready for its first offensive operation, working as the 'Mouse' for the first Oboe-led raid on a target in France, the docks at St Nazaire, at a range of 231 miles.[18]

For Oboe, bringing the Atlantic ports into its orbit represented a major change in target direction which was possible only by bringing 'on stream' this new ground station. Until then, though this was the intention strategically from the outset, the choice of objectives was roughly to the east, the first ground stations being situated on the east and south-east coasts with the Ruhr comprising the prime targets. Adding a south-facing pair (Sennen in Cornwall coming on stream to work with Worth Matravers), achieved little distinction for the Oboe system so far as attacks on those French ports were concerned. With just that one pair of ground stations available, the marking was subsequently judged to have been 'so sparse that it was probably without appreciable effect on the results of the operations, which were in any case extremely successful'.[19]

By now there had been a third calibration raid, this time at a cadet school at St Trond; this was within the Florennes complex in Belgium which was the location for the second such raid, the first having been the operational début of Oboe eight weeks previously, on 20 December at Lutterade in Holland. Four Mosquitoes carried out the St Trond attack, each crew releasing their bombs on the Oboe signal and thus achieving a hundred per cent Oboe success for the first time in the series – sweet music indeed to the ears of Hal Bufton who had been given the command of No. 109 Squadron earlier that month (February 1943) with promotion to the rank of Wing Commander. As had been scheduled for the Lutterade bombing, Bufton and Ifould were again first into the air; the pair had 'wheels-up' at 0330 hrs, Green with Douglass, Thelwell with Koester and Kleboe with Findlater following at ten-minute intervals. The estimated impact points were 40 yards to the south, 45 yards south, 80 yards south-west and 80 yards west, though the optimism of these 'guesstimates' was not entirely justified. Two sticks of 4×250-lb GP bombs and 2 sticks of 3×500-lb MC bombs were dropped and the positions of some of the bombs of each stick were plotted on photographs taken during subsequent aerial reconnaissance.* An illustration produced by Bomber Command ORS showed four definites and two probables within a quarter-mile radius of the aiming point (one was virtually on the aiming point), three more were within a half-mile and the last two were within three-quarters of a mile.[20]

Operational Research Section really had no more evidence than this to show how Oboe was performing against targets on the Continent. With the position of fall of only a small proportion of Oboe-released bombs or markers able to be plotted, something that could only be done by studying pictures taken from the air or with the benefit of intelligence sources on the ground, there was 'little information on the accuracy of Oboe'. Still, ORS was 'quite certain' from the results achieved that its accuracy had been 'entirely satisfactory' for marking, which was its most important task to date.[21]

The guesstimates continued to instil confidence: Oboe raids on Essen, Cologne and Bochum were rated 'no error', with other Oboe-released bombs judged to have landed within 100 yards of the aiming point at Essen, Bochum, Hamborn and Dortmund. Others were estimated to have fallen

---

* In *Mosquito at War*, by Chaz Bowyer (Ian Allan), Bufton recalls an intelligence report which referred to 'three or four hits on the school which killed a sentry at the gate and two officers in their rooms' and, perhaps more significantly, although its importance appears to have been missed at the time, a reference to 'two separate bombs from different aircraft' which had landed a kilometre from the target. This was 'unfortunate', Bufton wrote, as later on similar results 'cast doubt on the Oboe system'; it was not then known that when bombs were dropped in salvo (as two of the Mosquitoes had done in the attack on the St Trond cadet school) 'frequently two of them hit each other with a high risk of one of them spinning and falling back'. Scientists found a means to overcome this problem while TRE and ORS were carrying out a detailed study of the likely causes of inaccuracies in the Oboe system in the run-up to D-Day, an investigation so thorough as to embrace equipment at the ground stations and in the aircraft, working practices and specially devised test procedures. Slipstream interaction could indeed make a stick of TIs fall up to a mile apart but by increasing the time interval between their release, that distance could be reduced to some 200 yards.

considerably wider – one a half-mile from the aiming point in Cologne at a time when the Mosquito was held for thirteen minutes in a cone of searchlights and the anti-aircraft guns were putting up a heavy and accurate barrage. Additionally, there were equipment failures which caused crews either to bomb without the benefit of the system or, rarely, go back home without bombing either the primary or alternative target.

It was a promising time for Bomber Command, which had just started using another TRE-designed target-finding device, H2S, the radar ground-mapping system that provided crews with a TV-like screen projecting an image of the ground beneath the aircraft. As a moving picture, it was by no means clear but, with practice, operators would pick out the coastline, lakes and rivers inland and see built-up areas, all such features being indispensable to confirming the position of the aircraft. Pathfinder heavies were the first to carry this equipment, which was not limited in its range as was Oboe. With H2S, which was complementary to Oboe, Pathfinder Force squadrons with Halifaxes and Lancasters could lead Main Force bombers to more distant objectives with much improved prospects of finding and hitting the target. So, with more bombers at his disposal and H2S to help do a better job further afield than the Ruhr, which was fast becoming Oboe's home ground, Bomber Harris could face the future with increasing confidence. He wanted a target and a result that would justify that trust in his men and machines, and Essen would be the place for the world to see that Bomber Command now really was on the offensive.

There was no more obvious and accessible target in Germany's industrial heartland than the massive Krupps works in Essen, a fact that was equally obvious to the enemy, whose defences were strengthened in response to the initial threats posed by the British bombers. From the RAF aircrew viewpoint, Essen was just about the toughest target in 'Happy Valley', their name for the Ruhr, though the anti-aircraft gun barrages were not alone in hampering a successful attack on this part of western Germany. Heavily industrialized, Essen in particular enjoyed a further form of protection: there was habitually a haze which masked the target area, a natural smokescreen so that, when the bombers arrived, the prospect of getting anywhere close to the factories themselves was further reduced. To be in with a chance required larger numbers of aircraft than were available for earlier raids in 1940, 1941 and 1942, with specialist crews to lead them, pathfinders who could pinpoint Krupps irrespective of cloud or haze. No trouble with the resources in Main Force, they could draw from a first-line strength of some 660 heavies and 300 mediums[22] and Pathfinder Force had been functioning for six months, quickly gaining experience and confidence. It was the time now to start making full use of Oboe, with No. 109 Squadron's Mosquitoes streaking across the night sky, able to show 'the legion'* in Pathfinder Force and Main

---

* No. 109 Squadron's motto is *Primi hastati* – The first of the legion.

Force the location of the target with greater-than-ever precision, even if no one could even make out the ground, let alone Krupps.

In 1942, during fourteen major raids on Essen, Bomber Command had carried out 3,530 sorties, losing 179 aircraft in the process and achieving little more than a 'few scattered incidents' of damage to this prime target. The incentive to go for a landmark raid came from the knowledge that in just eight Oboe sky-marking raids on Essen during the past month (January 1943), as few as 418 sorties had produced more effect than all the raids in 1942 for a loss of eighteen aircraft. However, the results were 'still confined to scattered incidents of damage', according to the ORS unit at Bomber Command HQ.[23]

Nevertheless, imagine the effect that should be possible in a single, much heavier attack. The contemplation was sufficient for Harris to have his planners produce all that was necessary to get No. 109 airborne with the biggest-yet Oboe pathfinding force of 8 Mosquitoes and behind them specialist back-up markers and a bombing force that was more than 400 strong. It was the night of 5/6 March 1943, a night that would see Bomber Command's 100,000th sortie of the war; it was the night that would launch the Battle of the Ruhr, and, more importantly for Bomber Command's continuing benefit, it would be the night that 'made' Oboe.

Of the eight aircraft that No. 109 was required to provide, Campbell and Turnbull were first off, the wheels of their Mosquito leaving the ground at Wyton at 1855 hrs, the other crews being O'Neill/Maas, Thelwell/Koester, Raybould/Scott, Bufton/Ifould, Kleboe/Findlater, Griggs/O'Hara and finally, at 1925 hrs, Somerville and Douglass. All but three marked successfully, the five Mosquitoes' fifteen red-coloured target indicators (pyrotechnics in a bomb casing) being further marked by five Halifaxes and seventeen Lancasters with green-coloured TIs, the No. 109 crews experiencing Oboe equipment failure being Bufton/Ifould, Thelwell/Koester and Raybould/Scott. It was reckoned that some of the primary markers fell as close as 75 yards from the aiming point, which was within the Krupps works, but most landed inside 200 yards.[24]

To maintain the obvious need for secrecy – this was not the time to tell Main Force crews too much about this pioneering pinpointing innovation – briefing sessions ahead of the operation talked only about 'a new and very accurate' method of placing red markers at which Main Force was to aim 'with the greatest possible precision'. If no red markers were visible, the instruction was to go for the greens with equal care.[25]

In the event there was apparent acclamation for No. 109's efforts because, in Bomber Harris's words in his Despatch of War Operations, 23 February 1942 to 8 May 1945, the Oboe ground-marking technique was unanimously reported to have been very well executed by the pathfinders. Contemporary records affirm that the success of this raid depended on the Oboe Mosquitoes; they 'marked the centre of Essen perfectly', the backers-up from other Pathfinder Force squadrons carrying out their part of the plan too. Reconnaissance photos showed 160 acres of destruction with 53 separate buildings within the Krupps works hit by bombs.[26]

Looking more at the overall than the detail, Harris himself clearly regards that night of 5/6 March 1943 as having been an overture, a curtain-up on a performance still to come. He gave the event a measure of immortality, marking the date forever in the calendar of military achievements, when he attributed to it the definition that this was the 'precise moment' when Bomber Command's main offensive began – 'the moment of the first major attack on an objective in Germany by means of Oboe'. It was on that night of 5/6 March 1943 'when I was at last able to undertake with real hope of success the task which had been given to me when I first took over the Command at the beginning of 1942 – the task of destroying the main cities of the Ruhr'.[27]

It was a time for congratulations all round, to the aircrews who marked and bombed as well as to the people who provided essential support on the ground, among them the controllers and staff at the Oboe ground stations.[28]

Considering that this truly was a joint effort within Bomber Command, it was fitting that the praise came right from the upper echelons in Air Ministry, a message from the Chief of Air Staff, Air Chief Marshal Sir Charles Portal, to Bomber Harris stating that the reports and first photographs indicated that the Essen attack was one of the most successful of the whole war. It was, the CAS continued, 'an encouraging example of what can be achieved by hard work and keenness applied to training and operational development when coupled with the gallantry and determination in the air which have always characterized the work of Bomber Command. I congratulate you all and hope that you will achieve many such outstanding successes in the coming weeks'.

Harris passed on that message to all concerned in his own Command, PFF Commander Bennett adding to those all-round congratulations a personal message to Air Vice-Marshal R.S. Aitken, who was in charge of No. 60 Group which ran the ground stations. He expressed 'my very sincere appreciation of the intense and very satisfactory work carried out by your personnel in maintaining the Type 9000 stations during the last month'. This work had reached a climax on the night of 5/6 March when 'the most successful attack on Essen' was carried out. It was, Bennett explained, a target that had been 'a headache for Bomber Command for a very long time. With its heavy defences, searchlights, smoke screen and natural industrial haze it has proved a difficult target to hit with the old methods. By the proper use of Type 9000 Stations to mark the target, we have almost completely written it off'.

Subsequently, No. 60 Group had a message of congratulations from the Chief of Air Staff himself in which he told Aitken, 'The excellent results achieved by our aircraft in operations are due in no small measure to the assistance they receive from the ground personnel of your Group. The work they do, though vital, is monotonous and does not always receive the recognition which it deserves. I will be glad therefore if you will convey to them an expression of my great admiration and thanks for all they have done in the past and are doing now to help the Squadrons to achieve their successes against the enemy.' To which Wing Commander E. Fennessy, who had particular responsibility for the Type 9000 equipment, replied, 'My grateful appreciation for your kind message which will do much to stimulate the enthusiasm of all technical personnel in this Group in continuing to give of their best in the vital service they are performing'.★

By now, No. 109's Mosquitoes and No. 60 Group's ground stations – their joint efforts augmented by other squadrons in Bomber Command – had taken on a further crack at Essen, on the night of 12/13 March. It was, perhaps, overshadowed by the first attack, unfortunately so, because Essen No. 2 was more successful for Oboe and apparently caused greater damage. Squadron records confirm the first point and Bomber Command's War Diaries make the point about the results of this raid.

There were ten crews on this occasion, two more than previously, Ackland/Strouts, Flying Officer H.B. Stephens with Flying Officer F. Ruskell, Green/Douglass and Flying Officer T.E. Dodwell with Flight Lieutenant J.F.C. Gallaher in addition to those who were on Essen No. 1, these being Raybould/Scott, Campbell/Turnbull, Thelwell/Koester, Griggs/O'Hara, O'Neill/Maas – whose Mosquito was first off at 1925 hrs – and Bufton, this time with a change of navigator in Flying Officer I.F. Tamagno. There were only two instances of a non-attack due to an Oboe technical failure: Green/Douglass and Dodwell/Gallaher.[29] Statistically, this was an 80 per cent success for Oboe compared with 62.5 per cent the previous time. As for the results, the centre of the bombing area was 'right across the giant Krupps factory, just west of the city centre' and photographic interpretation assessed that it received '30 per cent more damage on this night than on the earlier successful raid of 5/6 March'.[30]

During those two raids in March and in a further one in the first week of the following month, some 985 Main Force aircraft out of the 1,175 detailed pressed home an attack and roughly two-thirds bombed the markers in each raid. There was 'great devastation' in the first and 'very severe damage' in the subsequent raids, nearly 25 per cent of the Krupps buildings suffering some form of damage. It was estimated that the equivalent of three months

---

★ The Wing Commander (subsequently Sir Edward Fennessy CBE), in an interview with the author, paid tribute to the 'remarkable job' done by No. 60 Group personnel who manned the ground stations. Although the officers were generally professionals in their specialist work – with a 'big intake from the BBC who provided stiffening' – the vast majority of those serving with them were 'off the streets, so to speak'. These were men and women straight from school or joining from jobs which bore little or no relationship to their eventual work in No. 60 Group. Yet these people were trained at RAF Yatesbury to understand the equipment, to install, maintain and operate it, complex tasks which they learned to tackle with enthusiasm, competence and speed. As well as their work at the ground stations, No. 60 Group personnel were sometimes called upon to lend a helping hand at TRE, building Oboe equipment.

production was lost as a result of these three Oboe ground-marked raids. Post-war German sources would provide lucid and definitive comment on both the effect of Oboe and the consequences of the bombing (see page 160).

In March, No. 109 lost its first aircraft and crew on Oboe operations, Ackland and Strouts failing to return from Duisburg when there was a last message exactly three hours after take-off on the evening of the 26th to say that the aircraft was being ditched – 'believed east of Southwold'. Over the North Sea at that time, they were no more than half an hour from home. It was a night to remember for all the wrong reasons: on a night when the squadron suffered its first setback in human terms, there were more Oboe failures than there were successes, only three other crews with Ackland and Strouts having achieved an Oboe release, compared with five who were unable to do so. The crew of a second No. 109 Mosquito was posted missing on 27 May (Flight Sergeants C.K. Chrysler and R.H. Logan), the pair having failed to return from an attack on Essen which required twelve of these aircraft to take part. Conjecture pointed to an engine cutting out over the target and the probability that this aircraft crashed in flames somewhere over Germany. In between those two losses outside the British mainland, a third crew was lost on 8 April as a result of a crash at Wyton on take-off; this would have been their first operational sortie with Oboe, flying as one of ten crews detailed that night to attack Duisburg.[31]

There was a brighter side, though it took a while for the facts and the findings to be presented in ORS reports which drew various conclusions on the squadron's first operations, spanning the period between the end of December 1942 and the middle of June 1943, and which passed an initial judgement on both sky-marking and ground-marking with Oboe.[32] Respectively, these techniques would become known as 'Musical Wanganui' and 'Musical Paramatta', Maori-based terms derived from two towns in New Zealand (Wanganui and Paremata), which lost their preface when describing these forms of marking without employing Oboe.

Although only a single sky-marking operation was able to be analysed, the results of the night photographs which were available for this one occasion indicated that 60 per cent of Main Force bombed within 3 miles of the aiming point – it was Essen on 9/10 January. This percentage figure was three times as great as the best so far recorded in any raid on Essen. On ground-marking it was found that using Oboe had at least trebled the proportion of the main force aircraft actually attacking the target. Furthermore, it enabled 'very successful attacks' to be made when previously it was almost impossible to find the target. Daylight reconnaissance confirmed Oboe ground-marking attacks as 'more consistently successful' than any previous attacks against German targets. The twenty operations studied included the heaviest and most successful of all the attacks ever made by the Command, the resulting damage being on a scale never previously achieved by night bombing.

It would have been surprising if those ORS reports did not also form some sort of conclusion about Oboe's performance in terms of precision.

The comment was guarded, presumably because there was still not much hard evidence to hand, and historical accuracy demands that it is best quoted verbatim. The particular ORS report (it was an early one, issued on 28 January 1943), reads as follows: 'Whilst there are indications that Oboe operational accuracy is of the order of 650 yards, there are signs that on occasions the overall error may rise to half to one and a half miles.'

Less controversial was the ORS judgement that the value of Oboe was 'considerably enhanced' by two factors. First, it became available at a time when Bomber Command was beginning to operate on a very considerably increased scale and, second, its introduction practically coincided with that of the target indicator bomb (TI). When PFF was formed, a first requirement was for some form of pyrotechnic which would not only illuminate the target area but provide a mark on which the Main Force aircraft could aim their bombs. For an aimable device there was a ready supply of 250-lb LC bomb casings; these were packed with 60 red, green or yellow 12-inch candles to become the first target-indicating ground marker – the first TIs. Early TIs burned for only three minutes but this illumination period was increased progressively to up to twelve minutes. PFF was given special powers to make a direct approach to the Ministry of Aircraft Production where the development and design of new markers was required, and there was even a PFF liaison officer installed permanently at the Ministry to 'coordinate PFF requirements and where necessary to circumvent official production and design channels when particular marker stores were required on high priority'.[33]

In the summer of 1943, Oboe was becoming the habitual marking device for targets within some 250 miles of the English coast and H2S was becoming accepted for those further afield. Front-line squadrons were re-equipping to put more powerful bombers into the offensive, bombers that could carry bigger loads for greater distances, higher and faster than was possible in its early days. And there were developments within No. 109 too, with the Mark IX Mosquito coming along. This later version would replace the Mark IV, whose ceiling was about 29,000 ft, and give the facility to operate at about 35,000 ft, the extra height increasing Oboe's range and reducing vulnerability to anti-aircraft fire.

But that wasn't all. Pathfinder Force's Oboe Mosquitoes were spawning and the expansion meant that No. 109 would no longer be the sole Oboe Squadron. It was going to move from Wyton to a new base at Marham in Norfolk and to 'swap' aircraft as well as crews with No. 105 Squadron – a squadron that had been flying Mosquitoes on daylight ops for longer than No. 109 had been operating with them. There would be a training unit created to bring along fresh crews to the unique standards required to operate with Oboe. There would be new and more distant targets, and there would be further marking techniques to introduce, so as to build on past successes and to try to utilize its full potential. The Oboe Squadron was on the move – and so was Oboe itself.

CHAPTER TEN

Pushing to the Limit

'In training, before ever we progressed into the Mosquito, we did "dry swims" in a Link Trainer, where we could simulate an Oboe-controlled operation without leaving the ground. Then we went up in an Oxford to get the feel of the system before going into the Mosquito.' Ron Curtis, navigator, who (with pilot John Burt) joined No. 109 Squadron at Marham from No. 1655 Mosquito Training Unit on 22 September 1943. Theirs was a partnership which completed an unequalled 104 Oboe operations, neither going on an op with anyone else.

Even before the first significant Oboe-led bombing raids were carried out over Germany in early 1943, Britain was already sharing the secrets of this device with America. It was done not simply because share and share alike was the order of the day, it was done for materialistic reasons, because Britain desperately needed American hardware and engineering expertise in order to further the development of Oboe. Certain equipment was available only across the Atlantic, as were scientists familiar with its development and application. Those products and that expertise would be necessary to maximize the integration of this hardware into the Oboe system. Furthermore, as the Allied leaders had agreed a joint bombing programme involving both the British and the American air forces, if Oboe was already benefiting the RAF, presumably it could also benefit their USAAF partners.

Senior officers at the US 8th Air Force Headquarters received, as did those at RAF Bomber Command HQ, No. 109 Squadron, No. 60 Group and TRE, a 'preliminary guide' describing the principles of Oboe. First it explained why the use of the system was presently limited to attacks on targets within some 270 miles of the ground station with the bomber at about 28,000 ft; then it went on to show how this performance would be improved by using a repeater system – which still needed to be tried out – where, with the aircraft flying at heights of 28,000 and 35,000 ft, theoretical ranges of respectively 570 and 620 miles became possible.[1]

Already, with a mixed force of up to a dozen USAAF heavy bombers equipped with Oboe Mark I to perform a pathfinding role, bombing trials had begun, the new ground station at Sennen, at Land's End, built and equipped over a three-week period in January/February, contributing to those trials within its opening week. The first took place on 17 February 1943, using the Stormy Down range, where just one out of three runs with a

Liberator bomber was logged as a success compared with three out of four successes that same day with one of No. 109's Mosquitoes.[2] It would be some months, however, before the Americans started using Oboe operationally, the hold up being the result of an agreement having been reached between the Chief of Air Staff and the Commanding General of the 8th Air Force to wait until sufficient aircraft were available to launch large-scale attacks against targets in Germany. This was an echo of the policy dictated by the Air Ministry to Bomber Command that Oboe was too precious a commodity to be put at risk with small-scale nuisance raiding over enemy territory.

At TRE, news came from the US Embassy in London that three Americans would be joining them, all having as their primary object 'the job of aiding Mr Reeves in the possible development of Oboe Mark II transmitters employing the American components'. The visitors promised to provide valuable and additional brain power at a time when concern was being shown by TRE representatives over the possibility that the 9PK2 klystron transmitters would have insufficient power, and the PK150 klystrons would be held up due to production difficulties.[3]

Whereas Oboe Mark I was homegrown in Britain, American equipment – in particular the ASGIII transmitter and modulator unit – became a key part of the Mark II version, both in the aircraft and at the ground stations. Originally, Oboe Mark I was to have been the means to demonstrate the system's potential under test conditions pending the introduction of Mark II, which was devised in tandem with Mark I but based on a known and as yet unavailable technology. In the event, once the performance of Mark I had been satisfactorily demonstrated on the bombing range, it was pressed into service to prove the principle of Oboe under operational conditions.*

In the summer and autumn of 1943, concurrently with the build up of 8th Air Force heavy bombers in readiness for large-scale operations against Germany, Oboe ground stations were in increasing use while the American pathfinder crews were gaining experience in tracking and releasing. Then, with the approach of winter, Hawkshill Down I reported a 'great increase' in training runs using USAAF Fortresses, as many as a dozen such tests having been carried out by that station alone in the first part of October, 'with greater success than of late, so much so that attempts have already been made to use the apparatus for operational sorties'.[4]

That initial use of Oboe on operations came on the afternoon of 18 October 1943, with ground-markers due to be laid for a following force of 240 heavy bombers detailed to attack objectives in the German town of

---

*Not only did Oboe Mark I enter active service, it remained operational right through to the beginning of 1945, Channel 3 'signing off' with a 100 per cent success rate on 14 January when Winterton II and Hawkshill Down III tracked and released respectively for target-marking on a German Air Force fuel depot at Dülmen and railway marshalling yards at Grevenbroich.

Duren, which had not so far figured as an Oboe target for the RAF. It was a disappointment, with Hawkshill Down III alternately keying the marker and the reserve until 'time on target' without responses from either aircraft, the term 'keying' meaning sending the aircraft call-sign for the recipient crew to switch on and so begin tracking on the ground station's signals. Two days later, Duren was again the target; again Hawkshill Down III keyed the two marker aircraft; and again there was no response. It was an inauspicious début for Oboe in the hands of USAAF crews.

In November, however, there came further Oboe-led attacks and the first successful release when, on 5 November, an eager (or unusually anxious?) US 8th Air Force B-17 Fortress pilot switched on to his tracking station, Hawkshill Down III, as much as twenty-one minutes before he was due to be called, making 'an excellent bombing run' which resulted in Swingate giving the release signal at 1314 hrs, 45 seconds for the first American target-markers to fall on Germany, the target being Gelsenkirchen. This pair's second aircraft failed, however, no release signal being given because this time the Fortress pilot was so far off track when he began the bombing run that he did not find the beam again until the target was behind him. For this attack there were two other marker aircraft in action, both controlled by a second pair of ground stations. With Hawkshill Down I tracking and Trimingham I releasing, both their Fortresses notched up Oboe successes, the first letting go his markers at 1315 hrs 10 seconds and the second at 1341 hrs 59 seconds, to produce an overall 75 per cent success rate.

On 7 November, in a raid on Wesel, the marking aircraft appeared when 40 miles from the beam and switched off, the reserve not coming on the scene despite being called; and in a subsequent raid on Wesel, on 11 November, the situation was even more bizarre when the aircraft responded while over the North Sea but then proceeded away from the target. In another instance, the aircraft was as much as 3 miles to one side when reaching target range; enough was enough, it seems, because this was the time when the crew chose to switch off! Practice, they say, makes perfect but perhaps not so far as the Americans were concerned. Throughout November, Hawkshill Down I handled daily training flights with US 8th Air Force Fortresses but these resulted only in a 'slight improvement'.[5]

Despite the American heavies subsequently abandoning Oboe, their comrades in twin-engined Marauders stationed in Britain with the US 9th Air Force would soon take up the system and use it to considerable advantage on D-Day and virtually right through to the end of the war in Europe. This is not to say that ultimately the Americans came to regard Oboe as a miracle to transform their bombing capabilities – far from it! One of No. 109's most experienced navigators, Flight Lieutenant F. Ruskell DFC, who held the Pathfinder Force Badge awarded permanently to him with effect from 9 March 1944 to mark the completion of his Oboe operational service with the squadron, moved into the RAF Sub Unit of the Americans 9th Bomber Command the following month to take on a liaison role with regard to its increasing use of Oboe for daylight raids. He would have a pretty sorry tale to tell, as would others, with accounts of commanders of Oboe-led formations taking over when their own navigator could see where he was (or thought he was), leaving the Oboe crew to watch helplessly as their gaggle went astray. In such circumstances, American Oboe pilots visiting an Oboe ground station would understandably be quick to point out that *they* were not the ones to blame.[6]

In the interim, questions continued to be posed as to the operational performance of Oboe, even to the extent of a formal meeting being convened at the Air Warfare Analysis Section, involving such parties as the Operational Research Section at Bomber Command HQ, the Senior Oboe Controller based at Trimingham and TRE staff, the purpose being to discuss the current state of knowledge on its accuracy. As the system 'might be used extensively' for precision bombing and its 'exact accuracy' was not known, it was desirable that this should be determined as soon as possible and if necessary improved. Although the meeting was 'most unwilling to commit itself', there was agreement that 'for practical purposes' the ORS estimate of a quarter-mile probable error could be used. In Northern France the accuracy should be better, with 200 to 400 yards the order of the errors to be expected 'from any given situation'.[7]

In the summer of 1943, besides the Americans, British crews in a squadron other than No. 109 – indeed, a squadron entirely new to the disciplines of Oboe flights – were busy in training and in carrying out their first operational sorties. These crews belonged to No. 105 Squadron, which had been flying Mosquitoes in daylight bombing raids and was by now re-formed as an Oboe Mosquito squadron.

The change over began in the first fortnight in June when six pilots and six navigators were detached from No. 105 at Marham to Wyton for training, Wyton still being the home of No. 109. At the beginning of that month, Marham itself transferred out of No. 2 Group to become a Pathfinder Force base, concurrent with that event being the transfer of its two squadrons, No. 105 and No. 139, into Pathfinder Force. It was a brief sojourn for No. 139, however, which switched to Wyton just over a month later, 4 July, in an exchange with No. 109 and going on to become a member of the Light Night Striking Force.★ The effect of these movements was to position the two Oboe squadrons on the same airfield: No. 109 – an operational Oboe squadron since the end of the previous year – with its eighteen Mosquito Mark IVs and six Mark IXs, and No. 105 – about to have its first taste of Oboe operations – with twelve Mosquito IVs.

★ A Blenheim of No. 139 Squadron was the first RAF aircraft to cross the German coast when, within sixty seconds of the outbreak of war on 3 September 1939, Flying Officer A. McPherson, with one crew member and a naval commander as passenger, received orders to take off from Wyton and photograph Wilhelmshaven and aerodromes in North West Germany, a mission that earned him one of the first two DFCs of the war.

To give the new squadron the asset of operational experience from the outset, a number of aircrew members of No. 109 were posted to No. 105 during the first fortnight of July. They included Flying Officer K. Wolstenholme and Squadron Leader J.F.C. Gallaher DFC, Flying Officer J.R. Hampson and Pilot Officer H.W.E. Hammond DFC, Flight Lieutenant Raybould DFM and Flight Lieutenant Tamagno DFC, Flying Officer Thelwell and Flying Officer Koester, as well as Flight Lieutenant L.F. Austin DFC and Flight Lieutenant C.F. Westerman. Certainly no time was wasted getting the two squadrons airborne on operations from Marham, No. 109 marking Cologne on 8 July and No. 105 going into action on 9 July when Squadron Leader W.W. Blessing DSO DFC and Flying Officer G.K. Muirhead DFC notched up a successful Oboe release of three 500-lb bombs and a single yellow target-marker on Gelsenkirchen, a second aircraft from No. 105 taking off just three minutes after Blessing's, at 0002 hrs, crewed by Flying Officer W.E.C. Humphrey and Flight Sergeant E. Moore. Four former No. 109 crews were in action later in the month as members of No. 105, Austin/Westerman, Raybould/Tamagno, Hampson/Hammond and Wolstenholme/Gallaher all completing successful Oboe releases when joining crews from their former squadron to mark Essen for more than 600 Main Force bombers on the night of 25/6 July.

There was a particular significance about that Essen attack. A third Oboe channel had just been introduced, which resulted in 'an immediate improvement' in the RAF's bombing effort, and this was the first raid where the three channels were used (Winterton II and Hawkshill Down III were now operating in addition to Hawkshill Down I/Trimingham I and Swingate/Trimingham II). The Oboe marking was almost continuous over a period of fifty minutes. Then, thanks again to there being this third channel (each channel theoretically capable of controlling one Oboe aircraft every ten minutes), continuous primary marking was achieved for the first time during a raid on Remscheid on the last night of the month. Both attacks were 'outstandingly successful'.[8]

The Remscheid attack was notable on a number of counts: it concluded the Battle of the Ruhr and was on a previously unbombed town, unlike the opener, which, it will be remembered, was Essen. Also, given that just 273 aircraft were detailed (including 9 Oboe Mosquitoes) and only 871 tons of bombs were dropped, the effect seemed out of all proportion – 83 per cent of the town devastated with reportedly 1,120 people killed and 6,700 injured. The Oboe ground-marking and bombing were 'exceptionally accurate'.[9]

By now there was 'on the job' training for novice crews, an example being an Oboe-led attack on Aachen on the night of 13/14 July when eight Mosquitoes including two reserves were detailed to position ground-markers at five-minute intervals from 0142 hrs, these aircraft to be followed immediately by three under-training Mosquitoes, each contributing 3 × 500 lb and 1 × 250 lb bombs to the overall effort. Those preceding the trainee trio displayed their experience to near perfection: the TIs were judged to have dropped between 30 and 200 yards of the aiming point and the reserves were not called.[10]

During the following month, August, there was a new experience for both squadrons when Oboe was used for route-marking during Main Force attacks on Berlin (which itself was well out of Oboe reach, of course), the Mosquitoes of No. 109 and No. 105 dropping a sequence of coloured flares at precise and pre-determined positions. An unexpected hiccup marred the marking intentions the first night it was used – Wolstenholme's aircraft hit a flock of birds on take-off so he had to abandon his participation and leave the ground crew to clean up the plane – but all went well for him on a subsequent night. Also that month, the results achieved in Oboe attacks on the Brauweiler switching station caused Syd Bufton, as Director of Bomber Operations at the Air Ministry, to send a handwritten note to the Assistant Chief of Air Staff (Operations) that this was 'the best evidence we have so far obtained of the accuracy of Oboe'. The potentialities of the direct destruction of precise targets were clear and, he wrote, such targets could be taken on once 'the 4,000-lb Mosquito is available, together with Oboe Mk II which can be used apart from Main Force operations'.[11]

When planning operations where Oboe was the precision tool either to mark the target for Main Force or for bombing confined to one of the Oboe squadrons, there was surely the temptation to argue that as there was no arbitrary figure governing the effective range of the system, if a particularly interesting target was marginally beyond the theoretical limit it was nonetheless still worth a try. There seems to have been agreement that Pathfinder Force Commander Bennett himself was 'a blighter' for this approach! One such proposition was the port of Emden in northern Germany, which was singled out for the Oboe Mosquitoes in the autumn of 1943, initially to use the conventional tracking/releasing aids and then to introduce the repeater method for the very first time. With this certainly, Bennett was in favour of taking a crack at Emden.

The nights of 22 and 27 September, when on each occasion six aircraft were detailed to attack with conventional Oboe, proved that unquestionably where Emden was concerned, the distances to the target from the ground stations at Hawkshill Down and Swingate, Trimingham and Winterton were in fact too great. The others, on the nights of 7, 18, 20, 21, 24 and 31 October, proved that even though the repeater method achieved what was intended and brought Emden into effective range, it was not possible to guarantee successful Oboe releases. In the two operations in September, only three of the twelve sorties bombed on Oboe signals; in the first, all six aircraft, which were flying at 31,000 ft, resorted to dead reckoning, while in the second, two of the three successful sorties were carried out higher still at 32,000 ft. Both were crews using the newly available Mark IX Mosquito (which had a improved ceiling and thus could extend the Oboe range), while the other three sorties bombed by dead reckoning. Ground control staff at Swingate, who performed a tracking role in the first attack and a releasing role in the second, condemned both operations as failures 'due to excessive range'.[12]

> The range of Oboe just permits
> The boys to blow the Ruhr to bits.
> But Bennett's own interpretation
> Dismisses Nature's limitations.
>
> He chooses targets for the boys
> When signal strength is less than noise.
> And yet the squadrons seem to cope
> When Nature said there was no hope.[13]

A further ground station had come into being at Cleadon, near South Shields, with the intention of using it in conjunction with one or more of the east coast or south coast stations for repeater operations. This was a means of extending Oboe coverage which, although envisaged among the Oboe group at TRE at the outset, nevertheless met with some scepticism. But Bomber Command wanted to give the scheme a try and, with Emden a specific target (370 miles distant from Cleadon), sought Air Ministry approval.

On 7 October, two Mosquitoes carrying repeater equipment were detailed to fulfill the role of the 'A' aircraft (Somerville/Turnbull the crew of one, plus a reserve aircraft), patrolling a pre-determined route at 28,000 ft over the North Sea and effectively adding another leg to the tracking station's capability. Meanwhile, five 'B' aircraft, all Mosquitoes from No. 109, were to track on signals coming from Cleadon via the 'A' aircraft and to release on signals received direct from the paired ground station. The first of the five 'B' aircraft to be called (Campbell the pilot, Scott the navigator) failed to pick up the signals satisfactorily and bombed visually on the docks at 2015 hrs (see page 157), however the others all attacked with Oboe – Griggs/O'Hara at 2028, Stephens/Ruskell at 2045, Cox/Bowman at 2058 and Jacobe/Tipton at 2119. There was a celebratory party on their return but this was, Tipton was to recall, 'Premature, I'm afraid! The repeater project was a patchy business which, if it had been successful, would have opened up great possibilities'.[14]

On the final operation in this Oboe repeater series of attacks on Emden, which took place on the evening of 31 October, three of the 'B' aircraft carried out an Oboe release and one bombed by DR from the last GEE fix. So the final tally stood at twenty-six sorties with eleven Oboe-releases (a forty-two per cent success rate), twelve releases on DR and one visual bombing – all of these were bombs aimed at the primary target – and there was one attack on an alternative target. In the one remaining sortie, the bombs were brought back to base.[15]

The next step could well have been a 'two-legged' repeater system with the release signals as well as the tracking signals going to the attacking aircraft via an airborne system. At Bomber Command Headquarters, inevitably, Oboe repeater operations were under scrutiny; the experimental series of repeater raids on Emden having come to an end, a decision on the future of the system itself was not long in coming. There was 'no operational requirement for Oboe Mark I repeaters' and TRE was to cease all work on this project, diverting all possible effort to the further development of Oboe Mark II.[16]

Other than Cleadon, which was used only for the repeater flights, the Oboe Mark I ground stations which had been selected, constructed, equipped, tested and had begun to control Oboe Mosquitoes operating over the Continent, were by now Trimingham I in Norfolk and Hawkshill Down I in Kent, which formed the first pair to come into use, controlling the release and tracking respectively for the Lutterade calibration raid on the night of 20 December 1942; Trimingham II and Swingate in Kent, which operated together for the first time on 3 January 1943; and the third channel provided by Winterton II in Norfolk and Hawkshill Down III, introduced mid-July 1943 to benefit further the operations against the Ruhr, their first success being recorded on 26 July. Additionally, Worth Matravers in Dorset and Sennen in Cornwall had begun operating as a pair on 28 February 1943 to launch a series of Oboe-led raids on the Atlantic ports.

Concurrently with Oboe Mark I coming on stream and in line with the development and testing of Oboe Mark II, a programme was in place to produce the first pair of Oboe Mark II ground stations. Although it was anticipated that these would be available by the end of July 1943, in fact it would be the night of 26/7 September 1943 before the first Mark II operations became possible. Even then, it appears, the introduction of Mark II was far from smooth. Winterton I and Hawkshill Down II were the stations and Aachen was the first target but unserviceability at Winterton aborted operations not only on that opening night but also on the night of 29/30 September, the blame being placed fairly and squarely on trouble which developed in the transmitter, trouble which 'could not be repaired due to lack of spares'.[17] It was not until the evening of 3 October that the first success was achieved, one out of the four aircraft detailed for a nuisance raid on Aachen scoring on this occasion. Still, there was a bright side to the introduction of Oboe Mark II: a subsequent operation against Brauweiler on 20 October was extended so that one of the aircraft could carry out a range test, the distance obtained being 284 miles. Meanwhile, going back to the problem that had caused disappointment with the opening sorties, the Rack 113 transmitter at both Mark II ground stations had been replaced with American equipment known as the ASGIII, the notable feature of this new gear being a tuneable magnetron. Performance was much improved too, according to Hawkshill Down II, where the replacement was effected on 16 October, just one week after the switch was made at Winterton I, its output being 'at least two and a half times' that of the previous transmitter.[18] Mark I was based on the 1½-metre wavelength with which it was expected the enemy would be able to interfere; it was intended for initial use – really to demonstrate the principle of Oboe – pending the introduction of Mark II, with its better engineered components and a shorter wavelength which would obviate interference.

Although the early crews in No. 109 learned their skills on the job, mid-1943 had seen No. 1655 Mosquito Training Unit come into being to meet a dual need beyond the core function of teaching pilots how to fly Mosquitoes: to prepare experienced pilots and navigators for the two Oboe squadrons (No. 105 having re-formed on 1 June to join No. 109 in Pathfinder Force) and to bring newly qualified pilots and navigators up to the requirements of both No. 139 Squadron (a member of the Light Night Striking Force) and the self-explanatory PFF Met Flight. For the Oboe squadrons, a minimum intake of four crews a month was envisaged initially, with pilots and navigators together spending twenty-seven hours in the Oxford and thirty hours in the Mosquito after an opening five hours of dual instruction.[19]

Flying Officer J.B. Burt, pilot, and Flying Officer R.E. Curtis DFC, navigator, were among the early crews joining No. 109 from No. 1655 MTU, their period of formal instruction having finished, although training would still continue as necessarily it would do for everyone moving to the squadron.

As Curtis recalled:

Unlike Main Force bomber crews who usually flew at least one operational sortie while at their Operational Training Unit, generally a 'Nickelling' raid [leaflet drops over enemy occupied territory], we did not take part in any operational flights until we were on the squadron – and then it was usually nuisance bombing on our own, to disturb the Germans' sleep and to keep them on their toes, rather than target-marking for a bombing force coming up behind.

In training, before we ever progressed into the Mosquito, we did what were called 'dry swims' in a Link Trainer, where we could simulate an Oboe-controlled operation without leaving the ground. Then we went up in an Oxford to get the feel of the system before going into the Mosquito. As I remember it, we didn't drop bombs on a practice range; instead we flew over North Wales where there was a method using an infrared beacon and a camera obscura that enabled us to do our run and to see how far we were off target. It was exactly as if we were on an op, as far as being called in by the ground station and the timings were concerned, however it couldn't give us any insight into the problems of getting to the waiting area before we came under ground control.

We had learned what to do and we had practised it too, but the period between take-off and getting ourselves into the right place at the right time to come under Oboe control was probably the most problematical, especially when the speed and direction of the wind proved to be not what was anticipated. At our operating height, having spent forty-five minutes or so climbing to this altitude before crossing the coast, I used to take fixes on the GEE box at six-minute intervals and work out our ETA at the waiting point based on the wind as forecast at briefing; inevitably we would be there early, having added a 10 per cent margin for wind variation, but we knew that a 60 degree dog-leg would lose one minute or a Rate 1 turn three minutes. With a 100-knot wind blowing at those heights, a real team effort was needed between navigator and pilot to get us to the waiting point neither too early nor too late. If you were a reserve crew it meant orbiting while finding out if the primary crew was 'on' or whether there was a problem – reserves who weren't required, returned feeling not exactly 'cheated' but certainly disappointed. Nevertheless this was, of course, part of the job!

When you were called, though, it became an intensive schedule that you had to follow irrespective of anything else going on outside or inside the aircraft. On the controlled run the navigator received Morse letters at timed intervals from the target – A's at ten minutes, B's at eight minutes, C's at six minutes and D's at three minutes. Then, at approximately two and a quarter minutes later, the release signal was received – five dots followed by a five-second dash and then silence . . . . The cessation of that five-second dash was the moment to press the button, note the time on your stopwatch to the second, switch off the Oboe gear and head smartly back to base. Recording the time was for your own benefit and as a double check – the ground station knew precisely when you had let go your load because your release ended their signals.[20]

The training period certainly must have paid off in the case of Burt and Curtis because their very first operation on transferring from No. 1655 MTU to No. 109 saw this crew bombing Knapsack with a good run made without error. Incidentally this flight was made in Mosquito DK331, a veteran of the Lutterade début operation (with Bufton and Ifould on board), which was now logging its fiftieth operational sortie. The next night saw a repetition of the target but, due to an Oboe equipment failure, it was decided to attack an alternative target in Cologne, releasing on dead reckoning. Op no. 3 was more to their liking because a successful Oboe release from 27,700 ft on Hamborn was possible – though less to their liking when their plane met very heavy flak and sustained a hit above the starboard radiator. This was a period when successive Oboe Mosquitoes were forced to run the gauntlet of severe anti-aircraft fire: Pilot Officer R.E. Leigh and Flying Officer J. Henderson were badly hit over the target at Bochum on 9 November, crash-landed on diversion to Wyton and suffered the ignominy of the tail falling off in the process. Two nights later, two more crews were hit after bombing, one in the wings, the other in the tail, while Pilot Officer R.H. Pattinson and Flying Officer D. Mackintosh were hit on successive sorties towards the end of that month. On the first occasion, Mackintosh was struck in the foot and the reflex action caused him to press the release button in error a minute before time, the next time being less dramatic but nonetheless memorable for the increase in the severity and the accuracy of the flak during and after the bombing run. Before the year was out, No. 109 had lost another crew who were posted missing on operations – Flying Officers L.F. Bickley and J.H. Jackson failed to return from Bochum on 2 December – and several other crews, though more fortunate, were forced to make the return journey with one or other of the engines disabled by anti-aircraft gunfire in the target area. Over Essen on 12 December, the plane carrying Warrant Officers B.E. Patrick and C.R. Matthewman was hit in several places and the port motor rendered unserviceable. Over Hamborn on 30 December, Flying Officers I.O. Breckon and A. Burnett diverted to Manston when their starboard motor was hit by flak, just ten days after an eventful experience over Rheinhausen in which they were forced to jettison their bombs when they lost control after being blinded by searchlights some 15 miles north of the target.[21]

The second of the Pathfinder Force squadrons flying Oboe-equipped Mosquitoes, No. 105 Squadron, had lost one aircraft in its first six months when Lieutenant F.M. Fisher DFC USAAF and Flight Sergeant L. Hogan DFM were killed in a crash at West Raynham on their return from ground-marking at Bochum on 29 September, and another on 16 November when one of the former No. 109 crews, Hampson and Hammond, baled out over Holland because of flak damage during a target-marking sortie to Düsseldorf (see page 147). It may have appeared that Düsseldorf was a bit of a jinx for No. 105 crews, judging by what occurred shortly afterwards on the night of 13/14 December. Seven aircraft were detailed but only two were able to mark the primary target; one of the remaining five had a hang-up which prevented the bombs from releasing, one jettisoned, one bombed on another crew's Red TIs and the other two chose last resort targets in the same area, all but the hang-up being the result of Oboe equipment failures.[22] Interference from German sources was possibly a contributing factor.

The closing weeks of 1943, particularly throughout November, saw enemy jamming exercising a disruptive influence on Oboe sorties, RAF and USAAF alike, with one of the ground stations, Swingate, finding the results of that month's operations 'disappointing compared with past results'. Enemy jamming was particularly severe, ninety per cent of operations apparently being affected by various types of interference, though there was a 'marked improvement' in the results obtained during December, a month in which – in Swingate's experience – enemy jamming slackened off considerably.[23]

On one night, 19/20 November, the worst happened and there was a total Oboe failure, all ten sorties to ground-mark Leverkusen (five aircraft from each of the two squadrons) suffering an Oboe failure in the target area. Never before had there been sorties into double figures where it proved impossible to carry out the mission in the intended manner.[24]

It was Black Friday so far as No. 109 especially was concerned, since the CO himself, Hal Bufton, and other Oboe pioneers including Stephens, Findlater and Ruskell had been flying that night, though the effect of the calamity spread far and wide in the coming hours and days with all and sundry endeavouring to come up with an explanation. Six fresh crews from No. 109, three with fresh aircraft, tried the same target three nights later; three 'coped' (their term for a successful Oboe release), two in aircraft that were on the earlier attack, while two bombed on DR and one returned early because of a failure of a different sort – a problem with the navigator's oxygen supply. There were, according to those on the squadron at the time, 'several bodies (civilian and service) around the place trying to investigate the troubles' and even a 'stand-down from operations so that aircraft and crews could make special test flights as part of these further attempts to establish the cause of the recent failures'. Interference notwithstanding, No. 109's operational sorties reached treble figures in a month for the first time during November – it was exactly 100 – and rose to a total of 108 in December.

As another year opened, the lately introduced ten-centimetre Mark II form of Oboe was in 1944 operating alongside the original 1½-metre Oboe I, which meant that there were now two Mosquito squadrons with two versions of this aircraft, each with equipment dedicated to one or other version of Oboe, with existing and new ground stations dedicated to either Mark I or Mark II. And depending on the equipment within the aircraft, the role of each type of Mosquito would vary to meet the special requirements which had been introduced to safeguard as far as possible the secrets of the latest version of Oboe. Basically, it was expected that should a crew flying with Mark I Oboe on board experience a technical failure, they would make every effort to find and bomb a suitable target in Germany, even if this meant entering a heavily defended area. However, to avoid losing an aircraft carrying Mark II Oboe, crews finding themselves in that situation were to adopt a different stance: here, the instructions were to drop their bombs, in Germany, but not to endanger their aircraft unnecessarily by entering a heavily defended area.[25]

Following first the Mark IV Mosquito and then the higher-flying Mark IX in service with the Oboe squadrons, the Mark XVI added a new capability in bomb-carrying, this latest version delivering the 4,000-lb 'cookie' which both squadrons dropped for the first time during March 1944. This was followed by preparations for both No. 109 and No. 105 to move to separate bases within the space of ten days. The departure of the Mosquito squadrons meant that the way was now clear to provide Marham with the concrete runways (the Mosquitoes took off and landed on grass) which were necessary for the much bigger warplanes scheduled to operate from this expanding airfield. First off on 23 March was No. 105, its aircraft leaving for Bourn between 1030 and 1130 hrs, during which time the departing crews 'treated Marham to a grand display of "beat-ups".'[26]

In a day or two, No. 105 would find a familiar face joining the officers' mess when Hal Bufton gave up the reins at No. 109 to become Station Commander at Bourn, Squadron Leader R.M. Cox AFC succeeding him as No. 109's Commanding Officer. Richard Cox, who had been flying Oboe ops with the squadron since Bufton's early days in command, took over the squadron with effect from 1 March, No. 109's move from Marham to Little Staughton, an airfield newly vacated by the USAAF, taking place on 2 April.

In No. 105, Squadron Leader J.S. Bignal AFC and Flight Lieutenant G.F. Caldwell DFM were the first crew to attack a primary target with a 4,000 pounder, the aiming point for this Oboe release being a target at

Hamborn on 12 March and the aircraft a Mark XVI Mosquito, ML938. Ten days earlier, No. 109 had dropped its first 4,000 pounder, the distinction going to Flight Lieutenant P.F. Woolland and Flight Lieutenant G.B. Tait, the target being Krefeld. In fact there should have been two of these 'cookies' delivered on that historic occasion but when Squadron Leader P.A. Kleboe's aircraft was being bombed up, the cable broke and the bomb fell, apparently nearly crushing one of the armaments team in the process.[27] Historical accuracy demands recognition of the fact that Woolland's was not the first Oboe-released 4,000 pounder – a technical failure meant that he chose to drop on the aircraft's ETA over the target – Flight Lieutenant R. Hartley and Flying Officer A. Burnett achieving this distinction, with a certain panache, in Mosquito ML956 on 5 March on Aachen, the crew being credited with an error of just 40 yards off the aiming point, which was a Nazi headquarters.[28]* By now, No. 109 had carried out its 1,000th sortie,† with Flight Lieutenant A.C. Carter and Flying Officer E.W. Garrett taking the honours among the ten crews detailed for an Oboe bombing attack on a flying bomb site at Bacqueville in Northern France, the others including a navigator who took part in the very first Oboe operation against Lutterade some thirteen months previously, Flight Lieutenant (he was then a Pilot Officer) Pat O'Hara, sitting alongside Flight Lieutenant R.E. Leigh.‡ Appropriately for such a milestone in the squadron, which pioneered the development and operational application of Oboe, this was a 100 per cent result, with all ten Mosquitoes dropping their 4 × 500-lb GP bombs through 10/10 cloud, a 'very successful operation to complete the squadron's 1,000th sortie' and an apparent maximum error of 100 yards.[29]

---

* In correspondence with the author, Peter Woolland explains that his navigator, George Tait, had been unable to obtain the signal from the 'Mouse' station. As there was 'no way a Mosquito could be landed safely with a "Cookie" on board', crews had been briefed that, if the Oboe equipment let them down, they must drop the bomb as accurately as possible in the target area. He goes on, 'I am confident there was a big bang in Krefeld that night.'

† It was flown on 29 January 1944 and included two Mosquitoes used in the Lutterade raid on 20 December 1942, DK331 (Burt/Curtis) and DZ319 (Carter/Garrett), which were flown on that Oboe début occasion by Bufton/Ifould and Thelwell/Koester as the squadron's first and sixth sorties respectively.

‡ O'Hara was by now a 'spare' navigator, Griggs having returned to his native Australia. He flew just this one op with Leigh (whose usual navigator had gone down with a cold) and 'slapped the markers right on the nose'. This encouraged Leigh to ask O'Hara to join him for the next operation but just ten minutes before it was time to climb aboard for take-off, the regular navigator (Flight Lieutenant M.R. Breed) turned up, saying that he was sufficiently recovered and would fly. O'Hara exchanged flying gear for his 'best blues' and travelled into town for relaxation. Next morning he learned that one of No. 109's Mosquitoes had gone missing. It was Leigh's – and he was known to have been shot down.

Approved

George R.I

J.D. Heaton-Armstrong

Chester Herald
and Inspector of Royal
Air Force Badges.

College of Arms,
January, 1944.

No. 109 Squadron badge, depicting a panther rampant incensed and incorporating the squadron motto, *Primi hastati*. Translated as 'The First of the Legion', the motto reflects the squadron's role as pathfinder-for-the Pathfinders, while the choice and posture of the black panther in the badge design symbolizes its night-hunting and attack function. Formed on 10 December 1940, No. 109 was unique in beam bombing. First it carried out a secret war against the radio navigational beams that the Luftwaffe was using to guide its bombers to their targets in Britain, then it spearheaded the RAF's use of the Oboe radar-based ground-controlled blind-bombing system in high-precision attacks on hitherto immune targets in Germany's key industrial centres. By the time the war ended in Europe, No. 109's pilots and navigators had carried out more than 5,500 Oboe target-marking and bombing sorties, gaining a VC and some 28 DSOs and 175 DFCs in the course of these operations. Postwar, No. 109's Mosquito aircraft were replaced with Canberras which the squadron flew during the Suez operations and retained until it disbanded on 31 January 1957. (Crown copyright/MOD)

Bombing-up a Whitley aircraft. This was the type that No. 109 Squadron used in its early attacks on the beam transmitters at Cherbourg and which 'Slim' Somerville flew during his tour with No. 10 Squadron in the second half of 1940. (Imperial War Museum: CH. 227)

A Stirling bomber from No. 7 Squadron, one of those which took part in bombing attacks on the *Scharnhorst* and *Gneisenau* sheltering in Brest, with pilots and wireless operators from No. 109 Squadron using an early form of Oboe for tracking and bomb release. (Imperial War Museum: CH. 3137)

A Mosquito IV as used for daylight bombing by No. 105 Squadron. One of these aircraft was transferred to No. 109 Squadron for conversion to carry the first Oboe equipment designed and produced by the Telecommunications Research Establishment (TRE). (Imperial War Museum: E [MOS] 884)

A close-up showing the carrier frames in the nose of the first Mosquito (a Mark IV, DK300) to be fitted with Oboe. Once the equipment was installed, the transparent plastic nose was painted matt black in the interests of security when the plane was on the ground and to avoid reflection if caught in the beam of an enemy searchlight. (RAF Museum, Hendon: P 019854)

At RAF Stradishall members of the fitting team work on DK300 during its conversion from daylight bomber to the first Oboe Mosquito. It had carried out low-level bombing in Germany but its new role would be to test the Oboe system and to train No. 109's crews. (RAF Museum, Hendon: P 019850)

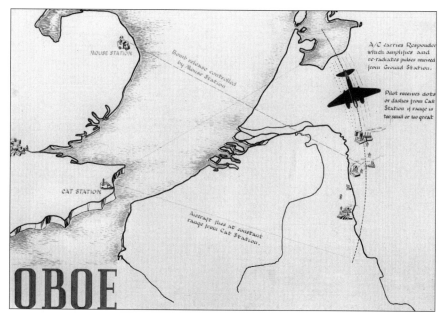

An illustration drawn when the first details were released showing how Mosquitoes equipped with Oboe were controlled from two ground stations in Britain, to track to their target and release either target-markers or bombs with an accuracy that was previously beyond possibility. Where German bombers were guided by a radio beam which gave away its presence by pointing directly towards the target, Oboe used signals passing between the Mosquito and each of two ground stations – typically, one was in Norfolk and the other in Kent – with the aircraft maintaining a set height and speed. In the illustration, signals from the 'Cat' station enabled the pilot to keep his aircraft along the arc of a circle which has that ground station at its centre, this constant range to bring him over the target calculated to one hundredth of a mile. Signals between the 'Mouse' station and the aircraft provided the navigator with the means to press the bomb-release button at the precise moment to achieve a theoretical direct hit on their target. (Imperial War Museum: E [MOS] 1439)

A.H. Reeves, an OBE for Oboe. (IEE Archives Dept)

F.E. Jones, an MBE for Oboe.

An Oboe Mosquito crew's view of the principal components comprising the airborne equipment of this ground-controlled blind-bombing system. It occupied the nose portion of the aircraft ahead of the navigator/bomb-aimer's position, who sat behind and to the right of the pilot, some of whose instrument dials and flight controls are seen on the left of this picture. (Defence Evaluation and Research Agency, Malvern [Neg. 4999 Folder 15]

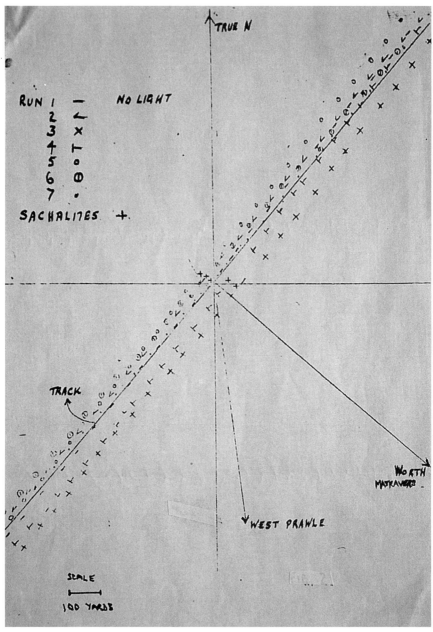

The consistency of the seven tracks plotted here, when a Wellington from No. 109 Squadron made repeated runs over a camera obscura located near South Cerney, Gloucestershire, coupled with the consistency of positional accuracy achieved during those runs, convinced the Air Ministry to permit a demonstration of Oboe-controlled bombing on the Stormy Down range (see p. 72). Tracking for the South Cerney experimental bombing runs was controlled by Worth Matravers ground station and release by the paired ground station at West Prawle. A TRE observer on the ground plotted the progress of the Wellington, while its pilot tracked in response to the Worth Matravers signals, as well as plotting the moment of 'bomb' release. This came when the navigator activated a camera flash in the bomb bay in response to West Prawle's signals. (Plots diagram via J.E.N. Hooper, TRE observer at South Cerney)

These five crew members of a Stirling bomber from No. 214 Squadron (plus a sixth who was unable to be photographed) each received the Distinguished Flying Medal for their individual and team effort when foiling the attacks of five enemy fighters, three of which the plane's gunners shot down, while returning from a raid on Bremen in June 1942. In the centre is Pat O'Hara who, with his pilot, Frankie Griggs (standing to his left), subsequently joined No. 109 Squadron as navigator and pilot respectively. (via A.P. O'Hara)

'Feet not Miles' is the emphatic contention in this unofficial Oboe emblem devised at TRE. It incorporates an oboe, codename for the system vital for accurate tracking and release, Cat and Mouse, symbolizing the ground stations which controlled each operation, and of course the bomb that was carried to the target and seldom brought back . . . . (via J.E.N. Hooper)

Nose art and bomb mission details were a feature on No. 109 Squadron aircraft, none more so than LR503, a Mark IX Mosquito that made its first operational sortie in June 1943 and its last (having subsequently been transferred to No. 105) in April 1945; this was its 213th, a record for an aircraft in Bomber Command. LR503 crashed during a goodwill tour in Canada with the loss of its two-man crew. (Mike Symons)

Commanding trio: Group Captain H.E. Bufton DSO, DFC, AFC, left; Group Captain G.F. Grant DSO and Bar, DFC, centre; and Wing Commander R.C.E. Law DSO, DFC, all led No. 109 Squadron during its time with Pathfinder Force. Hal Bufton, who was with No. 109 at its formation on 10 December 1940, held the position of Commanding Officer between February 1943 and March 1944, while the squadron was at Marham. George Grant, who flew pre-No. 109 sorties from Boscombe Down, as did Bufton, succeeded Richard Cox (who was No. 109's CO during the transfer from Marham to Little Staughton) in May 1944. Bob Law was in command at the 'finish' on 2 September 1945, having taken over from Grant in December 1944. (Imperial War Museum: CH.16205, CH. 16232 and CH. 16224)

No. 109 Squadron, May 1945. Seated on chairs, left to right: F/S Blizard, F/S Barber, W/O Burrows, F/L Mountain, F/L Slater, S/L Brown, S/L Curtis, S/L Sleep, S/L Fellowes, S/L Bowman, F/L Jones, W/C Cobbe, W/C Law, W/C Foxall, S/L Buckland, S/L A'Court, S/L Watson, S/L Boles, S/L Francis, F/L Rostron, F/L Neville, F/S Lendon, F/S Farley, Sgt Woolner and Sgt Dawson. Standing: LAC Whitehurst, LAC Bird, LAC Robinson, LAC Mills, F/L Davis, F/L Cresswell, F/O Langille, F/L Batchelor, F/L Shaw, F/S Leigh, P/O Pritchard, F/O Austin, F/L Carnegie, W/O Wicks, P/O Garratt, F/L Dykes, P/O Smith, P/O Wade, F/L Simpson, F/O Jones, P/O Reid, P/O McNay, F/L Relph, F/L Wigley, F/L Fernand, F/L Campbell, F/L Cleary, F/O Trigg, F/S Cutts, Sgt Dulmage, AC Milburn, Cpl Watson and LAC Williams. Seated on ground: LAC Angood, LAC Broom, LAC Rushton, Cpl Wright, Cpl Windmill, LAC Lewis, LACW James, LACW Keegan, LAC Trenerry, LAC Brown, Cpl Mahon, LAC Thorne, LACW O'Keefe, Sgt Nicholson, Cpl Starkey, Cpl Rutterford, Cpl Bridgeford, Cpl Alavoine, LACW Thompson, LACW Edwards, LAC Collins, LAC Brookes, ACW Mole, ACW Bassett, LAC Cornell, Sgt Lupton, Sgt Leete, Cpl Wilson, AC McLean, LAC Hogg, Cpl King, AC Welburn, Cpl Jones, LAC Ballentine and Cpl Lloyd. Standing on boxes: LAC Neal, LAC Lee, Cpl Reed, Cpl Bell, Cpl Smith, F/L Jenkinson, P/O Rogers, F/L Bowley, P/O Carter, F/L Jarvis, F/O Roberts, F/L Kirkham, F/L Parish, F/O Whittle, F/L Dalcom, P/O King, P/O Hope, F/O Young, F/O Harrop-Lomas, F/L Stevenson, F/O Bridgford, F/L Watkins, F/O Allan, F/O Rixon, Sgt Tennent, Cpl Burgess and Cpl Linfield. Standing on forms: AC Lynch, LAC Kingleby, LAC Greenhill, LAC Fowley, Sgt Wynd, Sgt Horrocks, F/O McIntosh, P/O Hopkin, F/O Neve, F/O Moorhead, Cpl Faithfull, Sgt Sanders, F/L Bond, LAC Fraser, LAC Garner, F/S Naylor, F/L Roseman, F/L Handley, F/L Powell, F/L Smith, F/L Liddle, P/O Harbert, F/L Birch, LAC Glew, LAC Pearce, LAC Barber, Cpl Redman, Cpl Harris, Sgt Klinkenberg, Cpl Funnell and Cpl Hofgartner. Standing on tables: LAC Reavy, LAC Hill, LAC Ward, LAC Hoskin, Cpl Wilson, LAC Pearce, LAC Langford, Cpl Sutton Smith, LAC Whitehurst, LAC Burnett, LAC Price, LAC Smith, LAC Henderson, Sgt Saunders, AC Reece, Sgt Savagar, Cpl Overy, LAC Langridge, AC Rattenbury, Cpl White, Cpl Pearce, LAC Mortimer, LAC Edwards, LAC Neal, LAC Coulson, Cpl Allen, LAC Jenkins, LAC Gossage, LAC Wright, Cpl Pygott, LAC James, LAC Grant, LAC Nicholson, Cpl Wright, LAC Ewen, LAC Brennan, LAC Morris, LAC Ward and LAC Haimes. (via A T Buckland, who was also responsible for arranging this photographic session)

An 'A' flight photograph taken in October 1944 included Bob Palmer, top row, centre, who won a posthumous VC, Bob Law, centre, Flight Commander and subsequent CO, as well as two navigators and a pilot well on their way to completing an eventual 100-plus operations apiece, Ron Curtis and Charles Brameld, left and right of Palmer, and John Burt, left of Law. (via R.E. Curtis)

Standing in front of a Mosquito Mark IX, ML907, on completion of its 100th operational sortie are pilot John Burt and navigator Ron Curtis, who would themselves notch up their 100th Oboe sortie in each other's company on 8 December 1944, as Oboe formation leader attacking Duisburg above 10/10ths cloud. ML907 was flown by this crew when marking the Maisy gun battery in Normandy on the eve of D-Day, one of the ten such targets that were detailed for Oboe-controlled attacks that night by No. 109 Squadron crews. (via R.E. Curtis)

Undated photograph of No. 109 Squadron, 'A' Flight, ground crews. Back row, left to right: Spencer, Trenerry, Cole, Ballingall, Walker, Tibbles, Jackson, Wills, Klinkenberg, Wiseman and Franklin. Middle row: Barber, Woods, Burnett, Morgan, Wheatley, Whitmey, Mahon, Gilmore, Hunt, Laing, Funnell, Wright and Brennan. Sitting: Jenkins, Broom, Brown, Lewis, Garner, Lendon, Henderson, Pilan, Collins, Evans and Brooks. (via R.E. Curtis)

No. 109 Squadron's radar section including Flight Lieutenant David Slater, the officer in charge, and (on his left) Sergeant Molly Nicholson, who was formerly at the Worth Matravers ground station. (via D.H. Slater)

One of the mobile ground stations that moved across to the Continent to track and release for Oboe target-marking and bombing operations once Allied troops were established in France. As the advance progressed, Oboe ground stations were located in France, Belgium and Germany. This one was photographed when in its final position at Gotha towards the end of the war in Europe. (via J.E.N. Hooper)

Lined up on the grass at Marham, No. 109 Squadron Mosquitoes are positioned in readiness for take-off on an Oboe operation. (Peter Woolland)

Bomb craters cover the site of a heavy gun battery at Longues on the Normandy coast where four out of five Mosquitoes from No. 109 and No. 105 Squadrons successfully released target-markers on Oboe signals as a prelude to an eve of D-Day onslaught by Lancaster bombers. One of the bombers that failed to return came from Little Staughton airfield, where No. 109 was also based, and its pilot was a former member of No. 109, Squadron Leader Raybould DSO, DFM, who flew in both major raids on Krupps in March 1943.

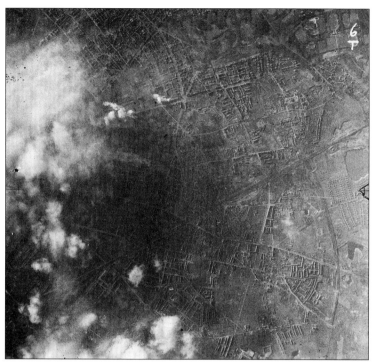

Photograph taken from Squadron Leader A.T. Buckland's Mosquito while carrying out a successful Oboe-release marking and bombing run at 28,000 ft on 2 March 1945, during the course of the last RAF raid on Cologne. The city was captured four days later by American troops. Some 500 heavy bombers took part in this highly destructive attack. The Pathfinder Mosquitoes each carried two TI smoke puffs and two 500-lb bombs, all twelve primary marker aircraft being backed up by a similarly equipped reserve.

Sitting on a 4,000-lb 'Cookie' in front of their Mosquito are one of No. 109 Squadron's crews in the closing weeks of the European war, Squadron Leader Buckland, pilot, and Squadron Leader Benson, navigator, with two members of their ground crew. (via A.T. Buckland)

A 4,000 pounder and a shower of incendiaries leave the bomb bay of a Lancaster during the daylight raid on Duisburg on 14 October 1944, when over 4,500 tons of high explosives and incendiaries were dropped within 25 minutes in the heaviest single attack yet made on any German industrial city. For that attack and for the even heavier night assault that followed, the two Oboe squadrons put up fifty marker aircraft and thus equalled the number employed to mark the Normandy gun batteries on the eve of D-Day. (Imperial War Museum: CL. 1404)

House-to-house fighting was still going on in Essen when an RAF official photographer flew over the city on 11 April 1945 and took this photograph of the devastation inflicted on the Krupps works, which stretched over an area measuring 2½ miles by almost 1 mile. More than two years previously Oboe-led bombing had begun the systematic destruction of this key industrial centre. (Imperial War Museum: CL. 2377)

In this 'still' taken from a film made by the RAF Film Production Unit, Bomber Command 'heavies' are seen here in silhouette against dense clouds on the night of 23/24 February 1945 during an attack on the important industrial and transport centre of Pforzheim. The white 'cascade' is caused by glowing target indicators dropped by Pathfinder Force aircraft. It was for his gallantry during that particular raid that Edwin Swales of No. 582 Squadron, which shared Little Staughton airfield with No. 109, received the VC. As Master Bomber, Squadron Leader Swales remained over the target issuing instructions, although his Lancaster had been crippled by an enemy fighter (see p. 132). (Imperial War Museum: C. 5007)

Air Vice-Marshal D.C.T. Bennett, Air Officer Commanding No. 8 (PFF) Group, seen here when introducing aircrew members to Her Majesty Queen Elizabeth during a Royal Tour of RAF Stations. He is wearing the coveted Pathfinder Force badge beneath his pilot's wings. (Imperial War Museum: CH. 9955)

Visiting TRE at Malvern, His Majesty King George VI and Queen Elizabeth are seen here flanked by the Superintendent, A.P. Rowe, and his deputy, Dr W.B. Lewis, while passing Preston Labs where the Oboe team members and other specialist groups spent much time. (Defence Evaluation and Research Agency, Malvern [Neg, 7982-83 Folder 36]

Grouped around 'Slim' Somerville at an Oboe reunion in 1983 are Don Bennett, foreground, left, and 'Ned' Fennessy, foreground, right, with 'Butch' Cundall, Harry Scott and F.E. Jones, left to right respectively. (Michael Ward, *The Sunday Times*)

The Oboe/Pathfinder reunion, Churchill College, Cambridge, 22 to 24 March 1993. Back row, left to right: Joe Larney, Harry Scott, Dick Smith, Frank Metcalfe, Ken Neville, Eric Dick and Jack Boucher. Middle rows: Ivor Edwards, Geoff Gilbert, Dick Strachan, Bill Green, Bill Humphrey, Owen Williams, Jack Worby, Charles Harrold, Jack Emmerson, John Pritchard, Arthur Buckland, Ron Curtis, Ken Wolstenholme, Ron Powell, Geoff Whitten, John Tipton and Pat O'Hara. Front row: Tom Thomas, Don Vardon, John Hooper, Sir Edward Fennessy, 'Slim' Somerville, Len Overy and Ralph Shonk. (via R.E. Curtis)

Another distinction goes to two crews who missed that occasion: that of having made No. 109's first daylight sorties. Flight Lieutenant F.W. Walton and his navigator, Squadron Leader E.R. Benson, and Squadron Leader R.C.E. Law with Flight Lieutenant W.J. Falkinder notched this up on 1 March 1944. The Walton/Benson combination, using Oboe to track and to attack, led a formation bombing mission at 20,000 ft where the formatting aircraft released on their signal through a blanket of cloud; the aircraft carrying Law/Falkinder was reserve to the formation leader and accordingly bombed on its cue.

There were other noteworthy occasions, for the squadron specifically and for Oboe generally, as D-Day approached. It lost its first aircrew member since moving to Little Staughton when, within forty-eight hours of arriving at the new airfield, a Mosquito flown by Flight Lieutenant E.W. Arnott lost the use of an engine while returning from operations. The aircraft flipped over on to its back and the navigator, Flying Officer P.E. Mitchell DFC, baled out over the sea. Although apparently he was quite close to the shore, he could not be saved and his body was subsequently recovered in the water. Arnott, staying with the aircraft, managed to land it safely at Bradwell Bay.[30]

The Americans resumed their use of Oboe, which saw eighteen twin-engined Marauders of the 9th US Air Force formation-bombing an airfield in Belgium on signals given by an Oboe-equipped aircraft controlled by Hawkshill Down IV (tracking) and Winterton III (releasing) on the afternoon of 21 February; the four-engined heavy bombers of the 8th US Air Force were no longer using the system. New ground stations were also coming into use, Treen handling its first range test on 14 April, Beachy Head hosting three mobile stations in readiness for use on the Continent – PFF Commander Don Bennett paid them a visit on 26 April – and Tilly Whim pairing with Beachy Head to handle another Oboe 'first' when two aircraft from No. 109 were detailed for an experimental operation using what might well be described as a 'no hands' release for a 4,000 pounder in the early hours of 2 May.★

Mark III Oboe was being introduced by now. An early concept, its principal purpose was to provide the facility for a number of aircraft to be

---

★ Initially a single Mosquito was detailed for this operation, No. 109 having just this one fitted up for automatic release, then PFF Headquarters increased the requirement to two aircraft and supplied the necessary parts. This introduction of the 'no hands' release capability worked in the case of the Thelwell/Scott combination but failed with Emmerson/Henry (a crew which nevertheless scored in another way by setting a squadron precedent with the completion of two ops in one day). The view expressed among the aircrews was that the 'auto' failure was no doubt due to the last-minute rush made by No. 8 Group to put on such an experiment. The following night, with a change of crew but against the same target (Achères, on the north-western outskirts of Paris), the same pair of aircraft achieved the same one-in-two success. The aircraft that failed on the first occasion did so again, Jacobe/Fredman finding that the automatic release was this time over-enthusiastic and allowed their 4,000-lb bomb to go at random. For that reason, if for none other, taking the release out of the navigators' hands was but a short-lived experiment.

controlled simultaneously on each radio frequency channel. Taking this capability to the next logical step, Hawkshill Down V, tracking and paired with Winterton IV, carried out the first simultaneous operation of two channels, which enabled two 4,000 pounders to be dropped within one minute of each other on Oberhausen (Squadron Leader E.V. Smith/Flight Lieutenant J.A. Simpson on Channel 32 at 0027 hrs, 55 seconds and Pilot Officer T.T. Thomas/Pilot Officer N.W. Wade on Channel 31 at 0028 hrs, 55 seconds), both using the automatic release gear which had made its début a week previously on 2 May. Within the fortnight that performance was eclipsed by the simultaneous operation of three channels (which added Channel 33), this time to control aircraft marking and bombing Duisburg.

There were two further developments which produced benefits specific to Pathfinder Force during the pre-invasion period. One was an adaptation of the 250-lb target indicator bomb, with tail-fusing enabling it to burst at lower heights and achieve improved accuracy when marking an aiming point, the other the introduction of a variant on the 'flash' equipment used when taking photographs from aircraft on the bombing run – the advantage here being that 'the point of cascade of the TIs can be accurately determined'.[31]

With this new development, No. 105 Squadron's Flight Lieutenant J.W. Jordan and navigator Flight Lieutenant J.R. Byles DFC set a new Bomber Command record for the highest night photograph when attacking railway yards at Osnabrück on 18 April 1944 with '3 x 500 MC and 1 x TI Red Photo Flash' released from their Mosquito Mark IX, ML 923. This photograph broke the previous record by 13,000 ft, at the same time providing 'an accurate check on Oboe marking'. Nine days earlier, Osnabrück itself was a record breaker; an attack on that occasion 'made history' because it was the first time Oboe had been successful 'at such long range'.[32]

In early 1944, No. 60 Group's Wing Commander 'Ned' Fennessy, being well aware that secret plans were being made for the Allied invasion of France, tried hard to engage Bomber Command in discussions on their requirements for GEE, G-H and Oboe coverage in support of this operation. He was advised that because of the C-in-C Bomber Command's deep commitment to pressing home the attacks on German targets, this was not 'a subject for immediate or popular discussion at Bomber Command'.[33] However, realizing the very considerable amount of planning and equipment preparation that was needed, and the probable limited time available for this major task, Fennessy drew his own conclusion as to the probable invasion area. He decided that it was likely to be on the sweep of the French coast to the east of the Cherbourg peninsula. He therefore drew up a series of plans for GEE, G-H and Oboe cover for this area. Having shown them to his AOC at No. 60 Group, he despatched them to the Directorate of Signals at the Air Ministry, marking them Top Secret.

What happened next bordered on the farcical. Instead of getting a call to discuss those plans with Group Captain Harry Foss, Fennessy received a summons from the Provost Marshal's Office! Led in to be cross-examined by an Air Commodore, Fennessy found himself coming immediately under hard interrogation for having sent documents that revealed the Allied landing zone under merely Top Secret cover. Fennessy protested that he thought that this was the correct procedure. 'But you are Bigoted', exclaimed the Air Commodore, to which Ned made some flippant remark about perhaps being that way inclined – a rejoinder which did nothing to mollify his interrogator.

By now it was becoming clear that the Provost Marshal had told Fennessy that his guess as to the invasion beach area was correct and that it was the Air Commodore, rather than Fennessy, who had committed a breach of security by confirming the location of the intended invasion area to someone who was not 'Bigoted'. This left only one course open in those circumstances: to put Fennessy on the 'Bigot' list, to be sworn to secrecy, to be told the place and time of the invasion and given a fine rubber stamp with 'Bigot' on it for use on all future occasions. Now legitimate, Ned was therefore cleared to discuss his plans with the Directorate of Signals – where they were fully approved – and the way was open to set in motion at No. 60 Group, the site selection process required by those plans.

Clearly the RAF and the American air forces operating in support of the invasion would require GEE, G-H and Oboe cover in step with the Allied armies advancing through Europe, so No. 60 Group drew up plans to form a fully equipped Mobile Wing ready to be deployed in France and advance with the front line, enabling the bombers to benefit from those radar navigational aids well forward of the fighting. Designated No. 72 Wing and coming under the command of Group Captain R.L. Phillips, in addition to GEE, G-H and Oboe it was to be responsible for a number of Type 11, 14 and 25 radar stations for use by RAF and American fighters. Engineering construction of the stations was carried out at TRE, RAF Kidbrooke and various contractors and all units were assembled for crewing and kitting out at RAF Cardington.

In the Oboe squadrons too, much of the work was specifically associated with the invasion preliminaries, the thrust of so many of the Oboe-led bombing attacks now turning away from Germany's industrial heartland and to a spread of new targets – new in location, new in the type of objective that was being selected. Soon the Allied troops would be going aboard the landing craft and soon, to help protect them in their progress, the Oboe squadrons would be flying record numbers of sorties.

CHAPTER ELEVEN

The Eve of D-Day

'You did famously last night . . . The next few days will necessarily be critical . . .
I know that you will do your damnedest to meet all assignments with that
efficiency and determination which has characterized the whole of your share of
Overlord to date.' Bomber Harris, in a congratulatory message sent through
the AOC, Pathfinder Force, on 6 June 1944. This was the morning of D-
Day, the day that Allied troops landed in Normandy, Oboe Mosquitoes
having marked ten coastal gun batteries threatening the invasion forces.

Ahead of D-Day, Oboe attacks were carried out on targets such as Trappes
on 6/7 March, the first of a series of raids on railway targets in France and
Belgium in preparation for the invasion; Vaires, near Paris, where two
ammunition trains were blown up and reportedly 1,270 German troops
were killed; Bourg-Leopold, where one Oboe-released TI fell right on the
target and the bombing which followed caused severe damage to this
military camp in Belgium; and Ferme d'Urville, the main German radio-
listening station near the coast chosen for the invasion.[1]

In his Despatch of War Operations, 23 February 1942 to 8 May 1945, Air
Chief Marshal Sir Arthur T. Harris, Air Officer Commanding-in-Chief,
Bomber Command, refers to large-scale attacks on the eve of D-Day on ten
batteries in the assault area, with 1,136 aircraft taking part and dropping a
total of 5,315 tons of high-explosive bombs. With a single exception, he
states, the batteries offered no serious resistance to the warships
approaching the coast or to the invading forces. Most of them were
completely silenced by the air bombardment.

The two Oboe squadrons each supplied twenty-five Mosquitoes to mark
those ten batteries during the night of 5/6 June, five Mosquitoes marking
each battery and achieving a hundred per cent Oboe-release success at three
of the ten batteries – St Martin-de-Varreville, Maisy and at Mont Fleury,
where the TIs went down with 'extreme accuracy'; at Longues, Houlgate and
La Pernelle, four out of five Mosquitoes obtained successful releases; at
St Pierre-du-Mont, Merville-Franceville and Ouistreham, the figure was three
out of five, while at Crisbecq, two out of five Oboe releases were successful.
Of those thirty-eight successful Oboe releases (seventy-six per cent), No.
109's Mosquitoes just had the edge over their colleagues from No. 105, with a
tally of twenty (eighty per cent) compared with eighteen (seventy-two per
cent). Squadron Leader R.C.E. Law and his navigator, Flight Lieutenant

C.W.J. Falkinder were first off in darkness at 2210 hrs, touching down at 0035 hrs, with Flight Lieutenant L.C. Jacobe and Flight Lieutenant J.H. Crabb bringing up the rear at 0400 hrs to return in daylight at 0625 hrs. At Maisy, Mont Fleury, Longues, Houlgate and Merville-Franceville, Pathfinder Lancasters backed up the target-marking for Main Force, while at St Martin-de-Varreville, La Pernelle, St Pierre-du-Mont, Ouistreham and Crisbecq, the Oboe Mosquitoes were alone in marking the targets for Main Force.[2]*

To assemble such a massive force of Oboe Mosquito target-markers meant bringing back into front-line service some twenty aircraft that still carried the Mark I 1½-metre equipment, each of them necessarily having to be controlled by a pair of equally veteran Mark I ground stations. By now Mark II Oboe was the routine for operational use, the ground stations dedicated to this centimetre system being supplemented for these eve-of-D-Day activities by the first of the Mark II mobiles that had been produced for service on the Continent and were presently positioned at Beachy Head. In the circumstances, the overall seventy-six per cent performance was to everyone's credit – thirty-eight releases on the Oboe signal among the fifty participants.

That night's operations are recalled by Flight Lieutenant Curtis:

> We knew that we were in the build-up period for the invasion but there wasn't a clue while we were being briefed during the afternoon of 5 June for the night's operations. Perhaps we might have guessed, though, when we found that the squadron had been given ten separate targets and that we would be putting up twenty-five aircraft. We had never had as many as ten targets before – and to provide twenty-five aircraft and twenty-five crews was starting to scrape the bottom of the barrel . . .
>
> Anyway, when the briefing was over I had a wager with Jock Turnbull, one of our senior navigators, that our task that night, which was target-marking ten gun sites between the River Seine and the Cherbourg Peninsula, would not turn out to be the prelude to D-Day. We had done gun batteries before, which meant that the type of target wasn't giving much away, so we made our bet: a pint and a whisky that this was not the invasion. I lost, of course, but I knew that he was a gentleman and that he would buy me the same in return!
>
> John Burt and I were in a Mosquito Mark IX, ML907 [interestingly, ML907 was an aircraft which survived the European war and, as did Burt and Curtis together in this and other Oboe Mosquitoes of 109 Squadron, it completed in excess of 100 ops]. It was already the morning of D-Day when we took off to mark the Maisy batteries, though I knew nothing about the invasion having begun until I heard the news in bed on AFN (American Forces Network) on my radio when I woke up after a few hours sleep following de-briefing. It was still dark when we flew back to Little Staughton, so we saw nothing of the ships in the Channel, but the boys who were on later than us had a grandstand view around dawn.

---

* Marking those same batteries, No. 105 equalled No. 109 with a hundred per cent success at five of the ten targets: St Martin-de-Varreville (three sorties), Maisy (three), Mont Fleury (two), Longues (two) and Houlgate (two). It was two out of three at La Pernelle, where the third aircraft had a 'hang-up'; one out of three at Crisbecq and at Merville-Franceville and one out of two at St Pierre-du-Mont and at Ouistreham. The respective Operations Record Books show that, on their separate airfields, a No. 105 crew (Flight Lieutenant L. Holliday DFM and Flying Officer C.L. French DFC) beat No. 109 into the air by two minutes, taking off from Bourn at 2208 hrs; No. 105's last touch-down was at 0628 hrs (Flying Officer J.A. Ruck and Pilot Officer L.B. Winsloe), three minutes after that of the last aircraft at Little Staughton.

All 'the boys' in the fifty Pathfinder Mosquitoes came back but ironically there was a former No. 109 Oboe pilot in those same operations and he lost his life.*

Squadron Leader Raybould DSO, DFM was captain of the first of sixteen Lancasters from No. 582 Squadron to take off that night from Little Staughton (which his squadron shared with No. 109) to attack two of the ten gun batteries. Longues was the target for Raybould's and ten other Lancasters, the remaining five being detailed against Mont Fleury.[3]

At Bourn, 'Butch' Cundall, the former No. 109 pilot who was now No. 105's CO, forecast that the invasion would mean 'a tremendous amount of extra work' for his squadron; all leave would be suspended, six crews would be on stand-by at thirty minutes' readiness, twenty-four hours to the day, and no one else in aircrew would be allowed away from the flights for more than three hours – and then only on condition that they stayed at the end of a telephone. All officers and airmen were to carry arms at all times,[4] an instruction echoed at Little Staughton for aircrew members of No. 109; there, when flying was in progress, sidearms were left in their lockers and an airman armed with a Sten gun accompanied the crews from the locker room to the aircraft for take-off and then met them at the airfield dispersal point on their return.[5]

Through the Air Officer Commanding, Pathfinder Force, Bomber Harris sent a message to those who marked and bombed targets on the eve of D-Day, in which he said that they 'did famously last night in the face of no mean difficulties'; fire from the coastal batteries was reported as 'virtually negligible' and 'all four radar targets were put right out'. 'I know that you will do your damnedest to meet all assignments with that efficiency and determination which has characterized the whole of your share of Overlord to date'.[6]

Among the ground-control stations, Beachy Head was paired with Tilly Whim to handle invasion-support operations carried out by both RAF Mosquitoes and USAAF Marauders. The three channels controlled thirty-two aircraft (twenty-seven successful Mosquito runs and four successful Marauder runs) between 2315 hrs on 5 June and 0617 hrs on 6 June, the Marauders taking over from the Mosquitoes at daybreak and contributing to a total for the month of June which comprised 428 sorties with 349 successful Oboe releases (a figure of 81.54 per cent).

---

* No. 109 Squadron's losses on Oboe operational sorties so far averaged less than one aircraft in three months, a remarkably low 0.003 per cent. Ackland and Strouts went down on 26 March 1943 (see page 104), Chrysler and Logan on 27 May 1943 (see page 104) and Bickley and Jackson on 2 December 1943 (see page 115). On 13 January 1944, the last contact with Flying Officer P.Y. Stead and Warrant Officer A.H. Flett was in the target area, on 6 May 1944 Stephens and Flying Officer N.H. Fredman were lost (see page 133) and on 2/3 June 1944, limping home from the Ruhr in a severely damaged plane, Carter and Garrett had to bale out over Kent. With D-Day now passed and the 2,000th operational sortie completed shortly afterwards, no further loss occurred until 31 August 1944 when Flight Lieutenant G.H. A'Court and Flight Lieutenant F. Waterman parachuted to safety behind Allied lines while returning from an attack on Leverkusen (see page 133).

Visiting Beachy Head on 25 June, Sir Robert Renwick, Controller of Communications at Air Ministry and Controller of Communications Equipment at the Ministry of Aircraft Production,* congratulated personnel on their performance during the month. It followed a message of appreciation from the Director General of Signals at the Air Ministry for the work done by all the ground stations on and subsequent to D-Day – a message passed via No. 60 Group Headquarters. By chance, Sir Robert's visit coincided with a comparatively close shave for Beachy Head in the shape of a V1 flying bomb which flew into the cliff face within a quarter of a mile to the east of the station, not sufficiently near to cause any damage. It was one that slipped through the net, many V1s being shot down by RAF fighters that month, the closing moments of these attacks providing a spectacular sight to station personnel.[7]

Less fortunate was one of the ground stations further round the coast, Swingate in Kent, England's 'Hellfire Corner', which was the part of the country closest to enemy occupied territory and within range of a number of heavy gun batteries on the coast of the Pas de Calais. A shelling duel over a 2½-hour period during the late evening of 20 March saw the Oboe equipment badly shaken, to the extent that there were intermittent faults for several days. Shelling had occurred before, in a cross-Channel gun duel on 10 February the previous year; shock from British guns dislodged the mechanical 'Mouse' and a splinter from an exploding German shell, weighing several pounds, all but struck the receiver, its path fortuitously diverted by one of the supports for a false roof. No longer would artillery exchanges threaten Oboe flights over the Continent, however, for in the second week of April 1944, Swingate gave up its operational status and became a training station.[8]

As a function of the pre-invasion planning, a number of mobile 'Cat' and 'Mouse' ground-control stations were prepared and formed into convoys, their role being to position themselves on the Continent so as to extend the range of Oboe and to facilitate attacks on significant targets deeper into Germany than the Ruhr, which was effectively the limit for ground stations in Britain. By the end of August, the first convoy was in France; known as Air Ministry Experimental Station 9432, it suffered a very rough crossing

---

* Privileged to have the ear of Churchill, Beaverbrook and the like, Renwick – a leading industrialist before the war – could be relied upon to cut through the red tape that often strangled lesser mortals. Within the disparate organizations he was charged with welding together to sustain the war effort, he was 'Uncle Bob'. Sir Edward Fennessy CBE, Wing Commander Ned Fennessy in those days, recalled in an interview with the author how once he sought Renwick's help to secure immediate commissioned officer rank for perhaps a dozen or more senior WAAF NCOs in No. 60 Group ground stations. It was to give them more muscle when dealing with RAF officers controlling Oboe operations on behalf of Pathfinder Force. When Uncle Bob rang back a day later, saying that he had arranged with the Director of the WAAF for this to be done, he added (fortunately with a chuckle in his voice!): 'Never do this to me again, Fennessy!'

which made it necessary to remain on board the landing craft for forty-eight hours before disembarking became possible on 22 August. The rate of the Allied advance meant that its first operations did not take place until 15 September when it was able to settle not in France but in Belgium. Its first operational location was at Florennes, the area where some of the early Oboe calibration bombs had fallen on New Year's Day 1943 now originating the first Oboe signals being sent to bombing and marking aircraft from Continental soil. A second mobile convoy, AMES 9441, carried out its first Oboe operations from Commercy in France on 25 September, working in conjunction with 9432 to control tracking and release respectively for what was intended as the début Oboe marking to be controlled entirely from ground equipment on the Continent. It was an unsuccessful venture, all six aircraft detailed for these first time Oboe attacks on Mannheim and Frankfurt failing 'due to poor communications'.[9] Whatever the precise cause, these would have been impossible targets for the UK ground stations, both being some 350 miles from the Kent coast. However, redemption came the following night when, at 2122 hrs, with the same pair of mobile stations performing the same roles, the first Oboe bombs were dropped at the behest of ground controllers based on Continental soil.

Bomber Command's work in the opening stages of the Normandy campaign earned praise from General Montgomery who passed on his 'grateful thanks' for the contribution of Pathfinder Force and Main Force aircrews in the tactical battle since the invasion troops first set foot on French soil. It was, he said, 'a most inspiring sight for the Allied soldiers in France to see the might of Bomber Command arriving to join the battle'.*

The squadron now had a new CO, Wing Commander G.F. Grant DSO, DFC, who was posted in from Pathfinder Force HQ on 21 June to succeed Wing Commander Cox, who moved to No. 82 OTU. Cox, who already held the AFC, would shortly add the DFC to this in recognition of gallantry and devotion to duty in the execution of air operations while serving with No. 109 Squadron. Grant was no stranger to No. 109; he was there in the summer of 1940 when beam bombing was in its infancy and he had taken part in Operation Trinity against the German warships sheltering in Brest in the days of the 'Broody Hen'.

The period shortly after D-Day emphasized the risks run by the Oboe Mosquito crews and the manner in which luck was either on, or apparently not on, their side. On a single night, for example, the night of 27/28 June, where one of No. 109's Mosquitoes was intercepted twice by an enemy night-fighter and was totally burned out in a crash-landing at Manston (Flight Lieutenant D.M. Russell and Flying Officer J.S. Barker both being

---

* Montgomery's message followed a particularly impressive Oboe-led attack on a defence strongpoint at Villers Bocage on 30 June 1944, when 250 heavy bombers, each carrying some 13,000 lbs of high explosives, blasted a massive tank concentration, the Target Indicators having fallen little more than thirty yards from the aiming point.

admitted to the station sick quarters with burns), another of its aircraft made an eventful landing on one engine – on an unfamiliar airfield – with its instruments unserviceable. The pilot was Flight Lieutenant R.M. Sleep, who was in only his first month with No. 109 since joining from No. 1655 MTU, and he made an historic landing in the middle of the night which left him and his navigator, Flight Sergeant W.C. Bridgford, unscathed in the incident. It was remarkable in that another pilot, a member of another squadron, almost literally held his hand in the descent to the ground. Wing Commander C.M. Wight-Boycott DSO from No. 25 Squadron took off, made contact with Sleep in the air, then guided him in through the clouds.[10] It was an exceptional demonstration of thoughtfulness, skill and patience that saved two crew members and their Oboe-equipped aircraft at a time when No. 109 could not afford such losses. It should be noted that this episode occurred towards the end of June, a month that saw a heavy call made on the Oboe Mosquitoes to mark a large number of small precision targets, 'often at rather short notice'.[11]

For No. 109, that month of June 1944 did indeed set a new level of demand for its services, with as many as 372 sorties being flown, but even that figure was surpassed in July, not by No. 109, which dropped back to 334, but by their friendly rivals in No. 105 with what would remain for them a best-ever monthly total of 412.

Among the most westerly of the Oboe ground stations, Sennen and Treen handled their last Oboe operational flights on 31 August, Worth Matravers continuing to be used (paired with Hawkshill Down) against Le Havre, Calais and Boulogne in softening-up operations against enemy forces still holding those ports. Worth Matravers' last operation was on 28 September, a month that saw a fresh and not-to-be-beaten record number of sorties by the crews of No. 109 (a total of 425) and as many as nine separate Oboe-led operations in a single day against a single location (against Le Havre on 10 September and Calais on 25 September, each time with the squadron putting up twenty-two aircraft to mark for Main Force).

An increase in the number of daylight raids during August provided the Operational Research Section at Bomber Command HQ with additional data to determine the efficiency of Oboe-led marking sorties. It was noted that 'considerable evidence' was consequently available on the accuracy of markers; these new findings indicated that 'our average error of 250 yards about the mean was achieved', a result which was said to represent a 'noticeable improvement' on that normally obtained at night.[12]

As winter neared, in addition to the well-established ground stations in the UK, which continued to be range-effective for many targets on the Continent, as many as five convoys of mobile stations were now deployed at various locations on the Continent itself, further increasing the Oboe catchment area, with a sixth and ultimate convoy yet to leave the UK. At the time of the Ardennes Offensive, which came when the year was drawing to its close, there were mobile stations still at Florennes and Commercy, to which had been added de Rips in Holland (it was established on an abandoned German GCI site, totally destroyed before the enemy's retreat) and at La Roche-en-Ardenne in Belgium, where AMES 9442 (two channels) with 9431A and 9412B (with one channel apiece) were positioned, operational since 22 October. However the Germans swift counter-blow was judged to put La Roche in jeopardy, so evacuation was ordered and those three units withdrew to Florennes, fortunately without repercussions any more serious than the loss of a number of vehicles which had to be left behind when the closing-down messages were transmitted at 1035 hrs on 18 December.

Before the enemy's action in the Ardennes became known, Wing Commander Fennessy had flown to Paris for meetings at the Supreme Headquarters of the Allied Expeditionary Forces (SHAEF) and subsequently at Reims where the Headquarters of the 9th United States Air Force was located. At SHAEF, his task on that occasion was to establish Bomber Command's requirements for GEE, Oboe and G-H so that preparations could be made to position the ground stations within the context of the next phase of the Allied advance. Next day, visiting the 9th US Air Force, which was always anxious to get the Oboe cover needed for its operations, the purpose was to determine where best the ground equipment could be located, the continuing push paving the way for Oboe-led raids on more and more distant targets. At Reims, however, Fennessy found that German forces were about to upset the best laid plans by counter attacking in force. It was a move that he appreciated could have serious consequences, especially for the fifty or sixty personnel of No. 72 Wing who were manning the GEE and Oboe equipment at La Roche.

In the Ops Room there was a map which showed the front line and I queried a V-shaped 'nick' in that line, to be told that this represented German reconnaissance movement into the positions held by Allied troops in the Ardennes. I was given to understand that patrols like this happened all the time, so there was no need to worry. That night, however, I was woken up around 3 a.m. by a telephone call from No. 72 Wing HQ at Mons, in Belgium, with the CO, Group Captain Phillips, telling me that La Roche was reporting information from the American forces in that area that German armoured columns were on the move. It looked dangerous, according to those on the spot, so the decision was made that if the CO considered it necessary, then La Roche was to be evacuated with nothing of value left for the enemy.

I drove to Mons, where Group Captain Phillips met me and the two of us went immediately to Brussels, to the Headquarters of the 2nd Tactical Air Force, to find out what was happening. When one of their top-ranking officers learned that we had given the CO permission to pull out of La Roche at his own discretion if the situation worsened, he blew his top, 'You can't do that,' he stormed, 'we need that ground station'. Then the phone rang, presumably with news of the German offensive, and we saw or heard no more of him! La Roche was evacuated – quite quickly afterwards it was overrun by enemy troops – and despite heavy snow which hampered the movement of equipment and personnel, the convoy was safe at Florennes within a day and soon set up and working again. Subsequently I heard that the Battle Orders of the German C-in-C, von Rundstedt, indicated that he had detailed a unit specifically to capture our radar unit at La Roche.'*

Closer to home, the end of 1944 saw the Mosquito Training Unit transferring out of Pathfinder Force, an occasion which provided Don Bennett with an opportunity to heap praise on Bomber Command, on the PFF itself, on the Mosquito aircraft which the two Oboe squadrons and other units flew, and on those within No. 1655 MTU who had trained their crews. In a Boxing Day message to its CO, Bennett stated, 'The work of Bomber Command led by the Pathfinder Force has been of vital importance in successfully waging the war against the Nazi criminal. The part played by the Mosquitoes has been a very vital one in the activities of the PFF.' He noted that the effectiveness of these very fast weight-carriers was being increasingly appreciated in all quarters and that the efficiency of their work was itself increasing. He recorded sincere appreciation and thanks to No. 1655 MTU personnel for the vital part they had played 'in making the Mosquito Force the magnificent weapon it is today' and asked them to do their utmost to maintain their spirit of cooperation, determination and total tenacity – the qualities 'they have already displayed so admirably'.[13]

While the experience of No. 1655 MTU personnel had been applied these past eighteen months to producing more Oboe crews, Oboe applications themselves had broadened, first with the increase in suitably equipped aircraft and in the availability of trained crews to fly them, which gave the opportunity for round-the-clock Oboe sorties, and then in a number of innovations which brought mixed fortunes and, on one notable occasion, tragic results both to Oboe and non-Oboe crews. There were 'musical' Mosquitoes marking for 'non-musical' Mosquito squadrons; there were Oboe Mosquitoes leading formations of Halifaxes whose bomb-aimers were instructed to release on visual signals given by the Mosquito navigator tuned in to Oboe, and there was Oboe-led formation bombing. Here the bomb-aimers released when the bombs were seen to fall from the formation leader, a Lancaster equipped with Oboe and carrying pilot and navigator 'loaned' by one of the Oboe squadrons, the deputy leader on those occasions being an Oboe Mosquito.†

---

* An entry in No. 72 Wing's Operations Record Book in June 1945 shows 'recent investigations' as having brought to light that Field Marshal von Rundstedt had in mind capturing the technical units located at La Roche intact, particularly desirable trophies being a Type 9000 (Oboe ground station), a Type 100 Heavy (G-H) and a Type 7000 (GEE). The enemy was 'in full possession' of the pinpoints of those sites and information as to the mobility of the convoys into which these technical units were formed.

† When, much earlier in the air war in Europe, the US 8th Air Force introduced Oboe formation bombing, the shortage of Oboe aircraft was such that as many as three Bomber Groups were led by a single marker plane. Inevitably, when upwards of fifty bomb-aimers were all supposed to be releasing at the same time as the one with Oboe, the resulting bomb spread could be well over one and a half miles.[14]

When Mosquitoes led Mosquitoes there was no problem with maintaining speed or height, with Mosquitoes leading four-engined heavies there certainly would be problems. Being considerably faster, it meant that the Mosquitoes must keep down their speed almost to the rate of knots likely to introduce stall conditions. Although this was something that could be accommodated by the pilots of No. 109 and No. 105, further problems arose which had not been anticipated. For example, when No. 109's Mosquitoes were leading formations of ten Lancasters in an attack on Coulon Villiers on 5 August 1944, weather conditions made it impossible for accurate formation bombing. One leader flew into cloud and iced up, firing the customary smoke puff at the moment of Oboe release. The reserve, trying to go round the cloud, lost the leader but found the ten Lancasters following him. Then, when passing the puff, the formation obediently bombed on cue.[15]

Contemporary records confirm that Oboe-led formation bombing was not the easiest form of attack to pursue, it was, however, one of the most rewarding in terms of operational efficiency within Bomber Command. An analysis of results achieved in the first month showed that with formations varying in number from six to sixteen heavy bombers, which took off at fifteen to twenty second intervals, 'an excellent concentration of bombs is being obtained, with a greater accuracy than with normal visual bombing'.[16] Although the use of those daylight Oboe formations was 'rather limited' in scope and scale, it was 'the most effective method of bombing' and produced 'better results per aircraft taking part than any other type of attack'.[17]

Using another form of comparative analysis – this was based on the 'Relative density of hits per acre at the AP per 1,000 bombs dropped' – Bomber Harris, in his Despatch of War Operations, 23 February 1942 to 8 May 1945, gives the figure of 7.44 for Oboe formation bombing on tactical targets in occupied territory, compared with 2.16 for Oboe ground-marking and 1.73 for formation GEE-H bombing. He refers to 'great difficulty' being experienced with Oboe Mosquitoes leading formations of Lancasters flying in pairs line astern, owing to the different speeds and heights of attack of the two types of aircraft, adding that all-Mosquito formations were used later with 'much greater success'.

The first heavy bomber formation attack with an Oboe-equipped Lancaster in the lead and an Oboe Mosquito as deputy leader took place on 11 July 1944, the target being a flying bomb site at Gapennes. In the first attack there was a single formation, the pilot and navigator in the leading Lancaster – they came from No. 109 Squadron (Somerville/Scott) – tuned in to Oboe, the Mosquito and the other six Lancasters bombing on the leader in good formation. The same principle was followed for a second attack in which this time there were three formations, all bombing as instructed although a reserve Mosquito took over from the Oboe Lancaster in one formation.[18] Subsequent operations of this sort were less successful:

in one on 14 July, the Mosquito followed the wrong formation and bombed with them while in another, just next day, the Mosquito returned early having failed to contact the formation. While those facts might be regarded as amusing now, Oboe-led formation bombing had its tragic side too. On 20 July, Squadron Leader F. Foulsham AFC and his navigator, Flight Lieutenant J. Swarbrick, leading a formation of Lancasters from No. 582 Squadron, came under anti-aircraft fire while running on to the target. The plane was seen to have been hit before release and caught fire, carrying on to bomb and then to break up in the air after leaving the target.[19]

The benefit of Oboe-led formation bombing was that it allowed the greatest possible tonnage to be dropped directly with a single Oboe release, each of the heavies letting go their bombs in company with those of the Oboe-equipped aircraft heading the formation. Regrettably, it was just such a method that produced No. 109's blackest day. The date was 23 December 1944 and the operation was one that brought about a devastating loss of life in quite unforeseen circumstances.

The attack was in daylight on marshalling yards at Gremberg (Cologne), a focal point for troop movements to fuel the enemy's Ardennes offensive. It was not a major raid – just seventeen Lancasters of No. 582 Squadron, ten Lancasters from No. 35 Squadron, two Mosquitoes of No. 105 Squadron and one Mosquito of No. 109 Squadron taking part – an Oboe Lancaster (with an Oboe Mosquito as reserve) leading each of three formations of eight aircraft. One formation was to follow the other with some four minutes separating them, No. 582 supplying the aircraft for the first and second groups and No. 35 for the third. The bombing height was to be 17,000 ft. Out of the thirty aircraft which set out, two Lancasters were lost within an hour of take-off, these aircraft and crews from No. 35 Squadron perishing as a consequence of a collision over the sea. As for the attack itself, when it became obvious that the absence of predicted cloud cover made conditions ideally suited to fighter intervention and that an Oboe run-in would make the aircraft unnecessarily vulnerable, change-of-plan instructions were broadcast over the R/T for the crews to bomb visually, in effect enabling the aircraft formating on their Oboe Lancaster leader to break away and to choose their own moment to let go their bombs.

Crew reports show that there were aircraft in all three formations which did not hear those instructions and continued to hold their position for an Oboe-led formation bombing operation. The first on the scene, the Oboe-equipped Lancaster crewed by No. 582 Squadron, maintained its run-in towards and over the aiming point, despite the formation having been jumped by enemy fighters four minutes before reaching the target area. The Oboe pilot was No. 109's Squadron Leader R.A.M. Palmer, whose completion of 100 operational sorties had earned him a second DFC, which was announced just fifteen days earlier, and the Oboe navigator was Flight Lieutenant G. Russell DFC, also from No. 109. For his actions that day at the controls of that Lancaster, Bob Palmer earned the Victoria Cross; the

134th VC of the war and the RAF's 23rd, it was one of three awarded in recognition of an act of valour while serving in Pathfinder Force, the only 'Oboe' VC and No. 109's only VC.* The citation stated that Palmer 'disdained the possibility of taking avoiding action', adding that 'his aircraft was last seen spiralling to the earth'.

The Oboe routine had been followed implicitly, right through to releasing the bombs that were being carried while they were ablaze (11 × 1,000 lb GP). Of those on board there was just a sole survivor, the rear gunner. He escaped by parachute as the plane broke up, counting himself incredibly lucky to be alive as would another whose place in that same Lancaster was taken at the last moment by the crew's regular gunner, the aircraft in the process of making its way from the dispersal point to the runway for take-off.

Over the target, the loss of the Palmer/Russell aircraft was quickly followed by that of its reserve, a No. 109 Mosquito carrying Flight Lieutenant E.C. Carpenter and Flying Officer W.T. Lambert DFC, which was glimpsed with an engine ablaze and four fighters on its tail. The toll mounted with one after another of the Lancasters in that first formation going down over the target or while limping home. One remained capable of flight as far as Belgium and the crew parachuted to safety, thus avoiding capture by the enemy, but their comrades from No. 582 in the other stricken planes either lost their lives or became prisoners of war.

Like Palmer and Russell – the Oboe pair heading the first formation – No. 105's Squadron Leader G.W. Harding DFC and Squadron Leader L.W. Millett DFC in the Oboe Lancaster leading the next formation (again comprising aircraft and crews from No. 582) also kept to their Oboe bombing run, the crew in this No. 35 Squadron aircraft seeing their own 1,000 pounders straddle the target. However the leader of the final formation, with No. 105's Flight Lieutenant R.E. Jordan and Flight Lieutenant J.W. Plunkett to track and release with Oboe, found it impossible to do their work effectively. Reluctantly their bombs were jettisoned instead of the intended precision release, the Oboe run spoilt by another Lancaster 'formating closely on us until the last moment and thereby not giving room to manoeuvre'.[20]

---

*Coincidentally, all three were posthumous awards and all were to pilots with Squadron Leader rank who were leading a bombing attack in Lancaster IIIs. Ian Bazalgette, No. 635 Squadron, lost his life when his aircraft exploded on the ground after marking and bombing a target at Trossy-St Maximim on 4 August 1944; the Lancaster had been hit by heavy anti-aircraft fire and was on fire but Bazalgette pressed on gallantly with the attack, remaining at the controls and even managing to land the aircraft. Edwin Swales, No. 582 Squadron, Master Bomber for a raid on Pforzheim on 23 February 1945, remained over the target issuing instructions although his Lancaster had been crippled by an enemy fighter and become easy prey to further attack. Swales tried to fly on but the aircraft crashed and he was found dead at the controls, the last crew member having jumped just before the aircraft plunged to earth.

With both those formations, the reserve aircraft was an Oboe Mosquito from No. 105 Squadron. Flight Lieutenant H. Almond DFC and Flying Officer C.R.A. Challis DFC, accompanying the Lancasters from No. 582, lost their hydraulics and the inability to open the bomb doors, which aborted their attack, while Squadron Leader G.W.A. Parker and Flight Lieutenant V.W.G. Musgrove DFC, flying with those from No. 35, bombed in cue with the formation leader.[21]

The two surviving Oboe Lancasters were so severely damaged that each diverted to Manston in Kent, crash-landing there within two minutes of each other. They were followed almost immediately by a further Lancaster, also from No. 35 Squadron, which, despite the fact that this last formation had begun breaking up some ten miles short of the target on hearing the R/T instructions, experienced hits in many places, including three of its four engines.

In the event, without taking into account those who died in the mid-air collision on the outward journey, which itself cost the lives of fourteen members of No. 35 Squadron, this raid was directly responsible for No. 582 losing thirteen crew members and five aircraft and No. 109 losing four crew members, two of them in one of No. 582's Lancasters and the other two in the single Mosquito to go down, a total of thirty-one aircrew members and eight aircraft lost in this one operation.*

There were losses of aircraft and crew with conventional Oboe operations too – inevitably. Sometimes crew members would find their way home again to Little Staughton and sometimes there would be confirmation of the worst, that missing aircrew had in fact died as was feared, though no one was inclined to give up hope while there was still the slightest chance of survival. With Stephens and Fredman failing to return on the night of 6 May, it was some months before there was official confirmation that both had lost their lives and that they were now buried in Venlo Cemetery. There was better news, in less time, with regard to another crew, Flight Lieutenant J.W. Shaw and Flying Officer J. Broadley; they both returned separately to the UK and reported to the Air Ministry some days after being listed as missing on an operational flight. A'Court and Waterman, whose aircraft was lost, baled out over France and turned up safe in the hands of American forces, while Warrant Officer J.A. Falconer, back from an unsuccessful

*According to an entry in Pathfinder Force Headquarters' Summary of Operations,[22] 'in the absence of cloud and in accordance with instructions, the [formation] leaders broadcast for the following aircraft to bomb visually'. The marshalling yards were clearly seen and all except five aircraft bombed on visual identification, those five bombing on the aircraft ahead. The summary shows that seventeen Lancasters and one Mosquito (from the twenty-seven Lancasters and three Mosquitoes detailed) attacked this target, doing so from between 15,000 ft and 17,300 ft. It describes the bombing as being 'very accurate', with numerous bursts seen on the marshalling yards and the aiming point being quickly obscured by smoke. The heavy anti-aircraft fire was also extremely accurate and many Me 109 and FW 190 fighters were seen in the target area.

operational sortie where his Mosquito caught fire on the return journey, force-landed at Woodbridge, his navigator, Sergeant R.W. Bradbury, touching down some miles away by parachute. There was a less happy return for another crew though, when, with Christmas 1944 less than a week away, Flying Officer W.T. Kerr and Flying Officer D.A. Weare DFC set off for their target, ran into trouble and returned early, crashed near Saxmundham and both lost their lives.[23]

The last year of the war began with record numbers of sorties by Allied bombers; it saw the British 1st Army moving into Germany at the end of January and the American 1st Army crossing the Rhine in early March; in the following month, on 25 April, it saw American soldiers sweeping forward from the west and Russian soldiers from the east who met and embraced each other at Torgau on the Elbe. In their own advance, the mobile stations that were required to extend the use of Oboe further and further east met opposition of another sort, however, which came not from the enemy but surprisingly from friendly sources.

At HQ No. 60 Group, Ned Fennessy was quickly made aware of this instance, which occurred when one of No. 72 Wing's convoys (No. 4 executing a top priority move from Florennes to Bad Homburg) had the misfortune to become entangled in the midst of American troops under General Patton, desperately trying to maintain their headlong dash for the Rhine. Vehicles carrying Oboe ground-control equipment were trapped in a massive traffic jam, the RAF blue uniforms standing out perhaps provocatively in a surging sea of US Army battledress. Patton wasn't going to have a non-combatant unit of any sort, let alone a 'Limey' unit, holding up his advance so 'he had our people taken into custody and it took three days to get them liberated, the result of a protest which started at Wing, carried on through Group, Bomber Command and Air Ministry, with Eisenhower himself having to intervene so that this Oboe mobile ground station could proceed to its next site'.[24]

Targets in cities as deep into enemy territory as Nürnberg (on 1 February 1945), as far north as Hamburg (31 March) and as southerly as Munich, No. 109's longest distance sortie (8 April), all came in for Oboe attacks. On 8 April Berlin was targeted for the first time, with four Mosquitoes of No. 109 Squadron and two from No. 105 achieving an overall fifty per cent success in releasing their markers for a small force of some twenty aircraft. This was the first of thirteen nights when nuisance attacks of this sort took place where one or other of the Oboe squadrons either marked for Mosquitoes of the Light Night Striking Force or released their own bombs, No. 109's Flying Officer A.C. Austin and Flying Officer P. Moorhead manning the aircraft credited with having dropped the last bombs on the German capital. Four 500 pounders, released on Oboe at 28,000 ft from a Mosquito XVI, MM929, fell through 10/10 cloud at 0214 hrs on 21 April 1945.[25] In a previous attack on Berlin, Squadron Leader R.M. Sleep reported seeing below him in the target area a Messerschmitt Me 262, the first jet-propelled fighter to go into operational service with the Luftwaffe. A single-seater, twin-jet aircraft reputed to be exceptionally manoeuvrable, it was capable of speeds in excess of 500 m.p.h. Less troublesome were the Focke Wulf FW 190s, two of which once chased a No. 109 Mosquito with Flight Lieutenant J.T. McCreal its pilot at the time. When he first saw them – this was on a daylight marking of Cologne on 2 March – the FWs were 1,000 yards behind him, however he opened up and 'neither of them gained any distance at all', the snub-nosed German fighters last being seen mixed up in a mêlée which he hoped contained predominantly Allied fighters.[26]

Failing to cause the demise of one Adolf Hitler in the Chancellery in Berlin, Sleep must have been particularly keen to have a go at doing so in the Nazi leader's mountain retreat at Berchtesgaden a few days later. On 25 April a daylight raid was ordered, in which he was to be flying one of eight Mosquitoes from No. 109, to drop red TIs from as much as 40,000 ft for a following force of 300 heavies. What might have been one of the most fascinating of all Oboe marking missions turned out to be among the most disappointing, not just for Sleep but for the entire squadron. From a personal viewpoint, he found that his aircraft was playing up shortly after take-off. So he landed and made another attempt, this time using one of the reserves, only to find that he could not make up time and had to concede an early return. It is unlikely that he would have been any more successful than the other seven Mosquitoes from No. 109 and the eight from No. 105 who were joining in for the Berchtesgaden raid, none of whom found Oboe working because the signals were blocked by the mountainous terrain.* Unhampered by such matters that were outside their control, No. 109 and No. 105 Mosquitoes were able to achieve successful Oboe releases when delivering leaflets to prisoner of war camps and marking for RAF heavies dropping some 6,672 tons of food under truce conditions at various still-occupied population centres in Holland, an activity known as Operation Manna, which continued for several days.[27†]

---

* In fact the target was the SS barracks at Wachenfels. With no Oboe markers down, the Master Bomber identified the aiming point by means of the lake and the town of Berchtesgaden, which he marked, subsequently directing the efforts of Main Force relative to the position of his own TIs. In No. 109 Squadron's Operations Record Book there is what can be regarded as an epitaph to this total Oboe failure. It says, 'Fortunately the target was clear so that our failure to mark it did not unduly affect the concentration of the attack.' The Oboe ground stations involved were those at Molsheim (No. 1 Convoy) and Gotha (No. 3 Convoy). No. 72 Wing ORB described Berchtesgaden as 'hopelessly out of range in view of the screening effect of the Black Forest', a fact, it is stated, that was 'known at No. 8 Group'.

† No. 109 Squadron's stablemates at Little Staughton, No. 582 Squadron flying Lancasters, took part not only in the Manna food drops but in another form of mercy mission named Operation Exodus. This began on 7 May with some 21 heavies from Pathfinder Force bringing home 483 ex-POWs from an assembly point in Brussels; this rose to 90 aircraft carrying 2,088 on 15 May and ended only when a total of 7,643 had been returned to the UK.[28]

In the final week of the European war, crews from No. 109 achieved a double distinction. The first was in an offensive mode when there were indications that German forces could be assembling in the Kiel region preparatory to a bid to continue hostilities in Norway. On the night of 2/3 May both Oboe squadrons were detailed to mark for the Light Night Striking Force attacking targets in Kiel itself and to bomb airfield targets in the same area on their own. At 0054 hrs on 3 May, No. 109's Flying Officer J.J. Rixon and Flying Officer O.W. Allan, aboard a Mosquito Mark XVI, RV316, carried out the last Oboe-controlled bombing of the war. Another crew, Flying Officer J. McIntosh and Flying Officer J.A. Neve released their 4,000-lb Cookie on Eggebek airfield virtually in tandem – but this was a release based on dead reckoning, this crew having unfortunately experienced a technical failure. It could be charitable to regard this episode as being a case of 'honours shared', because their aircraft established a record of its own as being the last one home from a bombing mission, touching down at 0240 hrs. The second distinction in that final week of war was more humane in its nature. Flight Lieutenant D.P. Dalcom and Pilot Officer C.J. King, whose aircraft, a Mosquito Mark IX numbered LR908, became, at 1520 hrs on 8 May, the last to land after completing an operational sortie. This was an Operation Manna flight in which this crew marked, from 29,500 ft with Oboe, at 1357 hours, an aiming point in Rotterdam for the food-carrying Lancasters. It was the final Oboe operational sortie of all time – and the 5,502nd carried out by the aircraft and the crews of No. 109 Squadron.

In the view of the authors of the definitive history of the de Havilland Mosquito[29] it is impossible to measure the contribution made by the Oboe Mosquitoes of 'a mere two squadrons' to the winning of the war; 'a handful of crews' contributed out of proportion to their numbers, making possible 'accurate and effective bombing with amazingly low losses'.

American bombers using Oboe made their final flights of the war on 1 May, four sorties achieving but a single success, a statistical result which was fortunately quite out of proportion to the USAAF's overall performance with Oboe. Its 893 successes among the total 1,663 sorties gives slightly under 54 per cent overall within the 627 operations flown by their Oboe-equipped aircraft since October 1943,[30] a period of 19 months compared with the 29 months that No. 109 operated with Oboe.

The mobile ground stations on the Continent handled the final Oboe-led bombing missions over Germany and those in the UK the mercy flights to Holland. For the Oboe squadrons, the ground controllers and the TRE scientists, however, the end of the fighting did not signal the conclusion of their work. There was still training to be undertaken (Bonn, Bremen, Cologne, Essen and Hamburg were all bombed in dummy missions after the war was over)[31] and there were the results of further bombing trials on the ranges to be determined. There was also an upsurge in the competitive spirit that had long existed between the two Oboe squadrons, the rugger matches of earlier days giving way now to bombing matches, though an historical account which belongs primarily to No. 109 Squadron is perhaps not an appropriate occasion to dwell on the results! For some, No. 109 ground personnel among them, the winding-down period presented an opportunity to join one of the Cook's Tours during May 1945, when sightseeing aircraft followed pre-set routes and altitudes to obtain an aerial view of the bomb damage inflicted on key German objectives – and on others such as Walcheren where the sea walls had to be breached and enemy gun positions flooded to put an end to bitter opposition at a critical stage of the Allied advance through the Low Countries.

Oboe participants marked in their own way the announcement of VJ Day on 15 August 1945, which brought at last an end to the Second World War. Typically, No. 6 Convoy, which left Mons on 4 February for its initial deployment at Tilburg and moved to Horstmar in time to handle the six aircraft marking Berlin with Oboe for the first time (and forty further sorties within the week), received the news of Victory over Japan Day 'with great joy' and 'all possible was done to celebrate this great day'.[32]

It was a time to offer thanks for lives being spared; it was a time to ponder over what was right to do in war and what ought not to have been done, and above all, this was a time to reminisce, to bring to mind the achievements, personal and otherwise, to think about what was, and what might have been.

CHAPTER TWELVE

When Luck runs out . . .

'I was lucky . . . I was never hit on the run-in, though some were less fortunate. You had enough to worry about in those critical few minutes, keeping your eyes on the horizon indicator, your hands gripped on the control column and your feet poised to move the rudder ever so gently to keep you on track.' 'Slim' Somerville, a veteran of the Blind-Bombing of Cherbourg (BBC) and Trinity operations, who flew on No. 109's first Oboe mission and later, on 25 September 1944, joined the second Oboe squadron, No. 105, as Commanding Officer.

How is a front-line squadron in wartime best remembered? By a single event that has dominated its history, for example No. 617 and the dam-busting raid, or by individual acts of valour; by continuous dedication to an operational theme, or perhaps by sustained effort demonstrated in the exceptional numbers of operations logged by its crews? In the case of No. 109 Squadron there was no singular occasion to excite national admiration, and its one member to be honoured with the Victoria Cross in fact won this award while flying an aircraft from another squadron. However, where No. 109 is in a class of its own is in respect of the unrelenting, single-purpose pursuit of its operational requirements, which were exclusively beam-based, and in the calibre of its aircrews whose members had to carry out their duties under conditions of tension and concentration which were quite unlike those experienced by the pilots and the navigators of other squadrons in Bomber Command. Furthermore, on average, aircrew members in No. 109 – the longest-serving Oboe squadron – could justifiably claim to be the most operationally seasoned among all the bomber crews because their losses were so much lower and the number of sorties flown was so much higher.

Bob Palmer won his VC posthumously on his 111th operational flight; he was a pilot, a Squadron Leader, and already he held the DFC and Bar. Squadron Leader E.R. Benson DSO, DFC and Bar, who was a navigator, came through with a probable record 145 ops which combined pre-Oboe and Oboe sorties, and Ron Curtis, another navigator, completed just one short of 140 ops, his 104th on Oboe having been preceded by an initial 5 on Hampdens and a further 30 on Lancasters. At least a dozen others in this squadron had 100 or more ops to their credit, the navigators by far outnumbering the pilots. The reason for this was that many of the pilots came from BAT (Beam Approach Training) Flights, with considerable specialist capabilities in beam flying but with little or no time on a front-line squadron, whereas the navigators had to come with operational experience and particularly be familiar with GEE.

Circumstances and a certain amount of luck dictated how many sorties a pilot or a navigator flew with No. 109. Zeal played no part in whether or not someone with 49 ops behind him actually reached the 'magic' half-century or a 99-er made it to become a centurion. One of no more than a handful of No. 109 pilots who completed 100-plus operations was John Burt. He and Ron Curtis flew all their Oboe ops in each other's company, neither of them ever going on an Oboe operational flight with anyone else.[1] It seems that it was Ron's aim to beat the 135 combined pre-Oboe and Oboe ops flown by fellow navigator Jock Turnbull, who was a squadron veteran having taken part in the Lutterade calibration raid on 20 December 1942 and both Oboe-marked Krupps attacks the following March. Curtis, on completion of his 136th, telephoned Turnbull – who had by then transferred to TRE's airfield at Defford – cheekily telling him, in the parlance of the day, to 'get some in'. A further three ops, the last of them being on the day after this navigator's twenty-third birthday, brought the Burt/Curtis Oboe tally to 104 and that of Curtis himself to 139 when combined with pre-109 ops on Hampdens with No. 144 Squadron and on Lancasters with No. 44 Squadron.*

Pre-109, both men had been stationed at Waddington for a time, when Burt was with No. 420 (Canadian) Squadron flying Hampdens, and their brief acquaintanceship was happily renewed when the pair arrived independently at Marham for Oboe training. There was no question of either of these Oboe centurions exceeding their individual 104 total: 'We were called into Don Bennett's office at Huntingdon, I remember,' said Ron, 'and while both John and I wanted to carry on, Bennett told us that if he were to agree, there would be questions asked in Parliament!'[2]

Like all other squadrons, No. 109 had its characters, for instance 'Slim' Somerville, who was in at the start.

When Flying Officer K.J. Somerville arrived at Boscombe Down in November 1940, a tour of bombing operations behind him and the much-coveted ribbon of the Distinguished Flying Cross newly sewn beneath the pilot's wings on his tunic, he joined a remarkable Oboe quartet. Individually and collectively, theirs was an outstanding performance; it was a quartet

---

* This 104th Oboe operation carried out by John Burt and Ron Curtis was on 6 March 1945. Six Mosquitoes from No. 109 were detailed to spearhead an all-Mosquito formation attack on Wesel in daylight: three formations, one apiece from Nos 128, 608 and 571 Squadrons, each with a leader and reserve supplied by No. 109. Burt/Curtis had great difficulty in finding their formation and picked them up only when those aircraft were close to the Dutch coast, fifteen miles off track. Matters improved and the No. 109 Mosquito successfully led the formation to bomb on Oboe, minus the reserve which lost touch early on because of a navigation instrument failure. Of the remaining formations, one bombed along with the reserve, which took over when the leader had technical trouble, and the other was left to do its best in the absence of both leader and reserve, these aircraft having collided in mid-air (see page 153).

whose members would each go on to display skills of the highest order and combine to achieve a distinction that was without doubt unique.

Of these four, Squadron Leader H.E. Bufton was already at Boscombe Down, setting the stage for a role that would unite the aircrews of the yet-to-be-created No. 109 Squadron with the scientists at the Telecommunications Research Establishment (TRE) in the evolution of the Oboe ground-controlled blind-bombing system. Less than three months previously, on 9 September, he had gained promotion from Flying Officer to Flight Lieutenant, with the acting rank of Squadron Leader. Flying Officer G.F. Grant had come from Dyce on a posting effective on 5 July and Flying Officer H.J. Cundall from St Athan, the effective date of his posting to Boscombe Down being 9 July. Somerville, the 'new boy', whose arrival now made up this exceptional quartet, stood apart because he was the only one who had been on ops with a front-line bomber squadron, the decoration being visible testimony to his courage under fire.

By the end of hostilities in Europe, all four would have moved up the promotion ladder to reach the rank of Group Captain, and all four would have become Commanding Officer of an Oboe squadron: Hal Bufton and George Grant taking charge of No. 109, Butch Cundall and Slim Somerville flying with both No. 109 and No. 105 and becoming Commanding Officer of No. 105. In both squadrons, unusually, this position carried the rank of Group Captain. This meant that Somerville, when he took over No. 105 on 25 September 1944, achieved a further distinction in being one of the youngest Group Captains in the RAF – he added the fourth ring on his sleeve and the 'scrambled eggs' on his hat when he was still four months short of his twenty-fifth birthday.

Somerville recalls:

When my posting came through to move me from No. 10 Squadron to become an instructor at Lossiemouth, the CO [Wing Commander S.O. Bufton] called me into his office and explained that his brother [Squadron Leader H.E. Bufton], who was running a special unit at Boscombe Down, would be keen on having suitably qualified pilots. Briefly, Syd told me what Hal was doing at Boscombe Down and this seemed far more interesting than instructing. So, there and then, Syd was on the telephone to the people who were handling the postings and mine was switched immediately – just like that! Which is how I came to join Hal Bufton, Butch Cundall and George Grant in what Syd always used to call his 'Little Oboe Family'.[3]

The job awaiting Somerville was to fly in search of the enemy beams that were laid across Britain to guide bombers to their targets; later on, he and others in No. 109 tried to bomb their source. He continued:

Sometimes we would go up in the Anson in the afternoon, when the Germans were positioning and testing their signals; we would criss-cross until we picked up the signals that confirmed the path of a particular beam. Then, when darkness came, we would fly down that same beam towards the transmitter on the Cherbourg peninsula. Having reached the 'cone of silence' – the point where the signals stopped, indicating roughly the position of the source – we would circle, bomb on the return, and head for home. We were ever-hopeful but unfortunately, from what I heard subsequently, it appears that we caused only minor damage.

He was on the Trinity sorties too, eternally grateful that while a No. 109 pilot was in charge of each Stirling on its straight-and-level flight along the beam to await the bombing signal, Wellingtons from other squadrons also attacking the *Scharnhorst* and the *Gneisenau* at Brest at the same time were doing so from a lower altitude and thereby attracting much of the anti-aircraft gunfire. On occasions, Stirlings would fly in formation across the target, one No. 109 pilot riding the beam with another on either side of him, this pair sticking as close as possible like satellites, to achieve greater concentration with their bombs.

To test the Oboe system throughout its development stages, Slim flew all of No. 109's mixed bag of aircraft including the pressurized Wellington VI.

I hated the 'Six' . . . it was an awkward plane to fly, especially because when you were taking off you couldn't see over the nose until your tail was up. This was a bit like Concorde except that those pilots were given the benefit of a nose that quite literally could be made to droop to provide the necessary visibility from the cockpit. We were so glad to get the Mosquito – an aircraft without vices that was a delight to fly!

When the first one arrived, Bufton and Somerville took it up on day one and next day it was Somerville's turn at the controls, accompanied by Pilot Officer A.D. Bates, an Oboe technician who was formerly a civilian on the TRE staff. 'It was trial and error, those first flights in a Mosquito. We had no instructions whatsoever on how to handle this aircraft,' he recalls.

Somerville flew on all stages of Oboe testing and trial bombing, up to and including the series of experiments intended to prove the validity of relaying one ground station's signals, by means of an airborne repeater system, to extend Oboe's range. It was rather like being able to pick up a ground station and position it at will, within effective range of new and more distant targets. The Oboe Mosquitoes detailed for marking/bombing would receive one set of signals via the repeater aircraft and the other direct from a suitably positioned ground station: 'We thought it was a good idea, which theoretically could have taken Oboe target markers to Berlin long before we were able to have mobile stations on the Continent, but the principle was abandoned after only a few sorties.'

Somerville gives his No. 10 Squadron CO, Syd Bufton, the credit for being foremost in recognizing the benefits of a dedicated pathfinding force and pressing for its creation, using his clout at the Air Ministry – he was Deputy Director of Bomber Operations – to gain the support of the Chief of Air Staff, Sir Charles Portal, and so win the day over Bomber Harris and others who were resisting the concept of an élite force. Syd Bufton, he says, was 'a man who would push, push, push to get something done'.

Operationally, when Pathfinder Force had come into being, with No. 109 one of the founder squadrons (with No. 156 Squadron from No. 1 Group, No. 7 from No. 3 Group, No. 35 from No. 4 Group and No. 83 from No. 5 Group), Slim Somerville flew the first and many subsequent Oboe sorties, completing a tour ahead of all others on No. 109.

What was it like for the pilot, this beam-flying? Here is Somerville's description:

> It was a stupendous feeling, crossing the North Sea and then, as we neared the target area, generally following the arc north to south, starting to pick up the dots and dashes of the beam. Most pilots, myself included, lowered the seat – we wanted to avoid distractions outside the cockpit and be able to concentrate 100 per cent on our instruments, on our controls and on the signals in our ears. We had no fear of night-fighters and none ever came near while I was flying, we were too high and too fast, but there was often gunfire from the ground which you could see and sometimes feel, once or twice you could even smell it. I was lucky, I was never hit on the run-in, though some were less fortunate. You had enough to worry about in those critical few minutes, keeping your eyes on the horizon indicator, your hands gripped on the control column and your feet poised to move the rudder ever so gently to keep you on track to the target. All this time your ears would be tuned to the dots and dashes, waiting for them to merge in response to the control that you exerted over the aircraft, so that then you knew you were making an accurate course. Once on track, you had to hold whatever speed was required; also, you had to maintain whatever height was necessary. The concentration was terrific, absolutely tremendous.
>
> Up to ten or fifteen minutes or so beforehand of course, you had the opportunity for verbal contact between pilot and navigator. Then, each of you had signals coming in which demanded total dedication to the task in hand. The navigator had his job to do, listening for the release, and I had mine. I would be waiting for him to pat me on the shoulder, which was his way of telling me that he had let go the markers – if it was a 4,000-lb bomb he was releasing, you didn't need him to tell you! – and I would put the nose down to increase our speed, turn and head for home. You reckoned that probably by then you could breathe a sigh of relief, though the only time I was ever hit by anti-aircraft fire was after we had put the target area behind us. The damage took out an engine but we landed at Manston on the 'good' engine without a problem.

By the time he left the squadron, going first to PFF Headquarters and then to Bourn to lead No. 105 Squadron, Slim had been credited with more than 100 operations, to which he added a further 15 with No. 105 to reach a grand total of 117.

There is an amusing story of a non-operational nature which links Somerville with the Pathfinder Force Commander, Air Vice-Marshal D.C.T. Bennett, at the time of the liberation of Paris in August 1944. It was Bennett's wish to fly into Le Bourget, then the French capital's principal airport, within twenty-four hours of de Gaulle's triumphant entry into Paris. Circumstances demanded that Bennett's rank seek higher authority to make such a flight and it transpired that he did, in fact, receive permission from Bomber Harris – the proviso being that he took a skilled Lancaster pilot with him. Taking up the story, Slim explains:[4]

Don Bennett was not too pleased as he was himself possibly the most experienced pilot in Bomber Command! Literally the first person he bumped into was myself. At which Bennett said 'Slim, we're off to Le Bourget in one hour's time!' We did just that, landing at Le Bourget and commandeering a Jeep to take us into Paris. We drove down the Champs-Elysées and through the Arc de Triomphe, the French people shouting '*Vive les Anglais*'.★

It was a most exciting occasion, certainly for Somerville who, a month later, joined No. 105 Squadron at Bourn, where the Station Commander was Group Captain Hal Bufton, a former CO of No. 109.

One of perhaps a handful of men on No. 109 Squadron whose job combined periodic flights in a Mosquito as well as pursuing his regular duties on the ground was Pilot Officer D.H. Slater, whose first experience of Oboe came with an unexpected posting to 'something called TRE'.

Dave Slater was a country boy who worked on a farm and little realized that he was destined to join a team which largely comprised boffins, whose scientific chatter – when he joined the RAF as a volunteer and began 'square-bashing' at Blackpool – would have been utter gobbledegook. The RAF, in its infinite wisdom, chose him for the first four-month course of its kind in Londonderry, where the unskilled and the unknowing learned as much about radar as the instructors were able to cram into them.

He was one of six radar mechanics joining TRE at the same time, the scientists necessarily guiding them always as to what to do next in the constant routines of building, adapting or testing the equipment that would one day go into an aircraft or to a ground station. Then, with the system reaching the point where more and more aircrews would be needed for operational flying, Slater was commissioned at the instigation of Reeves' team at TRE so that he would be better able to take on the next stage of his duties. This was to give the pilots and navigators of No. 109 an initial understanding of Oboe: 'Actually the orders were to keep them in dark so far as the technicalities were concerned, on the basis that if crews were shot down and interrogated, they could not give away what they didn't know,' Slater explains.[5]

In time, Slater's own unit expanded to include a Flight Sergeant, a couple of Corporals, half a dozen Leading Aircraftmen and even someone able to help handle his paperwork, the latter being a WAAF from Worth Matravers. Molly Nicholson had been transferred to No. 109 for liaison work between ground stations and air operations, as was Margaret Patterson from Trimingham, who went to No. 105 at Bourn.

★ Although seniority and position would have stopped 'Pathfinder' Bennett from taking part in an operational sortie, the PFF Commander was not going to be done out of an opportunity to get hands-on experience of Oboe under less hazardous conditions. So, when a new type of TI was being tested on the Orfordness bombing range (a 1,000-lb version in November 1944), according to the tracking station's Operations Record Book the pilot during the first runs was none other than Air Vice-Marshal Bennett.

Dave remembers the seemingly endless occasions when the Oboe equipment would be tested on the ground and work perfectly; then, in the air, something would go wrong.

> The crew would tell us that the set was 'running rough' – often that was all they could say – and we would need to go over the obvious and the not-so-obvious possibilities to track it down. Sometimes I would go up in the aircraft, sitting in the navigator's seat, and kneel as far forward as I could manage, it was all rather precarious, to get my hands on the set. The pilot would look askance because this was a case of practically taking the equipment apart while we were airborne, trying to sort out the problem. It might be nothing more than the need to wobble the leads or perhaps the culprit was my old friend the EF50 valve, which seemed to fail on account of vibration. And of course you know about the arc-ing problem [see page 72] which occurred before we were able to obtain pressurized sets that came with Oboe Mark II. In those early days some of us would wonder whether the sets were ever going to work properly! It was aggravating to say the least, sometimes the signals would be so clear, so perfect, and the next minute nothing. Remember, we didn't have the circuitry and the microchips that have come along since, we were relying on soldered wires and a dry joint could play havoc. We would hunt down the trouble on the workbench, rectify it, then an air test would produce a problem of a different sort. Those were the days!

In the immediate aftermath of hostilities, Dave Slater was in the surprising situation of making an Oboe drop of his own – no, not bombs! – which surely singles him out as being the only non-aircrew to fly in a Mosquito as 'navigator' and follow the release signalling procedure along the bombing run to the point when he himself pressed the button. It was a day to remember and also a day to remember for another special reason. The date was 5 May 1945 and the unconditional surrender of all German forces in north-west Germany, Denmark and Holland to Field Marshal Montgomery would become effective at 0800 hrs (with further capitulations elsewhere enabling VE Day to come on 8 May).

Flying with Flight Lieutenant D.P. Dalcom in a Mosquito XVI, Slater was airborne that morning at 0623 hrs, in one of two aircraft from No. 109 whose role was to mark the aiming point for RAF heavy bomber squadrons taking part in the Operation Manna food drops over key population centres in Holland. At 0740 hrs, just twenty minutes before that surrender became official, while flying at a height of 28,500 ft over a target that was completely hidden by cloud, he released red TIs to pinpoint the drop zone at Gouda. It was a successful conclusion to the penultimate Oboe mission before the fighting formally came to an end in north-west Europe – No. 109's Flight Lieutenant J.W. Shaw and Flight Sergeant K. Leigh, who were two minutes behind Dalcom and Slater in taking off from Little Staughton, marked the same aiming point at 0743 hrs.[6] Dave Slater would remember this extra-special flight as the aircrews' way of acknowledging, in a unique manner, the support that he had always given them in tuning the Oboe precision instrument to perfection, therefore enabling No. 109 to achieve results in which everyone on the squadron, fliers and ground staff alike took exceptional and lasting pride.

Being an aircrew member of a front-line squadron in wartime had its compensations. 'At least we came home to our beds and into clean sheets every night,' says Squadron Leader A.T. Buckland, a pilot with No. 109 from March 1944 to July 1945,

> and that's something the boys in the jungle were unable to enjoy. I would have hated being out there, I was so much more fortunate. I had decent food – I suppose you could say that I had a fair proportion of the comforts of home. Ours was a happy squadron and those were good times, due to the comradeship and the knowledge that the job was necessary and very worthwhile. Certainly for me, life was often so much easier than it was for many others in the RAF and in the other services.

It is arguable whether soldiers in the jungle, if equipped to do an aircrew job, would have relished the down side of life in No. 109. As with aircrew anywhere, whether in training or on active duty, a split second was all that it took to end a life – an aircraft failure, mid-air collision, bad weather, a prowling night-fighter or anti-aircraft fire the greatest threats. When 'Buck' began on the squadron, he endured quite literally a baptism of fire, returning from targets in the Ruhr with flak damage to his aircraft on each of his first four Oboe sorties. And if the enemy failed to hit you, there was always the chance that one of your own aircraft might do so instead. Completing a bombing run over Berlin, for example, he turned immediately and 'a black shape swept past, a couple of wing tips away', another Mosquito or one of the heavies, perhaps, because not once in some ninety-nine operations could he confirm ever seeing an enemy fighter, by night or by day. Collisions were just one of the countless number of risks that aircrew forced into the back of their mind, Buckland, particularly, since he had lost a brother, a flying instructor, in a mid-air collision in February 1942.

As well as the fatalities among No. 109 aircrew where there was a known cause, a number lost their lives in circumstances which were unclear. Buck recalls the time that his own flight commander, Squadron Leader D.H.S. Kay DFC, failed to return from operations where his Mosquito was carrying a 4,000-lb bomb. Even for an aircraft unencumbered by such a load, the weather conditions could not have been much worse. 'There was high cu. nimb. cloud,' he remembers, 'and there were thunderstorms. We reckoned that it must have been that frightful weather that brought him down. Only the previous evening we had been sitting next to him, my navigator and I, at a dance. Laughing and joking as we all were, the war seemed so far away that night.'[7]

Buckland's early sorties were all by night. After D-Day however, No. 109 was detailed for an increasing number of operations in daylight to supplement those taking place under cover of darkness. 'Being able to see quite clearly what was happening in the skies around us was a new experience. It was also rather unnerving sometimes, for instance, when you saw another aircraft coming straight towards you, closing at perhaps 600 or

700 m.p.h., and you didn't know whether it was one of theirs or one of ours.' On some of the daylight sorties the Mosquitoes' role was to mark and/or to bomb V1 launch sites while others were in support of Allied troops under pressure from enemy forces on the ground. Precision was necessary to ensure that the bombs fell in the right area, well clear of the Allied positions. 'Buck' notes, 'In a situation like that, it was the navigator who shouldered the main responsibility. He would have to get everything together – I was just the chauffeur, my job being to take us there on time and to get us back home in one piece.'

Getting a Mosquito back home again was not always as easy as Buckland makes it sound. In a 'rather elderly and underpowered Mark IV', for instance, returning from an early operation, he found the coolant draining away fast from the starboard engine. It meant 'feathering' the engine and heading for Manston, haven to many an aircraft in difficulties, whose convenient location and long runway were comforts not to be missed when, as was happening on this occasion, the sole remaining engine threatened to expire. This was, perhaps, the only time that Buck had the tiniest twinge of regret at having successfully requested a posting to No. 109, with its Mosquitoes, instead of staying where he was previously, crewed-up and ready to fly heavy bombers. These were Lancasters, and they had not two but four engines!

Unlike other squadrons, No. 109 had the supreme advantage of being able to pick and choose its pilots and navigators, at least during the formative period of 1942/3 when Oboe was proving itself first in tests and then in early operations. Bufton enjoyed 'a free hand to recruit anyone in Bomber Command' and – in his words – probably No. 109 could have had 'any willing customer from anywhere in the RAF'.[8] The beauty of this benefit was that there was seldom the need to transfer anyone out because he was not up to scratch. Just once or twice this did happen, though the reject rate was considerably below that of other units.

One pilot who was privileged to get a personal invitation was Flight Lieutenant J.R. Hampson. He was with No. 109 during the beam investigation era and later moved into radio countermeasures work, which saw that part of No. 109 being 'hived off' from the squadron to become a unit in its own right, No. 1473 Flight. It was there that he received a surprise telephone call from Bufton asking whether he would like to return to No. 109 now that it was in Pathfinder Force, flying Mosquitoes fitted with Oboe.[9]

Jeff Hampson first joined No. 109 in July 1941, straight from a flying training school, and carried out many searches of the 30's from Boscombe Down – the 30's were enemy beams transmitted on frequencies in the 30 megacycle band – before the Wireless Reconnaissance Flight, to which he belonged, moved to Upper Heyford. Then, back again with No. 109, Jeff was this time flying Oboe operations against targets in Germany. These were mainly in the Ruhr and on one of them, where as many as twelve of

No. 109's Mosquitoes were in action against Essen, Flight Sergeants Chrysler and Logan failed to return. Although this was not the squadron's first loss of an aircraft and its crew on an operational sortie, tragedies of this sort were not easy to put to the back of one's mind. Any lessons that could be learned were worthwhile, however, because one night you might find yourself in a similar situation.

On the night of 15/16 November 1943, Hampson, with seventeen sorties to the Ruhr behind him and navigator Flight Lieutenant H.W.E. Hammond DFC in the seat alongside as usual,* found the anti-aircraft fire causing rather more than the customary nuisance. The customary north–south approach was going well nonetheless with the right height, speed and timing to achieve a successful operation against an industrial plant at Düsseldorf. Then, a shell exploding nearby shattered that confidence. Hampson recalls:[10]

> 'There were bits of the cockpit cover flying all around, the engine temperature gauge was rocketing, we had no hydraulics, no flaps and no hope. There was no alternative but to abandon the aircraft. My navigator baled out first – it wasn't easy in the Mosquito, with the parachute, dinghy pack and all sorts of other protuberances to hinder a nice quick exit. I knew we couldn't afford to let an Oboe-equipped Mosquito fall into enemy hands so I did the only thing possible, which was to turn to the west and hope that the plane would glide sufficiently long enough to drop into the North Sea.

Having made his own escape from the crippled Mosquito, Jeff came down in the mud of the Schelde Estuary, just north of the Belgian frontier, which was a fair indication that this particular Oboe-carrying aircraft would have avoided enemy territory and hopefully disappeared beneath the waves, irretrievable and far from the coastline of the occupied Low Countries. He was unsuccessful in his endeavours either to find Hammond or to contact an underground group which might have been able to get him back to Britain. Instead, Hampson was picked up and taken first to the city gaol in Amsterdam and then to an interrogation centre at Frankfurt-am-Maine where he was reunited with Hammond. Eventually both were imprisoned in a camp close to the German–Polish border.

Unlike other POWs from the squadron, Jeff Hampson was fortunate that, despite the hardships of life in captivity, he did at least survive the war. In the final days, his prison camp was overrun by Russian forces and this seemed to be an appropriate time to slip away through a hole in the wire. Challenged once by a sentry, he found himself making friends with the Russian by using the only word he knew in that language – *Tovarich* (comrade). Begging for food, Jeff was astonished when his new-found

---

* Hampson and Hammond were among a number of sortie-seasoned pilots and navigators posted from No. 109 to No. 105 Squadron on 3 July 1943, to bring operational experience to this new Oboe squadron at the time of its formation (see page 110).

friend threw a hand grenade into a pond, the net result being probably enough fish to feed the entire camp. Realizing that the Americans would not be far away, he parted company from the Russian and made contact with a US transport company whose men were 'on the look out for guys like you', roaming escapees from POW camps seeking safe refuge. It was the first leg on the long way home, via a Canadian unit, a flight to Brussels and from there another plane to the UK.

Less fortunate were other prisoners in other camps, some of them having been compelled to endure physical hardship which broke them in body if not in spirit. Many returned home to bear for the rest of their lives the scars of captivity, while others, among them one of No. 109's pilots, Flight Lieutenant L.C. Bull DFC, and his navigator, Flight Lieutenant W.J. Grisman, who were taken prisoner when the loss of an airscrew forced all seven people aboard the Wellington to take to their parachutes over France on 5 November 1941 (see page 31), failed even to return home.

After the bale-out, Bull and Grisman eventually found themselves in Stalag Luft III at Sagan, where a mass escape of officer prisoners from the northern compound on the night of 24/5 March 1944 was effected by means of a tunnel close on a hundred metres in length that led beyond the camp fence. It is one of the better-documented POW camp episodes of the Second World War: it was anticipated that some 200 persons would be able to slip away but unfortunately the attention of a sentry was drawn to moving shadows and this prompted him to raise the alarm before even half that number had made their way through the tunnel towards freedom.

Nonetheless by then a total of eighty escapees had surfaced clear of the camp, all but the last four – spotted when guards arrived on the scene – managing for the time being to avoid detection. Although two Norwegians and a Dutchmen, all serving in the RAF, succeeded in the ultimate aim of reaching England, all the remaining seventy-three escapees were eventually rounded up after being on the loose on the Continent for varying periods of time, Bull and Grisman among them. Unfortunately, this brief account of that mass breakout from Stalag Luft III now takes a tragic turn because no less than fifty of those seventy-three escapees are known to have lost their lives under sinister circumstances (the remainder being sent to a concentration camp, to another prison camp or back to Sagan). The full facts behind this shocking story were revealed only as a result of long and patient investigations by multinational teams that led finally to a war crimes trial in Hamburg in November 1947. There, fourteen defendants were sentenced to death by hanging, two to imprisonment for life and the other two to imprisonment for ten years for their role in the 'Sagan shootings'.

For those who were in that prisoner of war camp in the aftermath of the mass escape, the grim news of the mass murder began to become public knowledge with the arrival of fifty urns towards the end of April 1944, each urn bearing the name of an escaper and assumed therefore to contain that person's ashes. In some cases too, personal belongings were returned to the camp. There was a brief, non-committal announcement from the authorities in Sagan yet this served only to provoke widespread disbelief. Then, as more information emerged, it became clear that the Nazi hierarchy had planned the shootings of the Sagan escapees with a specific purpose in mind. This was, of course, to discourage all future escape attempts among Allied prisoners of war: keeping the POWs under surveillance and preventing their bids for freedom tied up too much effort that the Germans would have preferred to use to greater advantage. Despite the atrocities being committed in different areas and at different times there was a common theme to the Sagan saga, which was the consequence of detailed instructions having been sent by teleprinter from Gestapo Headquarters in Berlin to the prisons in which the Stalag Luft III escapers were held. Those orders were explicit: to have each of the fifty escapers shot in the back, to give the impression that he had been running away.*

At Sagan, with the agreement of the authorities in charge of the camp at the time, a memorial would soon rise. The initiative of fellow prisoners, it would carry the names of the 'fateful fifty' among the eighty escapers from Stalag Luft III who had tunnelled a way out of captivity during that night of 24/5 March 1944, fifty names which will have been perpetuated in the printed word in the postwar years, fifty names which number among them, regrettably, Flight Lieutenant L.C. Bull DFC and Flight Lieutenant W.J. Grisman, both from No. 109 Squadron.[11]

---

* When the outcome of the mass escape from Stalag Luft III at Sagan became known within the Air Ministry, there was a proposal put forward for serious consideration that the first anniversary should be marked by a bombing raid on a particular Gestapo HQ, where rounded-up escapees had been taken, together with a leaflet drop referring to the executions and warning of the consequences to be expected from this and subsequent atrocities. The proposition was never actioned. It was no longer practicable because that part of Germany was being overrun by the advancing Russian forces before the year was up and to attack other Gestapo HQs was viewed as unwise because it could encourage last gasp reprisals against POWs still in enemy hands. As a note for the record within the Directorate of Bomber Operations at the Air Ministry puts it, 'It appears that we can take no further action in the matter and will have to abandon any idea of reminding the Germans of this particular crime on the anniversary of its commission.'[12]

CHAPTER THIRTEEN

A Time for Reflection

'So there we were, one of our Oxfords with odd propellers, the other with odd wings, and ours was a high-precision job of calibrating for accurate bombing. Surprisingly, we didn't have any trouble flying these "odd" aircraft.' Harry Scott, a No. 109 navigator with some eighty Oboe ops behind him (plus a succession of memorable Oboe 'firsts'), reminiscing about a new phase in his service career when he began calibration flights for the first mobile ground-control stations to be set up on the Continent in September 1944.

It fell to the wife of a fellow officer in No. 109, Flying Officer 'Roger' Reece, who shared a house with Les Bull and his wife, to break the news both to Cathy Bull and Marie Grisman that their husbands had failed to return from the flight over France that night of 5 November 1941. By an odd coincidence, just the previous night, Reece had also been across to the Continent on a similar Special Duties flight, as captain and pilot of that very same aircraft, Wellington T2565, detailed to do work for the 'Y' Service, which intercepted German wireless traffic.

Roger recalls:

> We were over the middle of France and the electrics failed us – we lost the use of our generator. There was some sort of trouble with the starboard engine but we managed to get back home. I reported the difficulties that we had experienced, the problems were apparently sorted out and an air test indicated that all was well with the aircraft. When the time came, Les Bull took off for what turned out to be his last flight, with – as it happened – the same TRE chap as had been with me the previous night. The squadron received a message about Les having experienced an engine failure and it transpired that he had lost his starboard airscrew, which left him with no alternative but to abandon the aircraft near Pontivy in France.
>
> I remember thinking to myself, 'There but for the grace of God'. . . .

In the first month of the war, Roger Reece had joined what was then the Blind Approach Training and Development Unit (BAT&DU), he and Hal Bufton having both been posted there as flying instructors on the same day, 29 September 1939, Reece coming from the School of Air Navigation and Bufton from No. 214 Squadron. As a beam pilot with No. 109, Reece took part in the Cherbourg blind-bombing raids and on 21 April 1941, while Les Bull, George Grant, Butch Cundall and Slim Somerville were bombing Cherbourg by conventional means, he carried out a unique function that night, that of testing and bombing on Oboe at Cherbourg.

Often on Oboe and other Special Duty flights,★ Reece had Jock Kyle as his wireless operator:

What a character he was . . . I remember being with Jock when King George VI presented him with the Air Force Medal. He already had the Distinguished Flying Medal, so naturally he was wearing the ribbon; unnaturally, though, there were no aircrew wings above the ribbon because he didn't qualify for them. The Monarch spotted their absence and in what was fortunately a light-hearted manner he asked for an explanation. Equally jocularly, Jock replied that he had reckoned he should go for the medals before he tried for an aircrew qualification!

It always seemed an unfair anomaly that No. 109's wireless specialists, whose skills were critical to whatever success we achieved as a squadron, merited an aircrew insignia only if suitably qualified in a conventional aircrew category, generally that of Wireless Operator/Air Gunner. Yet our people, who were experts in their own right and displayed a flair for the work which couldn't possibly be taught, probably flew operationally more than aircrew members who belonged to a front-line squadron. This set some of us thinking that it was about time Jock was able to show that he was aircrew!

He was much older than we were – and he looked it – but nonetheless he signed on for an air gunner's course, passing both this exam and his aircrew medical. How he did so, no one will ever know, but in getting through both of them he qualified for the badge that the Monarch's keen eyes had missed and consequently ceased attracting the attention of the Service Police who so frequently stopped him for improperly wearing medal ribbons.

Jock Kyle and his contemporaries were the 'stars', 'We just drove the aircraft,' says Roger Reece. It was the function of these wireless wizards to twiddle their knobs to pick up the signals coming from the enemy beams, which initially fanned out some 45 degrees like the beam of a torch, and then to transmit to waiting specialists on the ground the origin, direction and width of the much narrower, really fine beams which were contained inside them. Increasingly, therefore, it was possible first to locate the enemy's transmitters and then to determine the direction and strength of their beams, invaluable information which could be fed into the melting pot of intelligence emanating from so many sources, among them being intercepted radio messages, interrogation of prisoners and documents obtained from planes and ships falling into Allied hands.

Roger, having been in the 'hived-off' wireless reconnaissance duties component of No. 109, which moved to Upper Heyford at the beginning of 1942, continued with intelligence and other Special Duties work as a pilot with No. 1473 Flight. For example, he tested the radio-navigation system

---

★ In its time before joining Pathfinder Force, No. 109 performed from the outset a range of duties of a highly secret nature which took its aircraft over enemy territory on unaccompanied missions: as well as those to investigate the position of enemy navigational-aid beams directed across the UK, crews flew sorties where the unit's specialist wireless operators intercepted enemy radio messages and there were flights designed to test the efficiency of the various enemy radar systems intended to locate the presence of Allied aircraft. The term for such sorties was 'Ferret' (as in 'to ferret out' information).

known as GEE, he tested 'Window', which reduced the efficiency of German radar, and he tested 'Little Screw', the latter being an enemy device intended to enable their aircraft to home-in on RAF planes. In one test, 'stooging about in the North Cape, just waiting to be picked up', Reece did actually find himself the target of a German aircraft using the 'Little Screw' equipment: 'Fortunately our wireless specialists aboard knew what was going on and alerted me in sufficient time for us to head smartly for home before we could be intercepted.'

On two other occasions, Reece was threatened not by enemy planes but by RAF fighters.

> The trouble was that we were doing all this secret work and sometimes it appeared that too many people were in the dark about the presence of our aircraft. Once, three Hurricanes made that fact perfectly plain when, while I was flying one of our Ansons, they made it obvious that we were not welcome. Thinking that perhaps someone wanted to give us special instructions and couldn't make contact in the air, I did what I thought was intended and landed. On the ground, the pilot of the leading Hurricane asked if I had seen the warning shots he had fired in front of our aircraft. I said 'No', which was the truth, to which he replied that if I had not decided to land, he had been instructed to fire at us. He said – and I remember well his actual words – 'I would have aimed at the engines but I would have got you'.
>
> It was a similar situation another time with three Spitfires.
>
> For the 'Little Screw' flight, I was told only to go the Operations Room and give them a code word. On landing back an irate Station Commander was waiting for me. He would not listen to any explanation, and ordered me to take off immediately – he could not care where – and I had had no rest for 26 hours of which 19 hours were spent flying!

Deciding that a more positive role was preferable to the specialist wireless activities that formed the core of his work from the outbreak of war to the winter of 1942/3, Roger Reece volunteered for Bomber Command and as a Flight Lieutenant with a DFC and AFC to his credit, joined No. 149 Squadron via No. 1657 Conversion Unit in May 1943. Promoted to the rank of Squadron Leader, he flew repeatedly in raids against the Ruhr, Hamburg, Turin and Montlucon in Stirling 'A-for-Apple', an aircraft numbered EH883. In an uncanny repeat of the episode where Les Bull failed to return in a Wellington in which Roger Reece had experienced and reported problems just the previous night, he handed over EH883 to another pilot, Warrant Officer W.J. Leedham, Reece having by now exceeded for the time being his quota of operational sorties. Again, as had occurred with his Wellington, Roger reported a problem with one of the engines during previous operations. Again, as was the case with the Wellington, the Stirling was ground tested and found serviceable and Leedham was detailed for a raid in it that night on Mannheim. Remarkably, the aircraft that had brought Reece safely home despite its problems, failed to return when in the hands of its next pilot, EH883 being one of four Stirlings from No. 149 Squadron which were reported missing on the Mannheim raid. And again Roger would think to himself, 'There but for the grace of God'. . . .[1]

Losing a colleague would have been bad enough but actually seeing friends from the same squadron losing their life in the air must have been even more poignant. On record is a mid-air collision in daylight involving the crews of the two Mosquitoes from No. 109 who were detailed to lead one of six formations of six Mosquito bombers to attack Wesel on 6 March 1945, both men in one of the Mosquitoes being killed while the other pair survived. Those in at least one of the other aircraft (from No. 571 Squadron), saw the collision occur about 10 miles south-east of Southwold, the front portion and tailplane tumbling towards the sea in a spiral dive. Squadron Leader G.M. Smith, the pilot, and Flight Lieutenant W.A. Jones, navigator, who were to have led that formation, lost their lives; the pilot of the reserve aircraft, Flight Lieutenant J.F. Carnegie, also found himself hurtling seawards in a spiral dive, though his Mosquito was intact and he was able to land at Woodbridge. It was all but a double disaster, however, Carnegie having a jammed port aileron which he freed only at a height of 13,000 ft and substantial damage to the aircraft, damage to the port side of the fuselage, the port propeller unserviceable and the leading edge of the starboard wing damaged near the tip.[2]

The squadron lost aircraft and crews in different ways: in that collision before an operation; during operations, either brought down by anti-aircraft fire or enemy fighters or perhaps because of unusually severe weather conditions; while returning from an operation with a crippled aircraft; as well as an accident during training periods. Sometimes the crew survived, coming down by parachute over either enemy or friendly territory; sometimes they were not so fortunate and were known to have died or been posted missing until the facts could be established. There was the almost certainly unique instance within an Oboe Mosquito squadron where it had been decided that extra bombs were to be carried, on external wing racks that otherwise held overload fuel tanks. Due to icing, instead of those 500-lb MC bombs being released as would have appeared to the crew from the electrical control gear in the cockpit, they stayed put and dropped only when the aircraft touched down, the pilot losing his life and the navigator losing both legs in the resulting explosion.* And there was the

---

* Squadron Leader J.R. Emmerson DFC and Bar, AFM recalled, in correspondence with the author, that he was on ops that particular night, 22 March 1944, and there were bombs (some were delayed action bombs) 'strewn on the flarepath and around the airfield'. There were (according to the Operations Record Book of RAF Station, Marham) twenty-four Mosquitoes airborne on night operations against targets in seven separate locations. As instructed, Emmerson landed across the flarepath on this grass airfield but Flight Lieutenant C.F. Boxall (No. 105 Squadron) following him was 'either blown up by one of his own bombs shaking free on touch-down or hit a bomb on his landing path'. Boxall's navigator, Flight Lieutenant T.W. Robinson, suffered severe shock, burns and fractures. He was pulled from under the wing of the blazing aircraft by Squadron Leader P.A. Kleboe DFC, AFC, a pilot from No. 109 Squadron which that night put up two Mosquitoes to Oberhausen, two to Dortmund (which included Emmerson and his navigator, Flying Officer E.R. Henry), four to Venlo, two to Twente and two to Julianadorp. For No. 105 crews, these were their last operations from Marham, three to Venlo, four to Leeuwarden, three to Deelen (including Boxall and Robinson, whose aircraft set out with 6 × 500-lb MC bombs) and two to Julianadorp.

case of an aircraft believed to have been shot down which was not in fact lost through enemy action . . .

Ron Curtis explained:

> Long after the war was over, I was astonished to see a particular pilot come into the room where we were having a squadron reunion. In conversation later, I said that the last time I had seen him was in the crew room and we all thought he had been shot down. 'Shot down? Never! I should never have taken that plane off the ground – it was unserviceable,' he told me.
>
> It turned out that his Mosquito was giving him trouble from quite early on but that he managed to reach operating altitude and to cross the coast. Apparently the port engine suddenly revved and went on fire, the wing catching fire soon afterwards, so there was nothing more to be done but to bale out. Unfortunately the navigator failed to get out due to his dinghy jamming in the escape hatch; Willie, however, going out through the top, made it – just! It seems that his parachute had barely opened when he landed in the Zuider Zee. Luckily he was blown ashore; unluckily he became a POW. He did go back to the squadron in mid-July 1945, to see those who were still left, but by then I had moved on so I missed his visit.*

For Main Force crews who were in the wake of Mosquitoes Oboe-marking a target, memories were mixed. If you were a pilot, navigator or bomb-aimer, those memories were more liable to be centred on what was to be seen in the run up to the target; if you were a flight engineer, there was too much to concentrate upon inside the aircraft than to be concerned with what was going on outside; and if you were a gunner, you would probably recall the degree of alertness that was necessary in the event of interest being shown by enemy fighters or anti-aircraft gunners. However, if you were in a Lancaster crew belonging to No. 218 Squadron in No. 3 Group, flying out of Methwold on the night of 14/15 October 1944, your memories quite possibly revolved around what occurred at the briefing.

Flying Officer K. Bailey remembers it well:

> I was on my bed, reading a novel as I recall it, when one of the 'SPs' (Service Police) came banging on my door – a great burly chap he was – and his voice boomed out that everyone was wanted for a briefing. We all assembled in the Briefing Room and the Station Commander absolutely slated those who had been on the daylight raid on Duisburg earlier that same day. It had not achieved its purpose, he told us, so we would be going again. Furthermore, we would keep on going until we had done the job properly.[3]

---

* Flight Lieutenant M. Williamson DFC and Flying Officer A.E. Kitchen DFC were reported missing when detailed for operations on 27 November 1944 against a target at Neuss. The failure of this aircraft to reach the target area highlights the potential problems with a target-marking operation; at Neuss there was a reserve detailed as stand-in for two aircraft – Williamson's and another which had a technical failure – but both times the reserve was out of position and could not make a useful contribution. It was a busy night for the Oboe Mosquitoes with Main Force marking and 'spoof' raids that required a total of fifteen aircraft from No. 109 and a further twenty-one from No. 105.

Some 1,015 bombers had delivered the daylight attack, No. 218 Squadron providing twenty of them which dropped more than 100 tons of bombs in the space of four and a half minutes. The Station Commander's obvious disappointment was not difficult to understand: his crews had found the target area obscured by dense smoke and there were no PFF Target Indicators to be seen. The Master Bomber, whose customary role was to instruct Main Force which TIs were the ones to bomb, this time gave everyone a free hand so there was not much that could be done except to try to pick up the docks and use them as a pointer to where to drop your bombs.[4]

One in two of the pilots from No. 218 who were on the morning raid were in this latest attack; Kenneth Bailey, whose skipper had been sick for a while, found himself substituting for a missing WOP/AG in another crew which comprised a pilot, navigator, air bomber, flight engineer, mid-upper gunner and rear gunner who had all been together a week previously for a daylight raid on Cleves.

He continued:

The pilot was only a little 'un, who had to use a folded raincoat as well as his parachute in order to sit sufficiently high in his seat to see out of the cockpit. We took off and in making a turn when we were just about airborne the port wing was so near the ground that it almost caught an airman riding his bike down the perimeter track. I sensed that it was going to be one of those nights. We attacked from 20,500 feet on the Red TIs, which I suppose would have been dropped by Pathfinder Mosquitoes who were using Oboe for target-marking – not that those of us in Main Force (the 'Poor Blooming Infantrymen' we were!) knew much about it. As Wireless Operator/Air Gunner, I was positioned below the astrodome of our aircraft and I must have had the best all-round view of everyone on board. For me, the most vivid memory was the way that the flak was coming up that night, there was so much, you could have walked on it.

From the point of view of No. 218 Squadron crews (who were among the 1,005 crews detailed for the two-phase night attack on Duisburg, with other squadrons in No. 3 Group providing a further 163 Lancasters for the heavier, opening attack which spanned just 18 minutes), it was a much more promising raid than the one in daylight. All twenty aircraft, except for a single early return on account of a pilot's illness, found that this time the target area was completely cloud-free so saw and bombed the TIs. Despite what was generally agreed to be a fairly heavy flak barrage, the squadron's attack was judged to have been 'well concentrated' around the TIs.[5]

From Bomber Command's viewpoint, Pathfinder Force Mosquitoes and Lancasters had 'accurately marked' their aiming points in perfect weather and the subsequent bombing was 'highly concentrated', with 629 Main Force bombers in the first phase and 312 in the second reporting attacks on the primary area which, when added to the results in daylight, caused 'enormous damage throughout Duisburg'.[6]

From Kenneth Bailey's viewpoint, Duisburg by night with an unfamiliar crew was one operation that would stay longer in his memory than most of the twenty-nine which he flew with Nos 218, 514 and 195 Squadrons. He concludes:

> I thought we would never make it back home in one piece. We managed to avoid the flak all right but I was less sure about being able to dodge our own aircraft when we were in the vicinity of Methwold. For some reason we found ourselves doing the routine pre-landing circuit in the wrong direction. And if that wasn't enough, we even wandered into the circuit of Feltwell's returning aircraft, which meant that we had to avoid them too. What a night!

For the Oboe squadrons, when the daylight and night attacks on Duisburg were combined, this was as busy a period as the eve of D-Day, with No. 109 putting up twenty-six aircraft (one more than on the night of 5/6 June) and No. 105 a further twenty-four. For Duisburg, however, the marking requirement was halved and each of the twenty-five primary marker aircraft flew with a reserve, this stand-in to mark only if the primary was unable to do so. Significantly, in this series of operations against Duisburg, which saw the largest number of Oboe Mosquitoes airborne since the Normandy invasion, to mark the target for the greatest number of Main Force aircraft so far deployed in a twenty-four-hour period against a single location, the two squadrons achieved eight out of ten successful releases in the daylight attack and twelve out of fifteen successful releases at night – an overall eighty per cent success rate.

By the time the war in Europe was over, even that record number of Oboe sorties was beaten when, on a single day, 29 October 1944, some sixty-six Oboe Mosquito sorties were flown against Walcheren (thirty-six aircraft were employed for a succession of raids during that day, all but six of the Mosquitoes being required to go round again and mark twice), the fifty-one Oboe marker-releases producing a similar success rate approaching eighty per cent. On 6 March 1945, with Wesel the target for an eve of D-Day equivalent force comprising fifty Mosquitoes, all of them bombing on this occasion, there was a hundred per cent Oboe success compared with the seventy-six per cent obtained when marking the ten gun batteries that threatened the Normandy landings.

It is D-Day, though, which still evokes the most vivid memories among Oboe squadron crews, there being one exception – someone who couldn't retain memories of any sort connected with the event because he was absent from the proceedings.

Oblivious to the fact that the Oboe Mosquitoes were flying a record number of sorties while the Allied invasion fleets were nearing the Normandy beaches that historic morning, 6 June 1944, No. 109 Squadron navigator Harry Scott was tucked up in bed, fast asleep, with no inkling that dawn would bring news of such magnitude. He had gone on leave unaware, as was everyone else on the squadron, that when the weather became suitable, the first gliders and the first landing craft were to deposit entire armies on the enemy's doorstep.

For someone with a memorable collection of firsts behind him, the possibility of becoming the first navigator to drop markers on those critical gun emplacements would have been sufficient for him to give up his leave. He would have done so willingly, irrespective of the knowledge that he had earned it with the missions he had completed, and he would have ignored the fact that he needed this rest in order to prepare himself for whatever the future that No. 109 had in store. Scott knew nothing of D-Day, so this was a 'first' that was going to someone else.*

Harry Scott ran the gamut of Oboe operations: he was in the early bombing and sky-marking sorties; he led formations of heavy bombers, in a Mosquito initially and then, as a 'first', leading in an Oboe-equipped Lancaster; he flew in the repeater aircraft and he took part in missions where the ground signals to his own aircraft were relayed via equipment on board one of these repeaters; he was the first navigator to see his own bombs dropped entirely by ground-control, two firsts here because this happened both over a bombing range in Britain and over a target in Germany. He was also the first person inadvertently to bomb a back garden in Oxford – but that's another story.

During the series of repeater operations against Emden there was an occasion when, although the pilot heard the tracking signals perfectly, Scott was totally unable to pick up the releasing signals. It was a moonlit night, bright and clear, and the pilot – it was Squadron Leader C. Campbell this time – urged him to drop the bombs visually. The target was a set of dock gates, the water was reflecting the moon and in such inviting circumstances he was reluctant to return with the bombs. In full agreement, Scott did as suggested and released them more by instinct than judgement. Both men saw the flash of those high-explosives going off, apparently quite close to their target, but precisely how near emerged only when he was told: 'You don't need a bomb sight, you hit a pumping station alongside the dock gates.'

As so many Oboe bombing operations were carried out above the clouds, it was seldom that the Mosquito crews had an opportunity to see the point of impact. However, there was one occasion when the effect of Harry's marksmanship was not only visible, it was spectacular in the extreme. The bomb was a single one, a 4,000-pounder, a Cookie so heavy that it made the aircraft jump when released, and the target was an ammunition dump at Châteaudun. He recalls: 'It was a terrific sight – like all the Guy Fawkes parties in every town in Britain all rolled into one. It began with a huge white flash, further explosions following one after the other all around the

---

* Squadron Leader R.C.E. Law and navigator Flight Lieutenant W.J. Falkinder comprised the first No. 109 crew to take off from Little Staughton for target-marking on the night of 5/6 June 1944, releasing Red TIs over Crisbecq at 23.14 hrs, Law going on to earn a more significant distinction when, on 6 December 1944, he became the squadron's last wartime Commanding Officer.

target area, I reckon you could have read a newspaper even at the height we were flying, 30,000 ft. The pyrotechnics were still lighting up the sky when we crossed the English coast.'[7]*

Harry Scott was the first navigator to fly an Oboe-equipped Lancaster (Wing Commander K.J. Somerville was the pilot) when, in a daylight operation on 11 July 1944, he led a tight formation comprising other Lancasters whose instructions were to release their bombs when he dropped his; it was an alternative to leading in the so-nippy Mosquito. With a 'Mossie' at the front, it meant getting the wheels down and the flaps down too in order to reduce the speed sufficiently for the following Halifaxes to keep within a string which even so would extend perhaps up to one mile. In this kind of operation, those bombers would release on arriving beneath a smoke-puff marker that Scott had fired concurrently with dropping his own bombs. 'I remember thinking, someone is in for a surprise down below when that lot arrive,' he says, referring to the train of RAF heavy bombers approaching their objective, above a blanket of cloud that masked them from everyone on the ground.

When Harry Scott became the first navigator to use the automatic release system – a technique enabling the ground station not merely to signal the moment to push the button but actually to let go the bomb or bombs – he did see his bomb explode but alas, not on the Otmoor bombing range but in a back garden in Oxford. Fortunately this was 'just a small practice bomb', an 11½ lb missile containing only a detonator to release liquid in the tail section, emitting a puff of white smoke to indicate where the bomb had landed. Although no damage was caused, the incident was potentially much more serious. 'I had switched to auto-release at the start of the bombing run,' he explains, 'and I heard some sort of squeaking on top of the signal. Next time I made the switch only just before the time for release and this seems to have been the way to do it – it worked perfectly.'[†]

When the mobile ground stations began operating on the Continent, by which time Scott had flown eighty-odd sorties in No. 109's Oboe Mosquitoes, he was detached to an American air base to carry out calibration work with the mobiles, using an Oboe-equipped Oxford. In that

---

* An entry in No. 8 (PFF) Group Operations Record Book for that night, 3/4 May 1944, reports a 'violent and spectacular explosion', flames rising 'to a great height', a series of lesser explosions and fires that the returning aircraft could still see after 100 miles.

† The first automatic release on an operational sortie occurred on 2 May 1944 when Thelwell/Scott dropped a 4,000-lb Cookie on Achères (see page 119). Reference to the auto-releasing capability (where a ground station, instead of the navigator, triggered the moment for the bomb to fall) begs the question as to possibility of the tracking station taking over from the pilot when the time came to make the bombing run. Certainly the automatic pilot system in some aircraft was coupled experimentally into Oboe. Furthermore, no less an authority than Dr F.E. Jones is on record saying that there is 'no doubt' if the war had gone on much longer, 'the responsibility for the aircraft operation could have been taken from the aircrews'.[8]

winter of 1944/5 the airfield became a sea of mud, and it was so congested with planes that collisions while manoeuvring were inevitable. A duckboard over one area of mud flipped into the propeller of No. 109's Oxford, requiring a replacement prop, and a Fortress clipped a wing on another Oxford used by No. 105 Squadron. When the new prop was fitted, its diameter and pitch were found to be different, and when the new wing was substituted, that wasn't a match either, it had a different span. Scott notes, 'So there we were, one Oxford with odd propellers, the other with odd wings, and ours was a high-precision job of calibrating for accurate bombing. Surprisingly, we didn't have any trouble flying these "odd" aircraft.'

With the end of hostilities in Europe and no longer the opportunity nor the need for further Oboe operations, TRE and No. 109 resumed trial bombing in a fresh bid to establish the degree of accuracy achievable. The results were rewarding, as were the comments that came to light regarding the enemy's reactions to the introduction and use of Oboe. Equally interesting would be the views expressed postwar as to whether or not the unique merit of Oboe really was used to its best advantage in wartime.

CHAPTER FOURTEEN

Doubts and Deliberations

'Why did we go on killing our boys in heavy bombers when we had the two-man Mosquito, which could be made quickly and cheaply, and when we had Oboe, which enabled us to be more accurate with our bombing and more selective in our targets? It is as if strategic thinking died the very moment when those responsible should have been deciding what to do with this splendid new tool.' Frank Metcalfe, former bomber pilot and one of the first ground station controllers to be appointed within No. 8 (PFF) Group.

How much of an impact did the introduction of Oboe have on the heart of the German war machine? The definitive answer came from General Wolfgang Martini, the man in charge of the Luftwaffe's signals service throughout the Second World War, during a postwar visit to Britain. Martini's revelations about the astonishment over the dramatic improvement in the RAF's bombing efficiency can now stand as a lasting testimony to all who were concerned in the design, development and application of Oboe.

On the night of Bomber Command first using Oboe to lead a major attack on Krupps at Essen (the Oboe marking of the Krupps works in March 1943 opened what Bomber Harris called the Battle of the Ruhr) Martini was summoned by Herman Goering, head of the Luftwaffe, to fly with him to meet Adolf Hitler. The reason for this summons was to enable Hitler to question Goering on the reason for such destruction at Krupps and Goering desperately needed a means of getting off the hook; the only excuse he could offer was that a gap had occurred in the clouds and by mischance the moon had revealed the target to the bombers overhead.[1]

Although Martini was 'pretty certain' that the RAF must have had some new radar-based navigational aid to account for such a sudden and remarkable improvement in bombing accuracy, Goering insisted that Martini must keep his thoughts to himself. The outcome has been described by Winston Churchill in *The Hinge of Fate*, the fourth volume of the wartime premier's history of the Second World War, which was published in 1951, where he referred to the 'accuracy of the Oboe attacks' having 'worried the Germans considerably'. He has it that Hitler harangued the two men and described as 'a scandal' the fact that the British could hit individual factories on cloudy nights and the Germans could not – to which Martini responded that not only were the Germans able to do it but had done so with the X and

Y beam systems. Hitler demanded a demonstration, which was arranged, and in the meantime, Churchill writes, 'Bomber Command, guided by Oboe, had wrought great damage in the Ruhr'.[2]

The result of that demonstration has been noted in another postwar publication. Apparently, at a range of 225 miles, 50 per cent of all bombs fell within a radius of 900 yards, the demonstration having relied on the Y-Gerät system. Carried out without any British attempt to interfere with the signals, which had occurred when that system was used during the Luftwaffe's operations over England, it was a fair result for the range – but not up to Oboe's performance![3]

During the Oboe era, being based at Pathfinder Force Headquarters, J.A. Jukes was in an odd situation. His was, he recalled, a 'slightly different' position from all others whose role there brought them in close touch with PFF Commander Don Bennett. The first difference was that John Jukes was a civilian, 'everyone was in uniform but me', the second was that the job he had been given was a function in line management where his immediate superiors enjoyed a similar relationship with the person in charge at their place of work as he did at his, theirs being Bomber Command Headquarters where the man in the hot seat was the AOC-in-C, Sir Arthur Harris.

A graduate of Cambridge University, where he read physics, Jukes was among a number of scientists the Air Ministry enrolled just before the start of the Second World War, ultimately for various positions in Britain's radar defence organization. In the summer that war broke out he was coming to the end of his training period; he was at one of the radar stations in the Dover area while, as he put it, 'the RAF decided what to do with people like us'. Initially he became involved with the selection of locations for new radar stations within Britain and then, when Norway was under pressure from the Germans pushing up from the south, he was flown out there to see what prospects the Lofoten Islands, way to the north, offered as potential radar sites.

The welcome from the Norwegians was warm, unlike that of the crew of a German warplane who spotted the flying boat carrying him as a passenger, which was cruising around a bay looking for a suitable spot to offload everyone into a boat to take them ashore. With guns blazing, the enemy aircraft homed in on the taxiing flying boat whose pilot was weaving as erratic a course as possible so as to upset the enemy's target practice. Out of the ten people on board, five were hurt in the attack and needed hospital treatment; the aircraft's huge fuel tanks were peppered but fortunately there was no blaze, at least not until later on when, having been beached and abandoned, it was attacked again and this time completely burned out.[4]

Unharmed and without further trouble of that sort, John was soon able to set about his task of site selection in the comparative comfort of a commandeered craft which was well suited to island hopping. All this time, however, the Germans' hold on Norway was tightening and when the time came for evacuation – he left by air – he found himself in the annoying situation of having chosen where best to position a radar station, yet well aware that it would be the Germans building it, their needs replicating those of the British and suitable sites being in short supply in a region with geographical features as radar-unfriendly as the Lofotens.

After a spell at Bomber Command HQ, in the Operational Research Section (ORS) headed by Dr B.J. Dickins, Jukes was initiated into the work of the ORS, whose scientists began analysing the purpose and the performance of Britain's bombers with a view to proposing the ways and the means towards much improved results. During that time, he recalled, 'I recommended a proposal which was adopted called "Window". This involved the bomber aircraft throwing out strips of foil along their route that confused the enemy radar and considerably reduced the losses of our aircraft'. The formation of Pathfinder Force, which was itself a step along the long road to greater effectiveness of the bomber effort, saw him moving from Bomber Command HQ to PFF HQ with a loose job description which enabled him to adapt his role so that it best met Bomber Command's requirements as seen by his own superiors working with Harris and his top team.

John remembered:

We were scientists analysing the bombing raids to determine what was going right and what was going wrong, the idea being to see what changes in operational tactics were desirable. For my part, seconded from Bomber Command to Pathfinder Force, I was privileged to be given access to unrivalled sources of information to benefit my own work and that of ORS itself. As an indication, I was able to be present at pre-raid discussions at PFF HQ and I was able to go out to the airfields; I was able to listen to squadron aircrew members being briefed for an operation and to attend de-briefing on their return.

As the bombing campaign mounted under Harris, aspects of bombing methods, major attacks of particular importance and certain raids with a special significance were analysed in depth by Dickins' people at Bomber Command Headquarters, with Jukes feeding through to his immediate superior, G.A. Roberts, the relevant facts and comment gathered within Pathfinder Force headquarters. The ORS findings were not always to everyone's liking and certainly these published reports with their necessarily restricted circulation did not pull any punches. For example, where more than 200 Main Force aircraft bombed coastal gun batteries in the vicinity of Le Portel in northern France on the night of 8/9 September 1943 as Bomber Command's principal contribution to Operation Starkey, Pathfinder Force's marking for this two-phase Oboe-led attack was castigated as 'unsatisfactory' (ORS Report S126 dated 17 March 1944). These were detailed analyses, one beneficial source of material on which to base a judgement being the experts' interpretation of aerial pictures taken (by flash photography at night) in tandem with bomb release by Main Force aircraft. Often, besides the principal purposes of facilitating bomb plots and damage assessment, these would show the position of the Pathfinders' target indicators relative to the aiming point. Criticism from ORS reports was intended to be constructive, however, so another of their reports on the Le Portel bombing (ORS Report B173 dated 25 September 1943) observed that 'a very serious source of error in marking may be introduced owing to the fact that the TIs do not fall in salvo' (at Le Portel, a critical Oboe-released red TI had fallen as a stick, splitting into three parts, each burning some 800 yards from the next and straddling about a mile). ORS made the point that while this was 'not of great importance in area bombing', it became crucial in precision marking.*

Working for as long as he did at PFF HQ, John Jukes conceded that while Bennett 'could be a difficult person', his own relationship with the Pathfinders leader was enhanced by Jukes being 'slightly different' from others in that environment: 'He sought my advice and, yes, he used me a lot.' Jukes recalls how the pattern of night bombing evolved as a result of experience gained by those who ordered the raids and those who carried them out, to which practical knowledge was added the practised observations of ORS members like Dickins himself, Roberts, Jukes and others in their team.

When I started, the big raids were spread over a period of a couple of hours or so – Bomber Command didn't want aircraft bumping into each other so those who were doing the planning allowed them plenty of air space. Then, when we came to analyse it, in reality this was a very small danger compared with the far greater one that was a consequence of bombers spending so much time over a single target. The more time our aircraft were over the target, the more time the enemy had to organise his defences – particularly to marshal the night-fighters. It was preferable to concentrate the bombers over the target for a much reduced period of perhaps ten or twenty minutes, with all of them going in the same direction, though there was the odd occasion when a bomb dropped from one aircraft would fall through the wing of another flying at its prescribed lower altitude.

John Jukes was at the heart of Pathfinder Force for most of its existence. This was followed, once the ground fighting had moved further to the east, by visits to targets in the Ruhr in the immediate aftermath of the bombing onslaught. He was able to reach conclusions based on personal experience

---

* In *The Starkey Sacrifice: The Allied Bombing of Le Portel 1943* (Sutton), Michael Cumming draws on official documents and eyewitness accounts to reconstruct this little-known tragedy of a seaside town that was virtually wiped out with the loss of some 500 French civilian lives in a bombardment in which, over a period of sixteen hours, the RAF dropped 678 tons of high explosives by night and the USAAF 244 tons by day in the final stage of a British-led operation to make the Germans believe that a large-scale invasion of the Pas-de-Calais was imminent. At Le Portel, PFF relied on Oboe tracking and releasing for the primary marking of each of two coastal batteries little more than a mile apart, with the town between them. Subsequent to the publication of this book, even Oboe's staunchest supporters have conceded that with the geographical locations of the aiming points, relative to those of the controlling ground stations, the releasing station's signals could have been of doubtful quality.

of what Bomber Command intended to happen and the comments made to him by people who had been present during the bombing at the focus point of those intentions. John formed the view that PFF's ability for accurate target-marking fell short of expectations, though Oboe unquestionably achieved an improvement in bombing efficiency against targets within its range. It was his impression, too, that the effectiveness of the bombing offensive was 'really rather poor', the number of bombs reaching their target, or falling within a reasonable distance of it, appeared to him to be 'surprisingly small'. It was, he understood, the consequent worry over the inadequacies of the RAF's bombing performance that produced the decision to introduce area bombing.

When it became his function to assess the results of five years of Allied bombing, a campaign that he had seen grow increasingly more and more intense, Jukes found that his personal concerns were in fact justified: 'Factories which we had bombed and believed to have been put out of action were apparently soon up and running again.' This he gleaned from on-the-spot interviews which he himself conducted within the industrial heartland of Germany, though the devastating end results of the massive bombardment were there for all to see for themselves or in the vivid photographs widely circulated postwar.

Probably more than most, John Jukes acknowledged that sustained accuracy was scarcely more than a hope born out of a union of anticipation and determination. Too many factors existed to cast a disturbing influence on the best intentions of those who designed the bombing systems and those who delivered the bombs. Oboe was undoubtedly the best available product of its time and Professor R.V. Jones, the air intelligence specialist, called it 'the most precise bombing system of the whole war'.[5] Nonetheless, as a target-marking device, there was certainly no chance of Oboe even approaching 100 per cent accuracy when a basic ingredient such as wind speed and direction was no more than a guesstimate, when the ballistics tables essential to the system assumed that every bomb casing had a blemish-free surface,. and when, obviously, human beings too had their failings. That said, Oboe was the single most consistently effective means of placing a TI on a target which others could rely upon as their highly visible, clearly identifiable aiming point. Oboe was used to mark the tiniest targets – though not always with the greatest success; and it was used in area bombing, where the need to capitalize on its ability to pinpoint a definable part of a particular factory was perhaps an unnecessary refinement in the bombing effort. So, it is arguable whether Oboe was in fact employed to its best advantage in the hands of those whose job was to bring the enemy to its knees.

Many will share the view of Frank Metcalfe, former bomber pilot and one of the first ground station controllers, who came to the conclusion that strategic thinking 'sank without trace' when Oboe came into use in Bomber Command. The system was originally confined to use within some 250 miles of UK ground stations because of the height limit of prevailing aircraft of some 30,000 ft; with an intermediate aircraft to receive and re-transmit forward the Oboe signals, this would have effectively tripled the range, yet no real effort was made to persevere with the repeater system. But above all, he asserts, not enough was made of the principal advantage in that, for accurate marking of specific targets, Oboe was a precision tool without equal.

It did come into its own, however, on the eve of D-Day when applied in the marking of gun emplacements which threatened the approaching armada carrying troops who would be landing on the Normandy beaches. It was also used to advantage beforehand in the marking of key communications centres, railway marshalling yards and radar positions among them, and it was used subsequently with corresponding benefit against ammunition dumps and also even for ground-support bombing, though initially this idea was regarded with considerable apprehension, so much so that opportunities were probably lost that could have avoided the early hold-up at Caen. In fact Oboe's role in preparatory operations for the landings on the Continent were of 'inestimable value', the words of an HMSO publication which came out in 1963 (*The Origins and Development of Operational Research in the Royal Air Force*). This noted that 'small targets such as coastal batteries, railway centres and bridges were attacked with its aid'.

An important new Oboe opportunity arose when the ground-control stations were able to move on to the Continent and to reposition themselves progressively forward in step with the advance of the Allied armies. Certainly, in Frank Metcalfe's opinion, this presented a fresh possibility to attack distant smaller targets of strategic importance with smaller air forces, to shorten the war – targets including centres of communication, of oil storage and supply, of crucial engineering components and so on.

He posed the question: why did the RAF go on killing its own crews in heavy bombers when at one and the same time there was available the two-man Mosquito which could be made quickly and cheaply, equipped with Oboe? The casualty rate among the Oboe squadron crews was 'extraordinarily small' whereas an average four per cent casualty rate for the heavies represented, in just a single raid carried out by some 800 bombers, 'the tragic loss of up to 200 highly trained and intelligent men'. It is as if, he said, strategic thinking died at the very moment when those responsible should have been deciding what to do with this splendid new tool. In operational sorties alone, Bomber Command lost 47,268 members of aircrew,[6] the rate of loss being more than 4 per cent during 1942, falling to 3.7 per cent in 1943, to 1.7 per cent in 1944 and to 0.9 per cent in the last months of the war in 1945.[7] It was Frank's point that the sacrifice would have been less if greater emphasis had been placed on Oboe Mosquitoes, with their smaller crews and a far better survival rate, and if there had been more selective targeting which in itself would have reduced the extent of area bombing.[8]

The value that was to be obtained with the precision marking of key objectives was underlined in a particularly pertinent comment expressed by one of No. 109's pilots who was active around the D-Day period. He doubts that there would have been the opportunity for the Allies to invade at that time 'if it had not been for the work of Bomber Command in knocking out those guns on the night of 5/6 June and in hitting the production centres and the launching sites of both the V1 flying bomb and the V2 rocket. Targets so small in size yet so big in their significance were able to be attacked with such assured success because we had the means to pinpoint them for concentrated attacks by formations of heavy bombers.'[9]

Whether or not Oboe was used to best advantage, Reeves and his team at TRE would certainly have been putting their skills to maximum benefit individually and collectively in order to make the system do what Reeves himself, as the guiding light, intended it would achieve. If, on occasions, he was viewed as being perhaps less open than others would have wished, well . . . . It emerges that TRE and No. 109 were not always in accord, at least so far as Reeves, in his capacity at the head of the Oboe Group, and McMullen as the squadron's CO, were personally concerned. Aggravated by seemingly getting nowhere in trying to nail down TRE with regard to the operating heights needed for whichever aircraft would use Oboe, McMullen, who wanted this information so as to make sure that No. 109 had the most suitable plane at their disposal, resorted to tactics in which he chose to circumvent customary procedures and to put that particular gripe to someone at Bomber Command HQ he thought might be prepared to take up the cudgels – Dr Dickins, who ran the Operational Research Section (ORS).

In that approach, McMullen urged that pressure be put on TRE to make them be explicit in their requirements as to height and whether or not it was essential to use an aircraft with a pressure cabin. He considered that 'TRE have become shifty' and that 'friend Reeves' was 'a most difficult person to tie down because he refuses to make any kind of definite statement'. It was time, he pressed, for Reeves to be 'tied down' on this matter of operating heights. After the accuracy of Oboe had been proved at Stormy Down, McMullen thought that it was a mistake not to call a 'high-powered meeting' to decide the operational requirements of 'the gadget', a meeting where Reeves 'would have had to have been honest and straightforward'. Then, correct decisions could have been made to select the best aircraft and to arrange a satisfactory method of completing the practical tests and, as McMullen put it to Dickins, 'getting Oboe going'. Indicating that he was presently without access to those who would eventually deal with operational and tactical problems, McMullen apologized for sending 'this kind of stuff' but Dickins could, it was obvious, 'clear the air quicker than anybody'.[10]

Reeves and his No. 2, F.E. Jones, a man who was known better by his initials, or as Frank, than he was by his first name (Francis), tended to think and to act differently from one another, Reeves being more of a 'thinker' where 'F.E.' was a 'doer' (see page 72). A product as ingenious and as complex as Oboe needed someone like Reeves to conceive it; equally it needed someone like F.E. to get the most out of the total team whose role was to turn this imaginative brainchild into a practical system.* It seems to have been generally agreed that where Reeves appeared a remote individual, F.E. was visibly in the thick of it, his strong leadership qualities ensuring that responsibility was given where it was deserved; he kept everyone in the Oboe group fully informed of developments and in this way each member felt fulfilled.[11]

Where Reeves and F.E. were concerned – and here the pair were united both in thought and in action – Oboe was a scientific product which would perform within pre-determined parameters according to the degree of precision afforded to the data that had to be fed into the component hardware. In practice bombing, Oboe lived up to those expectations; it would never be constantly 100 per cent accurate, but generally the bombs could be relied to fall in the anticipated ellipse measuring some 200 yards by 100 yards. There was nothing to match this achievement, so understandably the excitement bubbled over when new crews arrived for training in readiness to join one or other of the two Oboe-equipped Mosquito squadrons. One already operationally seasoned navigator, Flying Officer C.P. Harrold, with twenty-two bombing raids behind him in the heavies, put it like this: 'We had this feeling that we were going to have the chance to do something really worthwhile. That was the spur when we came to No. 109 Squadron . . . it was war excitement at the most achievable level.'

What none of the crews would have appreciated on joining an Oboe squadron was that there were so many factors that could impact upon the accuracy of the Oboe system. Some were in the hands of those responsible for setting up the equipment in the ground stations, some were under the control of the pilots and the navigators in the run up to the target but some, unfortunately, lay outside the field of human endeavour. For example, bombs of a particular type could reasonably be expected to have identical properties and therefore to fall between aircraft and the ground in a given period of time; however, trials with a 500 pounder revealed that of three, one took 20 per cent longer and two took 50 per cent longer to reach the ground. It will be realized, of course, that with the Oboe system having to count on a given type of bomb falling in a given time, the greater the actual time, the greater the error in terms of distance from the aiming point. It is fascinating, now, to consider the effect of the several other factors that would have influenced the accuracy of Oboe – all these aspects and all these consequences having been appreciated by the scientists who spent every minute of their working day trying to get the best out of the system. It was known, for instance, that with an aircraft flying at 30,000 ft at 300 m.p.h., intending to drop a 250-lb bomb, an error of 10 m.p.h. in determining the ground speed would cause that bomb to fall 220 yards off target. A height error of 500 ft would result in a 130-yard error; an

---

* The Commission of Awards to Inventors awarded Reeves and Jones £3,000 in 1958 for their contribution to Oboe. Reeves, who was awarded the OBE for his work on Oboe, died on 13 October 1971 at the age of sixty-nine; Jones, who received the MBE for his part, died on 10 April 1988, aged seventy-four.

airspeed error of 10 m.p.h., a 3-yard error; an error in heading of 1 degree, a 95-yard error; and a drift error of 1 degree in 15 degrees, a 60-yard error.[12]

Initially when going on ops in heavy bombers, Charles Harrold had suffered the aggravation of seeing bombs go down with luck more than judgement; you weren't sure of your whereabouts, you couldn't be certain that you were in the target area and unquestionably you were fortunate to find that your bombs were within a couple of miles of the objective. This was true particularly in the Ruhr, with its smoke, fog, dummy fires and blinding searchlights. Then GEE came along, the first successful navigational aid, which Harrold used in its early days, though it had its limitations and in any event it was intended as a means of getting you to the target area, not as a bombing facility. Now, wonder of wonders, well within a year, there was this device called Oboe.

Harrold was well aware that Oboe was going to be an exacting task master. It promised the means to obtain hitherto impossible precision for the Pathfinders whose job was to mark the target for Main Force, so the specialist crews who did the marking with Oboe must get as close as possible, squeezing every yard out of the system by concentrating exclusively on the task in hand. Some were better than others at placing their markers on or alongside the aiming point, and sometimes it seemed as if even the best were not doing as well as their superiors expected of them.

> I remember all the No. 109 crews being summoned to a meeting in the Mess at Little Staughton one morning. Don Bennett was there to address us and it became clear that he was in a critical mood. He wasn't happy about our 'yardage' – the error rates that were creeping in – and he reckoned that we were getting slack. We knew that crews who were as much as 300 yards off-target would be taken off operational flying to spend day after day on the bombing range so we were concerned about what was coming next. He had this piece of paper in one hand, which he raised as if he was reading from it, and he told us that he wondered whether our performance was in any way coincidental with the fact that we were drinking more ale per head than any other squadron in Pathfinder Force. If there was this link, then he would make the necessary arrangements to see that our source of ale was stopped. He was serious, no doubt about that, and with that he turned on his heels and left the room.[13]

Charles Harrold was to see a lot more of Bennett when he finished with operational flying – he did seventy ops in his year with No. 109 – when he moved to PFF Headquarters at Wyton late in 1944 to take up an entirely new position in which, as a cub journalist before the war and now as a newly rested Pathfinder, he would have the opportunity to combine those experiences. He explains:

> Bomber Command decided that it was now time to lift some of the secrecy off the Pathfinders and that this would be done by having someone as a 'conducting officer' at PFF HQ whose job was to liaise with newspapers, radio, newsreels and so on. Bennett was hot on secrecy and didn't seem to welcome the idea; certainly he wasn't going to have someone from outside come into his headquarters, which is how the job came my way. In Pathfinders, they were always keen not to lose

people when it came to have them rested, and whenever possible placed them in a liaison role of some sort which they would enjoy.

We began with a few articles, which Bennett always wanted to see first, and soon we were getting visits from writers and cameramen. He was extraordinarily strict about where they could go and what they could see – particularly, he wasn't keen on them going anywhere near No. 109's quarters or its crews. And no one but no one was allowed close to the Oboe Mosquitoes. Before any visit, I had to spell out to Bennett what we would be doing – he was almost paranoid about secrecy.

With British forces pushing nearer and nearer the Rhine, Harrold moved from PFF Headquarters to Brussels, on attachment to the 21st Army Group and a role with the Air Information Unit which saw him conducting a media group to within a mile and a half of the Rhine on the afternoon of 23 March 1945. They would watch the final softening-up close-support bombing operations against the enemy garrison at Wesel just a few hours before the first British troops crossed the Rhine under cover of darkness.

Charles reports:

It was incredible to see the effect of some 200 heavies sending down their bombs on the Mosquitoes' markers.*

I had to get out of my mind the fall-back which used to occur during the course of an attack when Main Force bomb-aimers tended to get over-eager and press the release button a little early. I could see it happening here, when some of the later bombs began falling in the water, and I knew that if this continued, we weren't all that far from being caught up in the bombing ourselves. In fact we were untouched but I could well understand then why, early on in Normandy, there was so much resistance to the idea of Army cooperation attacks with so little distance between our lads and those of the enemy.

The war correspondents could see the markers being dropped on the other side of the Rhine and of course knew that the bombers were to aim on them. By now they were familiar with the role of Pathfinder Force but naturally no one was allowed to say anything about the methods that PFF employed to drop their target-markers. It was recognized that PFF crews were specialists in their work, which would explain the accuracy aspect, but no one ever queried with me how we were able to be equally efficient when there was cloud over the target. Oboe, which the Mosquitoes were using at Wesel, remained a secret for a long time – and sometimes I regret that this was the case. We've seen Bomber Command castigated for what some have called

---

* Although only five of the twelve Oboe Mosquitoes in action that night were successful, an entry in No. 8 (PFF) Group Operations Record Book states that the TIs were reported to have fallen 'in a good group' and the bombing was 'seen to be around them'. In an earlier onslaught on Wesel, packed with German forces retreating as the Allied armies advanced towards the Rhine, Oboe-led Mosquito formations in daylight on 6 March were followed by Main Force bombing at night led by twenty-five Mosquitoes from each of the two squadrons with a 100 per cent Oboe release. Little Staughton's Operations Record Book called it 'a really excellent achievement' and in the words of No. 109 Squadron's ORB it was 'a very good show all round . . . and it means a barrel of beer from the CO for this effort'. When British troops were across the Rhine, Field Marshal Montgomery sent Bomber Harris a message expressing his grateful appreciation for Bomber Command's 'quite magnificent cooperation'; he described the bombing of Wesel on the night of 23/24 March as ' a masterpiece' which was a decisive factor in making possible his troops' entry into the town before midnight.

indiscriminate bombing yet with Oboe we were able to pop a TI in a factory's backyard. I recall that in one raid where I was involved, at Louvain, I watched our red TIs falling directly over the marshalling yards . . . it was such a clear night, you could see the railway lines glistening and I know – because we were lower than usual and I could see it with my own eyes – we were absolutely spot on. This was confirmed when we returned because the first thing we always looked for on entering the de-briefing room was the marking error alongside the crew name.

Before Charles Harrold's time as a conducting officer was over, he was able to take a party of newsmen to Essen within forty-eight hours of the Americans entering and to stand with them amid the shattered remnants of the Krupps industrial complex, which had been scarcely touched until Oboe came on the scene. The group met one of the senior production directors who was there when the first markers went down back in March 1943. 'There were these great coloured lights,' he told them, 'hanging in the sky like the illuminations on a Christmas tree.' It was, he soon found out, the beginning of a raid the likes of which he had never before experienced and whenever those 'Christmas trees', as the Germans called the Pathfinders' target-markers, appeared in future, he knew that this was the time to try to get well away. That was the moment, Harrold has always believed, the right moment for the story of Oboe to be released to the world.

Inevitably there are still those members of the 'heavy brigade' who feel that any publicity about the benefits of Oboe overshadows their own endeavours – almost, it might appear, belittling the effort and the sacrifice that was so pronounced, especially in the first three years of bombing Germany. With the Krupps attacks alone, Bomber Command lost many crews for minimal gain and this is a fact that continues to disturb many people. If Oboe had become available earlier, perhaps some of those lives might have been saved . . . but what if there had never been Oboe?

At Little Staughton, Oboe Mosquitoes and Pathfinder Lancasters worked side by side in the bombing offensive in the last twelve months of the war. Postwar, Little Staughton Pathfinder Association has kept that camaraderie alive and enabled the members of the two squadrons, No. 109 and No. 582, to learn a little more about each other's activities during the war years. In battle, even on those limited occasions when Oboe pilots and navigators flew operationally in the Lancasters for specific Oboe-led bombing, the 'heavy brigade' knew nothing more about Oboe than its name and the fact that it was a means of placing markers accurately on the target. It must never be forgotten that, as well as backing up Oboe marking, Pathfinder squadrons other than No. 109 and No. 105 had to carry out much longer trips, using H2S, to reach and mark targets that were beyond the range of the Oboe system. And it must be remembered that, while conceding that latterly the Oboe Mosquitoes had to face accurate anti-aircraft fire even at their operating heights, Main Force squadrons with their bigger, slower aircraft, loaded with greater weights of bombs, could fly only at much lower altitudes where the flak was at its most severe.

CHAPTER FIFTEEN

The Demise – and the Debt

'What did the Germans know about Oboe? Enough to identify the signals as
a bombing aid, enough to jam the frequencies used for the early operations. If
there had been a concerted air attack on our Oboe ground stations, carried
out in a deliberate, and effective manner, who knows what the consequences
might have been to the bombing campaign.' Sir Edward Fennessy CBE,
recalling his time spent as a radar specialist in No. 60 (Signals) Group.

It is intriguing to ponder whether or not the enemy ever learned the secrets of
Oboe. Some say that the introduction of anti-aircraft guns capable of reaching
greater heights with increased precision was the result of knowledge extracted from
one source or another about the role of high-flying Oboe-equipped Mosquitoes.
This argument can be countered by recognition of the fact that USAAF heavy
bombers operated far higher than did the RAF heavies so those aircraft,
operating in numbers that filled the sky, equally warranted special attention from
the ground defences. Without doubt, though, there was what Charles Harrold
(the 1996/7 Chairman of Little Staughton Pathfinder Association) called
'unbelievable secrecy' surrounding Oboe; all that could reasonably be done was
done to safeguard both the knowledge and the equipment.

So far as keeping the airborne equipment from prying eyes was
concerned, it was equally important whether a disabled aircraft carrying
Oboe gear was in the UK or in friendly hands on the Continent; if at all
possible, all traces must be cleared from the plane and put into a secure
store with minimum delay.

One No. 109 crew, Flight Lieutenant J.B. Burt DFC and Flight
Lieutenant R.E. Curtis DFC, experienced a problem at 30 or 40 feet during
take-off for an operation some six weeks after D-Day and dropped into a
wheatfield on the far end of the runway at Little Staughton. It was especially
upsetting because (besides being the night of their squadron's 2,500th
operational sortie) this would have been the navigator's 100th op! By the
time the fuel supply was turned off and the Mosquito had screeched to a
halt, both men had smashed their way out through the cockpit top and were
down on the ground, shaking their heads in disbelief and ensuring that
neither had been hurt. No fire having materialized, it was then a matter of
waiting for the 'blood wagon' to arrive, and safeguarding the precious Oboe
equipment which was mostly in the nose of the aircraft. The crew knew
precisely what to do in such circumstances, they had the distinct impression

that protecting Oboe was rather more important than looking after themselves. Anyway, men and equipment all lived to fight another day, though doubtless the gear would have required emergency treatment, even if pilot and navigator exhibited no visible signs of needing it.[1]

There was a more serious incident on the Continent, however, which also occurred soon after D-Day, when Squadron Leader W.W. Blessing DSO DFC – an Australian pilot who had carried out No. 105 Squadron's first Oboe operation the previous July – lost his life. The Mosquito came down in an area where there was fierce fighting.* 'There was a real panic on,' recalls the then Wing Commander E.L.T. Barton, who had moved from a position in one of the radar departments at Air Ministry to become Chief Signals and Radar Officer at Pathfinder Force Headquarters. He recalled:

> It turned out that Bill Blessing's plane had been seen to come down and some of our lads were able to make it secure. Unlike us, they wouldn't have realized the value of the equipment inside but sensibly the Army let the RAF know that there was this aircraft and when we learned about it at PFF HQ, it was decided that we had to take swift action.
> The Mosquito was somewhere outside Caen and I was instructed to fly there without delay and to bring back the Oboe gear to Wyton, which was the PFF airfield nearest to our HQ at Huntingdon. Slim Somerville and I did just that, with Slim flying a non-Oboe Mosquito and me sitting alongside in the navigator's seat, with the salvaged equipment packed on board as best we could stow it. It was an episode that showed just how seriously everyone regarded Oboe. In this instance, had it not been for the good fortune of the plane coming down behind our lines rather than the enemy's, it is likely that the Germans could have gleaned much useful information despite the damage that the equipment had suffered.[2]

Although 'flying a desk' at PFF HQ, to which he had been posted on a request by Don Bennett (the two men had worked together before the war), 'Barty' once did what many people in his position would have liked to do but for lots of different reasons just couldn't manage it: he flew on an Oboe sortie over Germany. He did so in a Lancaster III, PB372, belonging to No. 35 Squadron, with Flying Officer J.A. Murrell its captain, for a raid on 4 December 1944 on the Urft river dam at Heimbach. This was an afternoon raid by three Oboe-led formations for which a total of twenty-seven Lancasters were detailed, each formation being accompanied by a Mosquito detailed as reserve Oboe leader.

The Lancaster with Barty on board made a successful attack 'by means of the precision device' (a term which was often used in operational reports

---

* Blessing's was one of twenty Oboe Mosquitoes marking the aiming point for more than 400 heavies on 7 July 1944 whose task was to blast enemy positions in the northern suburbs of Caen. Having started his run at 32,000 ft, the aircraft was hit by cannon shells. Blessing decided to land on one of the Allied air strips and radioed his intent to Biggin Hill. However the Mosquito suddenly entered a spin and he ordered his navigator, Pilot Officer D.T. Burke, to abandon the aircraft. According to the squadron's Operations Record Book, eye witnesses on the ground saw just the one man leave before the plane broke into pieces.

instead of Oboe or the equipment designation, AR5513) and the rest of his formation – including the Mosquito reserve leader – followed suit when seeing his bombs leave the plane, the Lancasters carrying a mix of 4,000-lb and 1,000-lb bombs and the Mosquito a single 4,000 pounder. With the other formations, however, in neither case did the operation go strictly to plan, the Lancasters on both occasions having to take their release cue from the Mosquito reserve leader 'who successfully attacked by means of the precision device in place of the Oboe Lancasters'.[3] In reality, one of those Oboe Lancasters (all three carried a beam pilot and navigator from an Oboe squadron) did a proper job only to the point of completing what appeared to be a successful release. When the time came for the navigator to press the button, none of the bombs left the aircraft; incredibly, it turned out that the main fuse was missing.[4]

As one of the three formation leaders that afternoon, Murrell's Lancaster would use Oboe to track and release, enabling Barty, flying as an observer, to experience its performance operationally in the best way possible short of personally handling the equipment. All those with him were, of course, performing the self-same roles as crews who took part in a number of subsequent operations, among them those on board a Lancaster of No. 582 Squadron whose beam pilot was No. 109's Bob Palmer, posthumous winner of the VC for his most conspicuous bravery during an Oboe-controlled bombing run on 23 December 1944 when, unlike the Urft dam raid which attracted nil defences, the formations met heavy flak, which was extremely accurate, as well as many enemy fighters in the target area. In that mission, from which five Lancasters and one Mosquito failed to return, Lancaster PB372 (which had taken Barty to the Urft dam and back without incident) suffered so much damage from the predicted heavy anti-aircraft fire that it crash-landed at Manston (see page 133).[5]

Barty considers the Urft dam op to have been part of his learning curve, a rare facility to observe Oboe in action because the Mosquito could not carry a third person. He was allowed to go by being able to convince the few who were aware of this flight that it was a necessary and practical way in which to further his knowledge of the job he was doing at Bennett's HQ, that of senior officer responsible for the signals and radar organization within PFF. 'You could say that I was over-eager,' he stated, 'but I suppose the excitement of the circumstances got the better of me, living and breathing ops all the time. Maybe, even, Don Bennett was unconsciously an example for me – he'd been an operational pilot before he took command of Pathfinder Force and he was always as keen as mustard – so when my chance came to see for myself how Oboe performed on ops, I took it! With hindsight, perhaps it was unwise – suppose, with the knowledge that came with my job, I had been taken prisoner by the Germans.'

Could the Germans ever have known about Oboe? It will be recalled that General Martini, who was in command of the Luftwaffe signals service at the relevant time, considered that there was a likelihood of the RAF having introduced a radar navigational aid to account for such devastation at the

Krupps factories in Essen. If, in time, it had become known that there was in use such a precision-bombing device as Oboe, and that sufficient technical information was in enemy hands, then surely more would have been done to nullify Oboe. The ways open were obvious: to jam the signals more successfully than was being done and to pay more attention to the single Oboe-carrying pathfinder aircraft. It was the practice for the Oboe Mosquitoes to climb to their operating altitude before leaving the English coast, to approach the target area at a certain height which would be precise for each individual aircraft, determined by the location of the target, and of course to spend the final seven or eight minutes on straight and level flight during the run-in towards the aiming point. If, as the war progressed, the Germans gained increasing knowledge about Oboe, how did that information reach them? There was nothing to indicate that any aircraft from No. 109 or No. 105 were ever lost in circumstances which would have enabled the Oboe gear to be successfully recovered; there was nothing to suggest infiltration or even careless talk; and nothing to point to the possibility that anyone with knowledge of Oboe may have passed it on while in enemy hands.

When the question was put to Ned Fennessy, who was closely involved with radar-based navigation systems in No. 60 (Signals) Group for much of the war, he recalled that the enemy knew enough to identify the Oboe signals as a bombing aid and to jam the frequencies used for the early operations. While expected from the outset, this enemy inspired interference with Oboe Mark I transmissions proved not to be especially effective, nonetheless, TRE was forced to develop further measures to overcome it. These required modifications to the equipment at the ground stations and in the aircraft, which would change the manner in which the signals were passed between them, in order to introduce additional levels of protection for these all-important transmissions.★

Nothing else was done, to his knowledge, to counter Oboe; if they had known more, he would have thought that blitzing the ground stations was the appropriate course of action. 'If', he said, 'there had been a concerted air attack on our Oboe ground stations, carried out in a deliberate and effective manner, who knows what the consequences might have been to the bombing campaign. No one can know but all of us who were involved with Oboe can guess at the possible outcome.'[6]

★ Dr F.E. Jones is on record that Oboe was 'not unduly worried by German jamming until towards the end of 1943, when, as the Germans told us after the war, they had about 2,000 people manning jamming stations trying to stop the effectiveness of 'Bumerang' – the German name for Oboe'.[7] Centimetre Oboe enjoyed freedom from enemy jamming until the closing months of the war, commencing 'in earnest' in early February 1945, according to No. 72 Wing records, which show that it occurred mainly in daylight during American 9th Bomber Command operations. Even when jamming was at its height the following month, four in five sorties were carried out with no interference being reported. Of the 524 sorties mounted, 32 failed and 27 were hampered but it was conceded that jamming remained 'troublesome' up to the second half of April. One jammer was pinpointed to a site near Mainz and there were others evidently operating in the Ruhr.

In print, the immediate post-D-Day period saw the first disclosure to the world at large that the RAF was using Mosquito aircraft to pinpoint bombers' targets. Writing about an attack at dawn on 18 July on the Caen battlefront, *News Chronicle* war correspondent Michael Moynihan described the arrival of a Mosquito at zero hour – 'marker for the greatest force of destruction in history' – and said how this was followed by a second Mosquito, showering 'the golden rain of its marker with deadly accuracy'. A steel factory at Monteville and four villages were to be obliterated, the factory was the Mosquitoes' target and 'it was going to be removed', because these were sections of the front line where enemy resistance was strongest.

Leaving aside further speculation about the extent of enemy awareness, with the war in Europe well into the closing stages there was still much about Oboe that remained something of a mystery even to the scientists who had spent up to five years in its introduction and development!

Inevitably there had been pressure to put each new technical advance into operational use, which meant that tests to the standards that the Oboe group at TRE would have wished were not always able to take place. One example relates to what was known as the Oboe Mark IIM equipment – the ground-control equipment required for the mobile stations to operate on the Continent (which handled some 3,383 sorties by RAF and USAAF aircraft by the cessation of hostilities). A consequence of the 'hurried completion' of its development in the first half of 1944 was the lack of opportunity for TRE to complete its trials of this system. Two prototype installations were completed at Malvern in early 1944, only to be pushed into service on the south coast, and these were followed by development and production equipment which was swallowed up by successive convoys moving forward through France, Belgium, Holland and into Germany, with Oboe penetration into enemy territory increasing with every new position. Not until towards the end of 1944 were the TRE scientists able to get their hands on Mark IIM equipment for experimental purposes, the first installation being set up at Flat Point, near Ilfracombe, and the second at West Malvern, Herefordshire. These facilitated tests under TRE supervision which led to a number of modifications being made to the operational stations, once the components were available.[8]

A series of bombing trials followed, with bomb drops from aircraft flying at various altitudes, some using the 'Delta' technique, which was an enhancement to the Oboe system enabling pilots to approach the final track more easily,* and

---

* It will be appreciated that an aircraft approached its target along what was theoretically a circular track, it was, of course, the circumference of a circle, the centre of which was the tracking ground station. Inaccuracies when using Oboe were often attributed to the effects of the aircraft weaving while trying to maintain course, so to minimize such errors, a change in the system was proposed. The depth of modulation of the tracking signal, instead of representing the distance that the aircraft was away from the centre of the theoretical circular track, would now represent the deviation of the aircraft's heading from its true direction. This enhancement was known as the Delta, or exponential, approach. Pen and paper plots produced on the simulator showed that even non-pilots could now 'fly the beam' with tolerable accuracy – and, as will be seen, it proved beneficial in operations.

others where the angle of cut between the two ground stations was reduced to as little as 23½ degrees, this in order to determine the extent to which Oboe accuracy was lost the closer together were the controlling ground stations.[9] It is significant that when ground stations at Hawkshill Down and Winterton were paired for the last of all Oboe operational flights, all with Delta tracking, five out of five Mosquitoes were successful on 3 May, five out of five on 4 May, five out of five on 5 May and three out of three on 8 May, the only failures being two out of five on 7 May, the overall success rate being more than ninety per cent.[10]

At TRE, once the war in Europe was over, the Oboe group disbanded – on a note of triumph, it would appear – judging from the result of a competition bombing trial against the latest version of H2S, which showed Oboe Mosquitoes getting as close as 45 yards compared with an average radial error of just over 150 yards for their opponents.[11]

For No. 109, practice bombing continued until 27 September, when one of the two Mosquitoes had a successful visit to the Otmoor range but the other was obliged to return early to base due to engine failure. For the record, this penultimate day for No. 109 as an operational squadron also included a fifteen-minute air test, two cross-country flights and – an event that is perhaps rather more dramatic, given No. 109's pioneering Oboe-led attack on the Krupps factories at Essen! – a simulation bombing of that very city. Next day, 28 September 1945, as the person responsible at that time for preparing the squadron's Operations Record Book put it for the then Commanding Officer, Wing Commander R.C.E. Law DFC, 'This is the finish – all our aircraft were flown to Upwood today.'*

It could be assumed, of course, that that departure of No. 109's remaining aircraft marked the demise of the squadron. It was not the end of No. 109, however, because within seventy-two hours, on 1 October 1945, on another airfield, Woodhall Spa, another squadron, No. 627 Squadron, which was first a Mosquito light bomber unit flying with the Pathfinder Force (it was founded at Oakington on 12 November 1943) and subsequently a low-marking specialist unit in No. 5 Group, experienced reincarnation as a new post-war No. 109 Squadron.

In RAF jargon, No. 627 was relieved of its squadron crest and presented with that of No. 109, becoming part of No. 1 Group with Wing Commander Scott AFC its Commanding Officer. It moved initially to Wickenby, the first

---

* Recommendations for honours to recognize individual achievements with No. 109 Squadron on active service were then still being processed, Bob Law himself becoming one of the last recipients when his DSO came through four months after VJ Day. The same award was announced at the same time for one of the flight commanders, Wing Commander W.G. Foxall DFC. By the year end, these had been followed by six more DSOs, four Bars to the DFC and – unique within No. 109 and a rare distinction indeed – a Second Bar to the DFC for Flying Officer Charles Brameld, the citation referring to him as 'a navigator of outstanding ability' and paying tribute to a 'long and distinguished record of operational duty'. Unofficially, this squadron has been credited with 1 VC, 27 DSOs, one Bar to the DSO, 112 DFCs, 62 Bars to the DFC, 1 Second Bar to the DFC and 1 DFM.

five of its Mosquitoes being flown there from Woodhall Spa as the advance party on 17 October with a further thirteen on 19 October and the final three on 20 October. The 'new' No. 109, equipped still with the Mark XVI until the Mark B35 came along, remained in service until 31 January 1957 when the squadron disbanded, the Mosquitoes having been phased out in the summer of 1952 and replaced by Canberra jet bombers. In the disposal of No. 109's aircrew, four members went to No. 9 Squadron and twenty-six went to No. 139 Squadron.

For anyone who was associated with either Pathfinder Force or the development and application of Oboe, it should be particularly interesting to read that for most of No. 109's postwar existence it continued to have an association with No. 105 – the Oboe-equipped Mosquito squadron which had transferred from Bourn to Upwood in June 1945 and disbanded on 1 February 1946, some four months after No. 109 itself had ceased to exist in its wartime role. The postwar connection between the two Oboe squadrons was underlined as an historical fact on 1 February 1949 when No. 109's 'number plate' was changed from No. 109 Squadron to No. 109/105 Squadron.[12] This was a noteworthy nomenclature indeed since it amalgamated what were of course the RAF's only Oboe squadrons. It would have been appropriate for the Canberras too to have carried Oboe but that was never to be.

It will be seen that No. 109/105 aircrews would nonetheless follow suit in one respect by being called upon to drop bombs in anger (towards the end of 1956 during the Suez operations), as their forerunners in No. 109 and No. 105 had done between 1942 and 1945 during operations against Germany and the countries it had occupied in Western Europe.

For the definitive assessment of Oboe as a precision blind-bombing and target-marking device in those wartime years, Report No. S236 of 24 August 1945 by the Operational Research Section at Bomber Command gives the marking errors noted in operational use as well as those recorded in bombing trials; also, it identifies the key factors affecting its accuracy as a target-marking system.[13] From December 1942 to February 1943 there was an average marking error of 650 yards; in attacks on marshalling yards during the period March/April 1944, it was 600 yards; and in attacks on gunsites in May 1944, 300 yards. In the period June/October 1944, during marking operations on the Ruhr and other long-range, heavily defended targets using ground stations in the UK (where the average angle of cut was 25 degrees), average radial errors were between 393 and 500 yards when attacking from 32,000 ft. In bombing trials, where the Delta enhancement was introduced, the inaccuracy ranged from 87 yards (at a height of 12,000 ft) to 150 yards (30,000 ft), the angle of cut here being 23 degrees. The predominant factors affecting Oboe marking accuracy were the effect of flying inaccuracies, especially at great heights, small angles of cut and the flare drift of high-burst TIs due to errors in the forecasting of ground winds. This ORS survey of Oboe accuracy recommended that any further development of Oboe as a target-marking device 'should be directed primarily towards improvement of the TI and the thorough testing of its ballistic properties from the heights above 30,000 ft necessary on most Oboe operations'.

Despite those performance figures, Oboe's shelf-life was fast running out. Vying for Bomber Command's affections in peacetime, Oboe had a rival in G-H, a radar-based navigation system that was without doubt less accurate and more liable to jamming, admissions conceded by Air Marshal T.A. Langford-Sainsbury when writing to the Assistant Chief of Air Staff (Operations) in October 1945.[14] Where Oboe lost points was that generally this was a device used by Pathfinder aircraft whose markers in large-scale attacks became the target for Main Force bombers which themselves were liable to create additional inaccuracies. G-H, on the other hand, could be used by each and every bomber detailed for whatever raid – there was no need for a dedicated vanguard force – and its range was comparable with that of Oboe. For the peacetime Bomber Command it would be a simple question of economics. In a choice between the two systems there would be no contest: where Oboe was seen as a specialist product serving a single squadron, G-H could soon be in the hands of the entire bomber force, Bomber Command getting 'far greater returns for smaller overheads'. Before the year was out, Bomber Command was authorized to discontinue the operational use of Oboe in No. 105 Squadron, which would carry on its target-marking role with G-H Mark II and the Mark XIV bombsight among its equipment. Development of what was described as 'the Oboe technique' would proceed at the Central Bomber Establishment 'on a limited basis commensurate with a peace-time economy' and just three of No. 105's Oboe Mosquitoes would be transferred there for such a purpose.[15]

While operational distances ruled out Oboe for potential shipment to the Pacific theatre in the final stages of the Second World War, seemingly it had missed the boat, figuratively speaking, with regard to alternative applications, whether war-based or peace-inspired. Certainly there were a number of possibilities of a non-military nature, as F.E. himself set down in a postwar paper for the Institution of Electrical Engineers, though none of them stood the test of time. There was radar survey with, instead of the bomb-release mechanism, an automatically operated camera photographing the ground; there was the prospect of using Oboe to obtain an accurate measurement of winds at any heights at which an aircraft would fly; and, rather more arcane though an application that was put into practice involving TRE scientists, for studying how the velocity of electromagnetic waves varies with height above the earth.[16]

Still in uniform, Ned Fennessy helped to form a survey unit, operating in Africa, which would rely on the G-H system and later, when back in civilian life, he tried with others – among them the radar pioneer Sir Robert Watson-Watt – to promote the adoption of GEE internationally as a navigational aid in civil aviation. Oboe, the third radar/navigation system with which Fennessy was involved throughout the war, occupied his thoughts too; though not a potential Oboe application, he proposed the Oboe carrier aircraft, the Mosquito, as an airborne TV relay station. He was of the opinion that patrolling Mosquitoes could overfly the UK in three-hour stints – this was before satellites were in use – and with their equipment floodlight the whole country with a signal that would take TV into every home . . . this at a time when ground-based transmitters covered only a small area of the UK.[17] It seemed a good idea at the time but, like so many others, it failed to get off the ground.

Alas, in the search for acceptance in the postwar world, Oboe missed the mark. The hardware vanished off the face of the earth, or so it appeared, ground stations and airborne equipment alike, which was in direct contrast to 'Oboe people', who were rightly proud of their contribution to 'one of the most important of Britain's secret weapons'[18] and who continued to meet in groups large and small, whenever opportunities arose.

> Now Oboe's dead – we meet tonight
> To pay a tribute to its flight.
> Let's lay a wreath upon its ashes
> A mixed bouquet of dots and dashes.
>
> A Phoënix rose in '83
> The Cat and Mouse stalk stealthily.
> The Oboe pipes its tuning 'A's
> As we recall its halcyon days.[19]

Efforts to keep the product alive as a blind-bombing contender were without success, not that there seems to have been much inclination towards any form of blind-bombing in the period immediately following the Second World War. At the Empire Air Armament School at Manby, for instance, bombing training was limited to ground instruction and elementary air practice in visual bombing methods, using the Mark XIV bombsight, Mark III low-level and stabilized automatic bombsights, with blind-bombing technique merely a subject of classroom lectures. In early 1948 the Commandant was pressing hard for the means to introduce training on H2S and G-H equipment ('Oboe', he stated, 'can be disregarded', though he did not offer his reasons). It was imperative, he concluded, that when training officers for the future, 'at least the methods of the immediate past should be taught'.[20]

Although it appears that there was a school of thought which considered that some 'universal blind-bombing aid' was necessary and that 'something of the type of H2S' would be 'the only way' to satisfy that requirement, as late as the summer of 1949 there was still no decision as to the way ahead for blind-bombing, if indeed it had any sort of future in the RAF.[21] H2S,

G-H and Oboe were still all that was available in those now long-gone days when the V-bombers were the new arrivals on the bomber squadrons.

While No. 109/105 Squadron retained its Canberras, the manner in which these aircraft would be used was, even in the mid-1950s, apparently still undecided. At first, once its current G-H commitment was completed, it seemed that the squadron would revert to its low-level marker role; that was welcome news, given that the squadron had been 'somewhat in the dark about its policy and role'. However, shortly afterwards, it emerged that 'this may be reconsidered' and it could be some time before No. 109/105 (which was then under the command of Squadron Leader J.M. Daniel) 'knows where it is going'.[22]

It stayed, in fact, as a squadron operating at the highest levels, taking part in the operational exercise Sky High in April that year, 1955. The exercise was in two phases, the first with targets on the Continent selected for simulated G-H attack, the second with simulated runs on various bombing ranges, dropping 25-lb practice bombs and again using G-H. Three months later, two crews converted to increased heights for G-H bombing – both to 35,000 ft – which was a fair indication of the path that was being found for the squadron. In April 1956, a detachment of eight aircraft with air and ground crews left the squadron's UK base for Malta to take part in Operation Medflex, which saw those Canberras carrying out 'attacks' from even greater altitudes, heights as much as 45,000 ft to 'bomb' ships in convoy, airfields and warships belonging to the US 6th Fleet. Then, in October that year, again operating from Malta, the squadron was engaged in Operation Gold Flake, which saw the crews practising shallow dive bombing, 'war load' take-offs and medium-level visual bombing, No. 109/105 now having reverted from marker squadron to Main Force squadron once again. As a consequence of this role change, the training emphasis moved from target marking to high-level bombing and cross-country flying, each crew consisting of pilot, navigator and observer.

This was, of course, the build up to the Suez crisis, which saw the Israelis invading Egypt, with Britain and France intervening to prevent an escalation of the fighting and to safeguard the passage of ships through the Suez Canal. In anticipation of the commencement of active operations against Egypt, seven crews from No. 109/105 Squadron were briefed on 30 October for a raid on Kabrit airfield which was then cancelled. Next day, which signalled the start of operations, three crews took off with the intention of attacking Cairo West airfield with a full war load comprising 6 × 2,000-lb MC bombs, but 20 minutes after wheels-up the raiding force was recalled. There was, it turned out, the chance that harm might be caused to American families who were using the road running past the airfield for evacuation purposes.

The squadron dropped its first bombs in an operational sortie that same day, 31 October, when three crews took part in a raid on Almaza airfield, bombing on TIs released by a Pathfinder force. In the course of the Suez intervention there were further raids on Cairo West airfield (1 November with three crews, the Pathfinder leader describing this attack as being 85 per cent successful), Cairo International airfield (1 November with two crews), al-Agami coastal gun emplacement (4 November with three crews) and Huckstep Barracks (4 November with two crews). When the ceasefire was announced, No. 109/105 was put on a four-hour standby; this period was extended first to twelve hours on 10 November and then, on 18 November, to twenty-four hours. By the end of the month the squadron was back to exercises and on 7 January its crews flew for the last time, 31 January 1957 seeing No. 109/105 disbanded.[23] The Canberra squadron whose combined numbering had perpetuated those of the only two squadrons in the RAF to have Oboe-equipped Mosquitoes had carried out its last air test, its last training flight, its last operational sortie and dropped its last bombs.

The high explosives delivered by No. 109/105 Squadron in its Main Force role in that Middle East 'mini war' were all released visually, tumbling down upon targets identified and marked in a manner quite different from that of the two Oboe squadrons in the 'big war'. The marking aircraft were both Canberras and Valiants, this latter type being the first of the family of V-bombers; comfortable operating heights were between 40,000 and 45,000 ft; 4.5-inch flares were in use for the express purpose of first illuminating the target area and there were 1,000-lb Target Indicators to go down (planted by an aircraft in a shallow dive) once the aiming point within the target area was identified. In the bygone days, No. 109's two-man crews in their twin-engined propeller-driven Mosquitoes opened the Battle of the Ruhr from no more than 30,000 ft in the first major Oboe-marking operation, using 250-lb TIs, so that Main Force bombers could savage the Krupps factories to a degree that had been totally impossible in pre-Oboe days.

In that big war, musical marking rose to a crescendo as time went on, its accuracy and its effectiveness improving through the united efforts of the scientists at TRE, the aircrews of No. 109 and No. 105, the personnel at the ground-control stations and the many others whose contribution was vital to the planning and the operational research activities that went on within Pathfinder Force and at Bomber Command Headquarters.

Oboe, as an instrument of war, sounded its final notes in comparatively insignificant operations against a number of airfields in northern Germany in the closing days of hostilities in Europe. In an overall performance that lasted for two years five months, its score was some 9,624 operational sorties by the RAF alone (a sortie being a single flight by an Oboe-equipped aircraft whether for marking or bombing) with an Oboe-release successfully accomplished on 5,908 occasions – a success rate of just over 61 per cent. In the hands of the Pathfinder Mosquito crews, Oboe helped orchestrate the role of the almost 120,000 Main Force bombers who released perhaps

720,000 tons of high explosives, 12 tons apiece for every civilian killed in enemy air raids on Britain during the Second World War.[24]*

In the Oboe squadrons, however, one operation has dominated and that was the first raid on Krupps (though the purists will insist that the Oboe-led attack a week later was even more successful). The former No. 109 navigator Charles Harrold, who subsequently picked his way through what was left of the Krupps works within a couple of days of American forces taking Essen, reckoned that that was the moment to tell the world about Oboe. Then, he says, was the opportunity to announce that Britain had produced a means of pinpointing a bombing target with hitherto unachievable accuracy – even when that target was obscured by a blanket of cloud. Consistently, target-marking was carried out to well within 300 yards of the aiming point, this was the 'maximum skill error' beyond which crews were taken off operational flying for intensive practice bombing. While typically the achievement with Oboe was considerably under 300 yards, even this sort of precision marking has paled in much later years with the introduction of laser-directed bombs.

Charles Harrold has drawn a parallel between the use of Oboe at Essen and the laser bombing against targets in Iraq. 'I'll never forget,' he said, 'the way that television showed us how our aircraft were able to slip a bomb through a doorway . . . incredible! But what our Mosquito crews were able to achieve half a century earlier was to my mind equally remarkable, given the extent of comparative technical know-how. In its day, Oboe was as important and as effective a bombing tool as the laser has proved to be when taking out key targets. As I see it, that's the scale of the debt that we all owe to Oboe.'

---

* Civilians who lost their lives in the UK due to enemy action totalled 60,595 (26,923 men, 25,399 women, 7,736 children under 16 and 537 unidentified), according to the HMSO publication *Medical History of the Second World War, Casualties and Medical Statistics*, edited by W. Franklin Mellor.

Sources

Chapter One

1. Public Record Office (PRO) document AIR 14/540. Summary of Events No. 8 (PFF) Group shows that in the month that the award of the Victoria Cross to Bob Palmer was announced (March 1945), gallantry displayed in air operations by no less than eighteen of his aircrew colleagues in No. 109 Squadron was recognized by the award of either the Distinguished Service Order or the Distinguished Flying Cross. One (George Grant, a former CO) received a second DSO; two, who already held a DFC, now added the DSO; two received a second DFC, and there were thirteen first-time recipients of the DFC, giving this squadron a hard-to-surpass nineteen individual honours (DFC and above) awarded in the course of a single month.
2. Despatch of War Operations, 23 February 1942 to 8 May 1945, by Air Chief Marshal Sir Arthur T. Harris GCB OBE AFC, Air Officer Commanding-in-Chief Bomber Command, October 1945, which provides some details of casualty figures and gives 4.1 per cent as the rate of loss for 1942, a percentage that then fell in each successive year.
3. PRO AIR 41/41. First draft of RAF Air Historical Branch narrative of bombing offensive June 1941 to February 1942 Para 7(i).
4. PRO AVIA 7/93. Bombing by RDF (1938/41), encl. 12B.
5. PRO AVIA 7/93.Bombing by RDF (1938/41), encl. 2A.
6. PRO AVIA 7/93. Bombing by RDF (1938/41), encl. 8A.
7. PRO AVIA 7/93. Bombing by RDF (1938/41), encl. 9A.
8. Bowen, E.G. *Radar Days*, Adam Hilger, 1987.
9. PRO AVIA 7/601. AMRE and TRE moves from Dundee to Worth Matravers, also to and from Worth Matravers (1939/42), part I, encl. 4A.
10. PRO AVIA 7/601. AMRE and TRE moves from Dundee to Worth Matravers, also to and from Worth Matravers (1939/42), part I, encl. 74A for initial report and ends 44A, 44B and 45A for report via Watson Watt.
11. PRO AVIA 7/601. AMRE and TRE moves from Dundee to Worth Matravers, also to and from Worth Matravers (1939/42), part I, encl. 84A.
12. PRO AVIA 7/602. AMRE/TRE moves from Dundee to Worth Matravers, also to and from Worth Matravers (1939/42), part II, encls 6A and 19A.
13. PRO AVIA 7/603. AMRE/TRE moves from Dundee to Worth Matravers, also to and from Worth Matravers (1939/42), part III, encl. 13A.
14. PRO AVIA 7/253. TRE Planning Conferences.

Chapter Two

1. PRO AIR 29/602. BAT&DU Boscombe Down ORB.
2. Interview with the Reverend Group Captain A. Reece DSO, OBE, DFC, AFC.
3. PRO AIR 26/580. No. 80 (Signals) Wing ORB, June 1940/December 1942.
4. PRO AIR 26/580. No. 80 (Signals) Wing ORB, June 1940 to December 1942.
5. Price, Alfred. *Instruments of Darkness – The History of Electronic Warfare*, Macdonald and Jane's, 1977.
6. PRO AIR 14/2905. Headache progress reports, nos 1–44, July 1940/December 1942, in which there is reference to Munro's flight in report 5 and to Blucke's in report 12.
7. PRO AIR 14/2905. Headache progress reports, no. 1–44, July 1940/December 1942, report 16.

Chapter Three

1. PRO AVIA 7/93. Bombing by RDF (1938/41), encl. 37B.
2. Interview with J.E.N. Hooper. For those unaware of the real reason for so naming Oboe and those who regarded the capital letter form as an acronym, several possibilities existed; there was Objective Bombing Of Enemy (which the author came across in material on file at the IEE) and even Objective – Bombing Of Europe. Doubtless there were various other alternatives in general or occasional use.
3. Interview with J.E.N. Hooper.
4. PRO AVIA 7/1331. TRE/Oboe Test Flight Reports, encl. 1A, report dated 20 April 1941.
5. PRO AIR 16/917. 'The History of Oboe, 1940 to 1945', compiled by HQ No. 60 Group, p. 18.
6. PRO AVIA 7/1331. TRE/Oboe Test Flight Reports.
7. PRO AVIA 7/3559. Oboe (1941/2) part II, encl. 8A.
8. PRO AVIA 7/3558. Oboe (1941/2), encl. 10A.
9. A letter from the BBC dated 10 September 1992 gives the wording and answer, forms of radar being of course Oboe, H2S (i.e., hydrogen sulphide with a smell of rotten eggs) and GEE. The programme notes said of Oboe: 'Oboe, developed from 1941 on, was a system for guiding an aircraft from the ground. Pilots followed a radio pulse over the target recognizing the correct course by a continuous note (of oboe-like quality).'
10. PRO AIR 26/580. No. 80 (Signals) Wing ORB, June 1940 to December 1942. Postwar, *Flight* (in an article in its 29 November 1945 issue) noted that in total 730 recorded attacks on Starfish sites there were only four cases where casualties occurred to people living in the neighbourhood.
11. PRO AIR 14/2905. Headache progress reports, nos 1–44, July 1940/December 1942, report 21.
12. PRO AIR 26/580. No. 80 (Signals) Wing ORB, June 1940 to December 1942.
13. PRO AVIA 7/3558. Oboe (1941/2), encl. 33.
14. PRO AIR 20/8953. *Radio Countermeasures – The Radio War: History of TRE* (1940 to 1945), monograph by Dr R. Cockburn.
15. PRO AIR 27/853. No. 109 Squadron ORB contains the posting; and PRO AIR 27/125 No. 9 Squadron ORB shows him missing.

Chapter Four

1. PRO AVIA 7/3558. Oboe (1941/2), encl. 33.
2. Biographical Memoirs of Fellows of the Royal Society, F.E. Jones (16 January 1914–10 April 1988), vol. 35, 1990.
3. Rowe, A.P. *One Story of Radar*, Cambridge University Press, 1948.
4. PRO AIR 16/917. The History of Oboe, 1940 to 1945, compiled by HQ No. 60 Group, p. 20.
5. 'Oboe – A precision ground-controlled blind-bombing system, F.E. Jones MBE, PhD, DSc, FEng, FIEE, FRS, a paper presented to an IEE Seminar entitled 'The History of Radar Development to 1945', held on 10–12 June 1985 to mark the fiftieth anniversary of radar. Professor Rankine's comment about sacking 'the man responsible for this fantastic Oboe' was contained in 'a Minute which appears on a Headquarters file', according to Dr Jones' paper.
6. PRO AVIA 7/3558. Oboe (1941/2), encl. 33.
7. Interview with J.E.N. Hooper.
8. PRO AVIA 7/3558. Oboe (1941/2), encl. 11.
9. PRO AVIA 7/3569. Oboe policy, encl. 39A.
10. PRO AIR 14/1781. Oboe – General Papers relating to (see JAJ/DHB memo dated 1 August 1941, comprising notes on the current position of Oboe). The document suggested that the 'very careful planning' on the operational side would 'obviously be a job in which ORS Bomber Command can be invaluable'. Later, the originator of that note, J.A. Jukes, as a member of Dr Dickins' ORS team at Bomber Command, would be based at the Headquarters of Pathfinder Force, the principal user of the Oboe system.
11. PRO AVIA 7/3558. Oboe (1941/2), Oboe schedule, 11 August 1941, FEJ/MT.
12. PRO AVIA 7/3569. Oboe policy, encl. 10A.
13. PRO AVIA 7/3569. Oboe policy, encl. 10A.

Chapter Five

1. PRO AIR 26/580. No. 80 (Signals) Wing ORB, June 1940 to December 1942; and PRO AIR 27/853 No. 109 Squadron ORB.
2. PRO AIR 23/1195. Employment of RCM Wellingtons against German Tank VHF, encl. 1A.
3. PRO AIR 23/1195. Employment of RCM Wellingtons against German Tank VHF, encl. 6A, report by Group Captain W.E.G. Mann, Chief Signals Officer.
4. PRO AIR 23/1195 Employment of RCM Wellingtons against German Tank VHF, encl. 12B.
5. PRO AIR 23/1195. Employment of RCM Wellingtons against German Tank VHF, encl. 46A, report by Group Captain W.E.G. Mann, Chief Signals Officer.
6. PRO AIR 26/580. No. 80 (Signals) Wing ORB, June 1940 to December 1942.
7. PRO AIR 26/580. No. 80 (Signals) Wing ORB, June 1940 to December 1942.
8. PRO AIR 26/580. No. 80 (Signals) Wing ORB, June 1940 to December 1942; PRO AIR 25/52 No. 3 Group ORB (January 1941 to December 1943); PRO AIR 28/607 RAF Station Oakington ORB; and PRO AVIA 7/3586 Trinity, encl. 8B.
9. PRO AIR 26/580. No. 80 (Signals) Wing ORB, June 1940 to December 1942.
10. PRO AVIA 7/3586. Trinity, encl. 6A.
11. PRO AVIA 7/3586. Trinity, encl 2B.
12. PRO AIR 14/3280. Trinity Operation, an ORS file, which includes a list of duties allotted to each crew member.
13. PRO AIR 14/3280. Trinity Operation, an ORS file, which includes a list of duties allotted to each crew member; and PRO AIR 27/98 No. 7 Squadron ORB.
14. PRO AIR 26/580. No. 80 (Signals) Wing ORB, June 1940 to December 1942.
15. PRO AIR 14/3280. Trinity Operation, an ORS file.
16. PRO AIR 26/580. No. 80 (Signals) Wing ORB, June 1940 to December 1942.
17. Interview with the Reverend Group Captain A. Reece DSO, OBE, DFC, AFC.
18. PRO AVIA 7/3586. Trinity, encl. 8F.
19. PRO AIR 16/917. 'The History of Oboe, 1940 to 1945', compiled by HQ No. 60 Group, p. 22, contains the first report; and PRO AIR 41/41, first draft of RAF Air Historical Branch narrative on bombing offensive June 1941 to February 1942, para 7 (iii), has the second. The third report comes from 'Oboe: History and Development', A.H. Reeves ACGI, DIC, and J.E.N. Hooper BSc, a paper published in the *TRE Journal* for October 1945 and included in a special issue on historical radar produced by the IEE in October 1985.
20. PRO AIR 14/1573. Ground Controlled Bombing – Trinity and Oboe, encl. 5a, draft minute from Director of Signals to Deputy Chief of Air Staff dated 5 January 1942.
21. PRO AIR 14/1573. Ground Controlled Bombing – Trinity and Oboe, encl. 4B.

Chapter Six

1. PRO AVIA 7/3569. Oboe policy, encl. 50A.
2. PRO AVIA 7/3569. Oboe policy, encl. 64A.
3. PRO AVIA 7/3569. Oboe policy, encl. 77A, Oboe Plans and Progress up to February 1942.
4. PRO AIR 14/1573. Ground Controlled Bombing – Trinity and Oboe, encl. 27A.
5. PRO AVIA 7/3558. Oboe (1941/2). See de Burgh letter of 16 February 1942; and TRE Superintendent's letter of 13 March 1942.
6. PRO AVIA 26/233. Oboe Mk I Trials, in which TRE Report 4/R.103/JENH, dated 7 June 1942, refers to runs made by a Wellington on 24 and 25 April and on 1, 3, 19 and 21 May (perfect visibility on the first four days and at least 8/10ths cloud on the final two days), its airspeed 160 mph and flying generally at 10,000 ft.
7. PRO AVIA 7/3558. Oboe (1941/2) – A Highly Secret document dated 18 June 1942 entitled 'Notes of an informal meeting to discuss a possible operational use of Oboe'.
8. PRO AVIA 7/603. AMRE/TRE moves from Dundee to Worth Matravers, also to and from Worth Matravers (1939/42), part III, encl. 68A, paper by D. Watson, 31 March 1942.
9. PRO AIR 25/679. No. 60 Group Headquarters Unit ORB for details of the bombings; and *The Origins and Development of Operational Research in the Royal Air Force*, HMSO, 1963, for explanation of the move.

10. PRO AIR 14/1573. Ground Controlled Bombing – Trinity and Oboe, encl. 25A, ORS (BC) Report (Memorandum S.53) dated 14 June 1942; and PRO AVIA 7/3569, Oboe policy, encl. 114A, note from A.P. Rowe to Sir Henry Tizard dated 15 June 1942.
11. PRO AIR 14/1573. Ground Controlled Bombing – Trinity and Oboe, encl. 32A.
12. Bowyer, Chaz. *Mosquito at war*, Ian Allan, 1973.
13. PRO AIR 27/826. No. 105 Squadron ORB.
14. PRO AIR 14/1574. Oboe Operational Development, encl. 1A, SASO letter dated 21 July 1942 to OC No. 109 Squadron.
15. PRO AVIA 7/1331. TRE/Oboe Test Flight Reports, encl. 78A, where Worth Matravers' general log shows that this test flight took place on the afternoon of 1 August, earlier trials, on the afternoon of 30 July, having been inconclusive (the first two tests not proceeding because of equipment failure in the air and on the ground respectively, while the third and final test lacked sufficient time to obtain 'any real idea' of the Mosquito's performance).
16. Interview with Flight Lieutenant A.P. O'Hara DFC and Bar, DFM.
17. PRO AIR 20/1418. RDF Chain Executive Committee 'B' Oboe, Minutes of Meetings, 23 July 1942 to 26 July 1944.
18. PRO AIR 14/1781. Oboe – General Papers relating to . . ., encl. 40A, memorandum from McMullen during his time at Stradishall as OC No. 109 Squadron.
19. PRO AIR 14/1573. Ground-Controlled Bombing – Trinity and Oboe, encl. 38A.
20. Interview with Sir Edward Fennessy CBE.
21. PRO AIR 20/1418. RDF Chain Executive Committee 'B' Oboe – minutes of meetings, 23 July 1942 to 26 July 1944.
22. PRO AIR 14/1573. Ground-Controlled Bombing – Trinity and Oboe, encl. 38A.
23. PRO AIR 14/1573. Ground Controlled Bombing – Trinity and Oboe, encls 40 and 41, Saundby/Harris correspondence, 16 and 18 August 1942.
24. PRO AVIA 7/1548. Oboe 1½-metre Ground Equipment, encls 100A and 116A refer respectively to an armed escort and to the panels nominated for destruction.
25. PRO AIR 14/1574. Oboe Operational Development, encls 9A and 20A.
26. PRO AVIA 7/3569. Oboe policy, encl. 176A.
27. PRO AIR 14/1575. Oboe Interference, encl. 1A.

Chapter Seven

1. PRO AIR 27/141. No. 10 Squadron ORB.
2. PRO AIR 27/141. No. 10 Squadron ORB.
3. PRO AIR 27/141. No. 10 Squadron ORB.
4. Interview with J.E.N. Hooper.
5. Interview with F. Metcalfe CBE.
6. Interview with L.W. Overy.
7. PRO AIR 27/1319. No. 214 Squadron ORB.
8. Interview with Flight Lieutenant A.P. O'Hara DFC and Bar, DFM.
9. PRO AIR 27/853. No. 109 Squadron ORB.
10. PRO AIR 27/125 No. 9 Squadron ORB.
11. Personal account of Bufton's experiences during the period 26 August to 20 December 1941 made available to the author.
12. *Ibid.*

Chapter Eight

1. PRO AIR 14/1574. Oboe – Operational Development, encls 7A and 38B.
2. PRO AIR 14/1575. Oboe Interference, encls 62A and 30A.
3. PRO AIR 14/1574. Oboe – Operational Development, encl. 55A.
4. PRO AIR 14/1574. Oboe – Operational Development, encl. 67A.
5. PRO AIR 14/1574. Oboe – Operational Development, encl. 30A, 1 October 1942 letter to Saundby from DB Ops.
6. PRO AIR 14/1574. Oboe – Operational Development, encl. 41B, 5 October 1942 letter from McMullen to Commander PFF.

7. PRO AVIA 7/1548. Oboe 1½-metre Ground Equipment, encl. 151A, TRE Report G1/202/DAW dated 1 October 1942 which identifies paired ground stations by these names; Cunningham is credited in an interview with J.E.N. Hooper; and PRO AIR 14/1574 Oboe Operational Development, encl. 53A, Most Secret Memo dated 16 November 1942 from Bennett to HQBC, headed Stations Type 9000 – Naming of Duties.
8. PRO AIR 14/2704. Oboe – Operation, Research and Development Reports, encl. 13A, 7 November 1942, letter from SASO Bomber Command to Bennett.
9. PRO AIR 14/1574. Oboe – Operational Development, encl. 71A, Message AX311Serial No. Y1650 dated 7 December 1942.
10. PRO AIR 20/8655. Reports of PFF Results and Technique, November 1942–May 1945, see Review of Pathfinder Techniques, Appendix A.

Chapter Nine

1. PRO AIR 29/168. Trimingham ORB.
2. First report Webster, Sir Charles & Frankland, Noble. *The Strategic Air Offensive Against Germany, 1939–1945*, vol. II, HMSO, 1961; second report Middlebrook, Martin & Everitt, Chris. *The Bomber Command War Diaries*, Viking, 1985.
3. PRO AIR 27/853. No. 109 Squadron ORB.
4. Jones, R.V. *Most Secret War*, Coronet Books, Hodder & Stoughton, 1979.
5. PRO AIR 14/1574. Oboe – Operational Development, encl. 90A, ORS (BC) report no. S. 78, The Operational Use of Oboe Mark 1A, 20/21 December 1942 to 16/17 January 1943.
6. PRO AIR 14/2704. Oboe – Operation, Research and Development Reports, encl. 36A, has the Bennett report; and PRO AIR 14/1574 Oboe – Operational Development, encl. 90A, ORS (BC) report no. S. 78, The Operational Use of Oboe Mark 1A, 20/21 December 1942 to 16/17 January 1943.
7. PRO AIR 14/1574. Oboe – Operational Development, encl. 90A, ORS (BC) report no. S. 78, The Operational Use of Oboe Mark 1A, 20/21 December 1942 to 16/17 January 1943.
8. Interview with Sir Clifford Cornford, KCB, F. Eng.
9. Webster & Frankland. *The Strategic Air Offensive Against Germany, 1939–1945*, vol. II, HMSO, 1961.
10. Author's compilation based on crews' records.
11. PRO AIR 20/4776. Oboe and H2S Results, in which see the section relating to Oboe results prior to 29 May 1943 showing 'Dead accurate' on 7/8 January 1943, a 1,200-yard error on 9/10 January 1943 and 'Spot on' marking by two Oboe-controlled Mosquitoes on 12/13 January 1943.
12. PRO AIR 27/853. No. 109 Squadron ORB.
13. PRO AIR 14/2703. Oboe Policy, encl. 16A, Bennett's letter dated 12 February 1943.
14. PRO AIR 29/145. Hawkshill Down ORB.
15. PRO AVIA 7/3559. Oboe (1941/2), Part II, encl. 259A.
16. PRO AVIA 7/3559. Oboe (1941/2), Part II, encl. 260A, TRE response letters dated 15 February 1943 and encl. 275A, letter dated 16 March 1943, signed by J.E.N. Hooper and F.E. Jones respectively.
17. PRO AIR 14/2704. Oboe – Operation, Research and Development Reports, encl. 37A, Bennett letter dated 11 January 1943; PRO AIR 14/2703. Oboe Policy, encl. 18A, Saundby letter dated 20 February 1943; PRO AIR 14/2704. Oboe – Operation, Research and Development Reports, encl. 40A, Bennett letter dated 11 February 1943; and PRO AVIA 7/3559. Oboe (1941/42), Part II, encl. 258A, RDC12 note dated 9 February 1943.
18. PRO AIR 29/169. Worth Matravers ORB.
19. Despatch of War Operations, 23 February 1942 to 8 May 1945, by Air Chief Marshal Sir Arthur T. Harris GCB, OBE, AFC, Air Officer Commanding-in-Chief Bomber Command, October 1945.
20. PRO AIR 14/1574. Oboe – Operational Development, encl. 123A, ORS (BC) report no. S. 102, The Operational Use of Oboe Mark 1A, 20/21 December 1942 to the introduction of K Oboe in mid-June 1943, ORS illustration BC299A, dated 6 August 1943.
21. PRO AIR 14/1574. Oboe – Operational Development, encl. 123A, ORS (BC), report

no. S. 102, The Operational Use of Oboe Mark 1A, 20/21 December 1942 to introduction of K Oboe in mid-June 1943, para. 30.

22. Saward, Dudley. *Bomber Harris, The Authorised Biography*, Cassell/Buchan & Enright, London, 1984.
23. PRO AIR 14/1574. Oboe – Operational Development, encl. 123A, report no. S.102, The Operational Use of Oboe Mark 1A, 20/21 December 1942 to introduction of K Oboe in mid-June 1943, para. 21.
24. PRO AIR 20/4776. Oboe and H2S Results, see section relating to Oboe results prior to 29 May 1943.
25. Webster & Frankland. *The Strategic Air Offensive Against Germany, 1939–1945*, vol. II, HMSO, 1961.
26. Middlebrook & Everitt. *The Bomber Command War Diaries*, Viking, 1985.
27. Saward, Dudley. *Bomber Harris, The Authorised Biography*, Cassell/Buchan & Enright, London, 1984.
28. PRO AIR 29/145. Hawkshill Down ORB.
29. PRO AIR 27/853. No. 109 Squadron ORB.
30. Middlebrook & Everitt. *The Bomber Command War Diaries*, Viking, 1985.
31. PRO AIR 27/853. No. 109 Squadron ORB.
32. AIR 14/1574. Oboe – Operational Development, encl. 123A, ORS (BC) report no. S.102, The Operational Use of Oboe Mark 1A, 20/21 December 1942 to introduction of K Oboe in mid-June 1943; and encl. 90A, report no. S. 78 covering the period to 16/17 January 1943, Appendix A.
33. PRO AIR 24/206. HQ Bomber Command ORB January to June 1944.

Chapter Ten

1. PRO AIR 14/2704. Oboe – Operation, Research and Development Reports, encl. 50A, see notes signed by Wing Commander Brittain, RDF (Nav), dated 31 March 1943.
2. PRO AIR 29/168. Sennen ORB.
3. PRO AVIA 7/3570. Oboe Policy, Part II, encl. 147A, letter from Scientific Liaison Officer, Office of Scientific Research and Development, US Embassy, dated 28 June 1943.
4. PRO AIR 29/145. Hawkshill Down ORB.
5. PRO AIR 29/145. Hawkshill Down ORB.
6. Wing Commander J.E. Tipton DFC and Bar in correspondence with the author.
7. PRO AIR 14/2704. Oboe – Operation, Research and Development Reports (see Minutes of 3 September 1943 meeting on Oboe accuracy).
8. Despatch of War Operations, 23 February 1942 to 8 May 1945, by Air Chief Marshal Sir Arthur T. Harris GCB, OBE, AFC, Air Officer Commanding-in-Chief, Bomber Command, October 1945.
9. Middlebrook & Everitt. *The Bomber Command War Diaries*, Viking, 1985.
10. PRO AIR 20/4776. Oboe and H2S Results, see section relating to Oboe results prior to 29 May 1943.
11. PRO AIR 20/4776. Oboe and H2S Results, Bufton's note prompting a response that 'The Hun must surely suspect Oboe, it is amazing to think he has not discovered it'.
12. PRO AIR 29/168. Swingate ORB.
13. Verses from the 'Oboe Poem', produced and updated for postwar reunions of 'Oboe people', reproduced here by kind permission of its originator, J.E.N. Hooper, a member of the Oboe group at TRE from creation to disbandment.
14. Wing Commander J.E. Tipton DFC and Bar, in correspondence with the author. Tipton, a Flight Lieutenant at the time, took part in five operations to Emden besides eight test flights between 7 September and 13 October 1943, as navigator to the then Flight Lieutenant L.C. Jacobe.
15. PRO AIR 27/853. No. 109 Squadron ORB; PRO AIR 29/168 Cleadon ORB; and PRO AIR 25/152 No. 8 (PFF) Group ORB.
16. PRO AIR 14/2704. Oboe – Operation, Research and Development Reports. Memo dated 16 November 1943 from Director General of Signals.
17. PRO AIR 29/169. Winterton ORB.
18. PRO AIR 29/145. Hawkshill Down ORB.
19. PRO AIR 14/2719. No. 1655 MTU.
20. Interview with Squadron Leader R.E. Curtis DSO, DFC and Bar.

21. PRO AIR 27/853. No. 109 Squadron ORB (which subsequently carries an entry that the formerly 'missing on operations' pair Bickley and Jackson had 'arrived back in this country on 15 September 1944' and been reclassified 'safe UK').
22. PRO AIR 27/827. No. 105 Squadron ORB.
23. PRO AIR 29/168. Swingate ORB.
24. PRO AIR 27/853. No. 109 Squadron ORB and PRO AIR 27/827 No. 105 Squadron ORB.
25. PRO AIR 14/2703. Oboe Policy, encl. 104A, letter dated 27 March 1944 letter from Pathfinder Force SASO to Officers Commanding nos 105 and 109 Squadrons, copied to No. 1655 MTU.
26. PRO AIR 27/827. No. 105 Squadron ORB.
27. Entry from diary made available to author.
28. Entry from diary made available to author.
29. PRO AIR 27/854. No. 109 Squadron ORB.
30. PRO AIR 27/854. No. 109 Squadron ORB.
31. PRO AIR 25/153. No. 8 (PFF) Group ORB.
32. PRO AIR 27/827. No. 105 Squadron ORB.
33. Interview with Sir Edward Fennessy CBE.

Chapter Eleven

1. Middlebrook & Everitt. *The Bomber Command War Diaries*, Viking, 1985.
2. PRO AIR 25/153. No. 8 (PFF) Group ORB.
3. PRO AIR 27/2052. No. 582 Squadron ORB.
4. PRO AIR 27/827. No.105 Squadron ORB.
5. Interview with Squadron Leader R.E. Curtis DSO, DFC and Bar.
6. PRO AIR 27/827. No. 105 Squadron ORB.
7. PRO AIR 29/168. Beachy Head ORB.
8. PRO AIR 29/168. Swingate ORB.
9. PRO AIR 29/192. Entry in AMES 9432 ORB.
10. PRO AIR 27/854. No.109 Squadron ORB.
11. PRO AIR 25/153. No. 8 Group ORB.
12. PRO AIR 14/540. No. 8 (PFF) Group, in which ORS member J.A. Jukes was shown as the contributor to the August Summary. Jukes was seconded from Bomber Command HQ to Pathfinder Force HQ (see page 162).
13. PRO AIR 14/2719. No. 1655 MTU.
14. PRO AIR 14/2703. Oboe Policy, encl. 98A, notes on fourth meeting of the Allied Air Force Bombing Committee, held on 14 January 1944 to discuss radio aids for heavy bomber operations.
15. PRO AIR 27/854. No. 109 Squadron ORB.
16. PRO AIR 14/540. Summary of Events No. 8 (PFF) Group.
17. PRO AIR 20/8655. Reports of PFF Results and Technique, November 1942–May 1945, see notes on methods of target-marking, prepared for the guidance of operational crews.
18. PRO AIR 25/153. No. 8 Group ORB.
19. PRO AIR 27/854. No. 109 Squadron ORB.
20. PRO AIR 27/381. No. 35 Squadron ORB.
21. PRO AIR 27/827. No. 105 Squadron ORB.
22. PRO AIR 14/3075. No. 8 (PFF) Group Summaries – Day, December 1944.
23. PRO AIR 27/853. No. 109 Squadron ORB.
24. Interview with Sir Edward Fennessy CBE.
25. PRO AIR 27/856. No. 109 Squadron ORB.
26. PRO AIR 27/856. No. 109 Squadron ORB.
27. PRO AIR 25/154. No. 8 (PFF) Group ORB.
28. PRO AIR 25/154. No. 8 (PFF) Group ORB.
29. Bowyer, Michael J.F. & Sharp, Martin C. *Mosquito*, Faber, 1967/71.
30. PRO AIR 16/917. 'The History of Oboe', produced by No. 60 Group, p. 135.
31. PRO AIR 27/856. No. 109 Squadron ORB.
32. PRO AIR 29/169. No. 6 Convoy ORB.

Chapter Twelve

1. A document dated 23 March 1945 in the author's possession lists, as at that date, all aircrew who were either still serving on the squadron or on a temporary detachment with another unit; at that time there were only 3 pilots with 100 or more total sorties (Flight Lieutenant F.C. Petts DFC with 100, Flight Lieutenant A.P. Mountain DFM with 106 and John Burt with 129). There were, however, 9 navigators with 100 or more total sorties: Flight Lieutenant N.W. Wade DFC with 106 (101 sorties while with Pathfinder Force), Squadron Leader N. Bowman DSO DFC, 106 (74 with PFF), Flight Lieutenant R.W. Powell DFC, 110 (81), Flying Officer C. Brameld DFC, 110 (78), Squadron Leader J.A. Mahood DFC, 113 (78), Flight Lieutenant C. Matthewman DFC, 117 (88), Squadron Leader F.G. Davy DFC, 118 (70), Squadron Leader H.A. Scott DSO DFC 131 (95) and Ron Curtis with 139 (104). A further eight pilots and three navigators were credited with seventy or more PFF sorties.
2. Interview with Squadron Leader R.E. Curtis DSO, DFC and Bar.
3. Interview with Group Captain K.J. Somerville DSO, DFC, AFC.
4. Group Captain K.J. Somerville DSO, DFC, AFC, in correspondence with the author.
5. Interview with D.H. Slater MBE.
6. PRO AIR 27/856. No. 109 Squadron ORB.
7. Interview with Squadron Leader A.T. Buckland DSO, DFC, Croix de Guerre.
8. Bowyer, Chaz. *Mosquito at War*, Ian Allan, 1973.
9. Interview with J.R. Hampson.
10. Interview with J.R. Hampson.
11. Crawley, Aidan. *Escape from Germany, A History of RAF Escapes during the War*, Collins, 1956.
12. PRO AIR 20/4757. Special Ops, POW Camps.

Chapter Thirteen

1. PRO AIR 27/1003. No. 149 Squadron ORB; also interview with the Reverend Group Captain A. Reece DSO, OBE, DFC, AFC, in which he acknowledged that those two incidents had been particularly significant when reaching a decision postwar to offer himself as a candidate for Holy Orders.
2. PRO AIR 27/856. No. 109 Squadron ORB.
3. Interview with Kenneth Bailey.
4. PRO AIR 27/1352. No. 218 Squadron ORB.
5. PRO AIR 27/1352. No. 218 Squadron ORB.
6. PRO AIR 24/297. Bomber Command ORB, vol. 3 Appendices, Night Raid Report No. 741.
7. Interview with Squadron Leader H.A. Scott DSO, DFC and Bar.
8. 'Oboe – A precision ground-controlled blind-bombing system', by F.E. Jones MBE, PhD, DSc, FEng, FIEE, FRS, a paper presented to an IEE Seminar, 'The History of Radar Development to 1945', held on 10–12 June 1985 to mark the fiftieth anniversary of radar.

Chapter Fourteen

1. Interview with Sir Edward Fennessy CBE, who met General Martini when he and a number of his former staff officers were in England at the invitation of Sir Robert Watson-Watt.
2. Churchill, Winston S. *The Second World War*, vol. 4, 'The Hinge of Fate', Cassell & Co. Ltd, 1951.
3. Price, Alfred. *Instruments of Darkness – The History of Electronic Warfare*, Macdonald and Jane's, 1977.
4. Interview with J.A. Jukes.
5. Jones, Professor R.V. *Most Secret War*, Coronet Books, 1979.
6. Messenger, Charles. *Bomber Harris and the Strategic Bombing Offensive, 1939–1945*, Arms and Armour Press, 1984.
7. Despatch of War Operations, 23 Feb. 1942 to 8 May 1945, by Air Chief Marshal Sir

Arthur T. Harris GCB, OBE, AFC, Air Officer Commanding-in-Chief, Bomber Command, October 1945.
8. Interview with F. Metcalfe CBE.
9. Interview with Squadron Leader J.R. Emmerson DFC and Bar, AFM.
10. PRO AIR 14/1781. Oboe – General Papers relating to . . . encl. 45A, letter dated 9 July 1942 from McMullen at Stradishall to Dr Dickins at HQBC, encl. 45A.
11. Interview with J.E.N. Hooper.
12. 'Oboe: History and Development', A.H. Reeves ACGI, DIC, and J.E.N. Hooper BSc, a paper published in the *TRE Journal*, October 1945 and included in a special issue on historical radar produced by the IEE in October 1985.
13. Interview with Flight Lieutenant C.P. Harrold DFC and Bar.

Chapter Fifteen

1. Interview with Squadron Leader R.E. Curtis DSO, DFC and Bar.
2. Interview with E.L.T. Barton CBE, OBE (Mil).
3. PRO AIR 25/154. No. 8 (PFF) Group ORB, which reported that cloud conditions prevented an assessment of the bombing results.
4. PRO AIR 27/855. No. 109 Squadron ORB.
5. PRO AIR 27/381. No. 35 Squadron ORB, which shows Flying Officer E.J. Rigby as captain and pilot of PB372 on that occasion; this aircraft was delivered from Wyton on 14 November 1943 and carried out only one other sortie as an Oboe leader, its first, on 21 November, when Murrell led a formation attack on Wesel.
6. Interview with Sir Edward Fennessy CBE.
7. 'Oboe – A precision ground-controlled blind-bombing system', by F.E. Jones MBE, PhD, DSc, FEng, FIEE, FRS, a paper presented to an IEE Seminar, 'The History of Radar Development to 1945', held on 10–12 June 1985 to mark the fiftieth anniversary of radar.
8. PRO AVIA 26/847. Oboe Mark II Bombing Trials from 12,000 ft, see report no. G4/106/JENH, analysing forty-seven bomb drops in March 1945 from a Mosquito (airspeed 270 mph) where the arriving point was on a sea range to Hellsmouth Bay, near Pwllheli, North Wales, 112 miles from Flat Point and 108 miles from West Malvern, the angle subtended being 53 degrees. Fifty per cent of the bombs fell within 75 yards of the Mean Point of Impact (compared with a 140-yard radius in the April/May 1942 tests).
9. PRO AVIA 26/918. Oboe Mark II Bombing Trials from 30,000 ft using small angle of cut. See report no. G4/108/JENH dated 23 July 1945.
10. PRO AIR 29/145. Hawkshill Down ORB.
11. Oboe group's final report to A.P. Rowe, 13 July 1945.
12. PRO AIR 27/2810. No. 109/105 Squadron ORB.
13. PRO AIR 14/901. Operational Use of Oboe (Blind-Bombing) vol. II, encl. 22.
14. PRO AIR 14/901. Operational Use of Oboe (Blind-Bombing) vol. II, encl. 23A.
15. PRO AIR 14/901. Operational Use of Oboe (Blind-Bombing) vol. II, encl. 26A.
16. 'Oboe – A Precision Ground-Controlled Blind-Bombing System', F.E. Jones MBE, BSc, PhD, which appeared in the Journal of the IEE, vol. 93, part IIIA, no. 2, 1946.
17. Interview with Sir Edward Fennessy CBE.
18. PRO AIR 16/917. The 'History of Oboe', compiled by HQ No. 60 Group, p. 4.
19. Verses from the 'Oboe Poem', produced and updated for postwar reunions of 'Oboe people', reproduced here by kind permission of its originator, J.E.N. Hooper, a member of the Oboe group at TRE from creation to disbandment.
20. PRO AIR 20/6886. Blind-Bombing – Future Policy, EAAS/9/19/AIR dated 1 January 1948.
21. PRO AIR 20/6886. Blind-Bombing – Future Policy, loose minute S. 345/ACAS (TR) dated 8 August 1949.
22. PRO AIR 27/2810. No. 109/105 Squadron ORB.
23. PRO AIR 27/2810. No. 109/105 Squadron ORB.
24. Statistics for sorties and successful releases are based on tables included in No. 60 Group's 'History of Oboe'.

Bibliography

Bowen, E.G., *Radar Days*, Adam Hilger, 1987

Bowyer, Chaz. *Mosquito at War*, Ian Allan, 1973

Churchill, Winston S. *The Second World War*, vol. 4, 'The Hinge of Fate', Cassell, 1951

Crawley, Aidan. *Escape from Germany, A History of RAF Escapes during the War*, Collins, 1956

Cull, Brian, with David Nicotte and Shlomo Aloni. *Wings over Suez*, Grub Street, 1996

Cumming, Michael. *The Starkey Sacrifice: The Allied Bombing of Le Portel, 1943*, Sutton, 1996

Jefford, Wing Commander C.J. MBE. *RAF Squadrons*, Airlife, 1988

Jones, R.V. *Most Secret War*, Coronet Books, Hodder & Stoughton, 1979

Lee, Air Chief Marshal Sir David, GBE, CB. *Wings in the Sun, A history of the RAF in the Mediterranean, 1945–1986*, HMSO, 1989

Messenger, Charles. *Bomber Harris and the Strategic Bombing Offensive, 1939–1945*, Arms and Armour Press, 1984

Middlebrook, Martin, with Chris Everitt. *The Bomber Command War Diaries*, Viking, 1985

Moyes, Philip J.R. *Bomber squadrons of the RAF and their aircraft*, Macdonald & Jane's, 1964

Price, Alfred. *Instruments of Darkness – The History of Electronic Warfare*, Macdonald and Jane's, 1977

Rowe, A.P. *One Story of Radar*, Cambridge University Press, 1948

Saward, Dudley. *Bomber Harris, The Authorised Biography*, Cassell/Buchan & Enright, 1984

Sharp, C. Martin, with Michael J.F. Bowyer. *Mosquito*, Faber, 1967/71

Tavender, I.T. *The Distinguished Flying Medal, A Record of Courage*, 1918–1982, J.B. Hayward & Son, 1990

Webster, Sir Charles, with Noble Frankland. *The Strategic Air Offensive Against Germany, 1939–1945*, vol. II, HMSO, 1961

Papers and Other Publications

Cockburn, Dr R. Monograph entitled 'Radio Countermeasures – The Radio War: History of TRE, 1940 to 1945'

Harris, Air Chief Marshal Sir Arthur T., GCB, OBE, AFC, AOC-in-C Bomber Command. Despatch of War Operations, 23 February 1942 to 8 May 1945, published October 1945

Jones, F.E., MBE, BSc, PhD, FEng, FIEE, FRS. 'Oboe – A Precision Ground-Controlled Blind-Bombing System', a paper which appeared in the *Journal of the IEE*, vol. 93, part IIIA, no. 2, 1946

——. 'Oboe – A Precision Ground-Controlled Blind-Bombing System', a paper presented to an IEE Seminar entitled 'The History of Radar Development to 1945', held on 10–12 June 1985 to mark the fiftieth anniversary of radar

Reeves, A.H., ACGI, DIC, and J.E.N. Hooper BSc. 'Oboe: history and development', a paper published in the *TRE Journal* for October 1945 and included in a special issue on historical radar produced by the IEE in October 1985

'Biographical Memoirs of Fellows of the Royal Society', F.E. Jones (16 January 1914–10 April 1988), vol. 35, 1990

'The History of Oboe, 1940 to 1945', compiled by HQ No. 60 Group

'The Origins and Development of Operational Research in the Royal Air Force', HMSO, 1963

Index

Caen 165, 172, 175
Calais 65, 127
Caldwell, G.F. 117
Campbell, C.F. 89, 91, 93, 94,
    101, 103, 112, 157
Canberra aircraft 177, 180,
    181
Carnegie, J.F. 153
Carpenter, E.C. 132
Carter, A.C. 118, 124
Cartwright, J. 49
casualties, Oboe Mosquito
    crews, *see* Oboe
casualties, RAF Bomber
    Command 4, 96,
    101, 165
casualties, UK civilians in
    Second World War
    182
Cat, Tracking Station, *see also
    by name* 58, 85, 97,
    125
CH 10, 34, 65, 66, 71, 72
Challis, C.R.A. 133
Châteaudun 157
Cherbourg 12, 20, 21, 22, 23,
    24, 25, 26, 27, 28,
    31, 35, 36, 45, 46,
    51, 56, 71, 79, 120,
    123, 138, 140, 150
Chivenor 30
CHL 9, 10, 24, 36, 98
Chrysler, C.K. 104, 124, 147
Churchill, Winston S. 125,
    160, 161
Clayton, S. 63
Cleadon 112, 113
Cologne 31, 57, 62, 79, 80,
    84, 97, 99, 100,
    110, 115, 135, 136
Commercy 126, 127
Cornford, E.C. (Clifford) 92,
    93
Cox, R.M. 112, 117, 126
Crabb, J.H. 123
Crampton, W.F. 80
Cundall, H.J. (Butch) 18, 25,
    26, 56, 124, 140,
    150
Cunningham, Dr L.B.C. 59,
    85, 92
Curtis, R.E. 106, 114, 115,
    118, 123, 138, 139,
    154, 171

D-Day, 6 June 1944 99, 108,
    119, 122, 123, 124,
    125, 126, 145, 156,
    157, 165, 166, 172,
    175

Dalcom, D.P. 136, 144
Daniel, J.M. 180
de Burgh, D.H. 58
de Gaulle, Charles 142
de Havilland, Geoffrey 62
de Rips 128
Denman, R.P.G. 43
Dickins, Dr B.J. 59, 61, 67,
    162, 163, 166
Dodwell, T.E. 103
Dortmund 98, 99, 153
Douglass, A.C. 95, 96, 99,
    101, 103
Downing, E.T. 25
Duisburg 70, 79, 85, 88, 89,
    91, 94, 96, 104,
    120, 154, 155, 156
Dundee 1, 7, 8, 9, 34, 60
Duren 98, 108
Düsseldorf 84, 92, 94, 95,
    116, 147

Eggebek 136
Eisenhower, General 134
Emden 98, 111, 112, 113,
    157
Emmerson, J.R. 119, 153
Essen, *see also* Krupps Works,
    1, 62, 84, 86, 87,
    91, 92, 94, 95, 96,
    97, 99, 100, 102,
    103, 104, 110, 115,
    136, 160, 170, 174,
    176, 182

Falconer, J.A. 133
Falkinder, W.J. 119, 123, 157
Feltwell 80, 156
Fennessy, E. (Ned) 65, 66,
    103, 120, 121, 125,
    128, 134, 171, 174,
    178, 179
Fernbank, E.P.M. 49, 79
Fighter Command 8, 15, 60,
    65, 66
Findlater, R. 90, 94, 99, 101,
    116
Finn, B.W. 83
Fisher, F.M. 116
Flares, *see also* target
    indicators (TIs),
    77, 94, 95, 111,
    181
Flat Point 175
Flensburg 63, 86
Flett, A.H. 124
Florennes 90, 94, 98, 126,
    127, 128, 129, 134
Foss, H. 121
Foulsham, F. 131

Foxall, W.G. 176
France, invasion of 120, 121,
    122, 125, 126
Frankfurt 126, 147
Fredman, N.H. 119, 124, 133
French, C.L. 123

G-H 66, 120, 121, 128, 130,
    178, 179, 180
Gallaher, J.F.C. 103, 110
Gapennes 130
Garrett, E.W. 118, 124
GCI 71, 128
GEE 3, 53, 66, 92, 112, 114,
    120, 121, 128, 139,
    152, 168
Gelsenkirchen 59, 84, 86, 87,
    108
George VI, King 151
Gneisenau 40, 45, 51, 52, 141
Goering, Herman 160
Gold Flake, Operation 180
Goodier, J. 25, 27, 71
Gore, R. 15, 19
Gotha 135
Gouda 144
Grant, G.F. 25, 26, 49, 57,
    126, 140, 150
Gray, J.A. 41, 53
Green, F.A. 96, 99, 103
Gremberg 131
Griggs, F.M. 64, 65, 77, 78,
    79, 89, 94, 95, 101,
    103, 112, 118
Grisman, W.J. 148, 149, 150
ground-markers 94, 95, 101,
    104, 105, 107, 110

H2S 3, 100, 105, 170, 176,
    179
Halifax 96, 100, 101, 129,
    158
Hallicrafter 15, 46, 48, 52
Hamborn 91, 92, 99, 115,
    116, 118
Hamburg 79, 134, 136, 148,
    152
Hammond, H.W.E. 110, 116,
    147
Hampson, J.R. 110, 116, 146,
    147, 148
Harding, G.W. 132
Harris, Sir Arthur T. 1, 57,
    62, 63, 66, 67, 81,
    96, 98, 100, 101,
    102, 122, 130, 141,
    142, 160, 161, 169
Harrison, F. 34
Harrold, C.P. 167, 168, 169,
    170, 171, 182